Citadel in the Wilderness

The Fesler-Lampert *Minnesota Heritage* Book Series

This series is published with the generous assistance of the John K. and Elsie Lampert Fesler Fund and David R. and Elizabeth P. Fesler. Its mission is to republish significant out-of-print books that contribute to our understanding and appreciation of Minnesota and the Upper Midwest.

The series features works by the following authors:

Clifford and Isabel Ahlgren

J. Arnold Bolz

Helen Hoover

Florence Page Jaques

Evan Jones

Meridel Le Sueur

George Byron Merrick

Grace Lee Nute

Sigurd F. Olson

Charles Edward Russell

Calvin Rutstrum

Robert Treuer

EVAN JONES

Citadel in the Wilderness

The Story of Fort Snelling and
the Northwest Frontier

University of Minnesota Press
MINNEAPOLIS

First University of Minnesota Press edition, 2001
Published by the University of Minnesota Press
111 Third Avenue South, Suite 290
Minneapolis, MN 55401-2520
http://www.upress.umn.edu

Printed in the United States of America on acid-free paper

Library of Congress Cataloging-in-Publication Data
Jones, Evan, 1915–
Citadel in the wilderness : the story of Fort Snelling and the northwest
frontier / Evan Jones.— 1st University of Minnesota Press ed.
p. cm. — (The Fesler-Lampert Minnesota heritage book series)
Includes bibliographical references (p.) and index.
ISBN 0-8166-3879-9 (pbk. : alk. paper)
1. Fort Snelling (Minn.)—History. 2. Frontier and pioneer life—Minnesota.
3. Frontier and pioneer life—Northwest, Old. 4. Northwest, Old—History—
1775–1865. I. Title. II. Series
F614.F7 J6 2001
977—dc21
2001023474

The University of Minnesota is an equal-opportunity
educator and employer.

11 10 09 08 07 06 05 04 03 02 01   10 9 8 7 6 5 4 3 2 1

For
Judith

CONTENTS

Illustration will be found following page 98

Publisher's Note

The Fesler-Lampert Minnesota Heritage Book Series is designed to renew interest in the state's past by bringing significant literary works to the attention of a new audience. Our knowledge and appreciation of the culture and history of the region have advanced considerably since these books were first published, and the attitudes and opinions expressed in them may strike the contemporary reader as inappropriate. These classics have been reprinted in their original form as contributions to the state's literary heritage.

PROLOGUE

A THOUSAND MILES north of New Orleans and the same distance west of New York the Mississippi is joined by an eastward flowing tributary. In the early nineteenth century this confluence was renowned among western Indians. They rode in from the prairies or came downriver in canoes to be awed by a limestone stronghold which rose from the river bluffs. Fort Snelling, as this citadel came to be called, reminded some visitors of a Rhenish castle. It could be seen for miles, and the sight of it eloquently announced that the United States had taken possession of the lands of the Sioux and the Chippewas. Within its walls as many as two hundred and fifty soldiers formed ranks daily to be put through close order drill. From its sally ports they marched to police unruly tribesmen; they manned the cannons which commanded both the Mississippi and the St. Peter's rivers. Their bastion stood high above the two streams, crowning a massive promontory as the Gibraltar of the West. If war whoops echoed against its parapets, no scalper ever forced his way within the citadel—its stone walls proved as impregnable as they looked. Until the tide of settlement crossed the ninetieth meridian Fort Snelling—for years the army's strongest western post—secured the wilderness. But its very existence, conceived of before the War of 1812, was long delayed, for the successive events which made its erection inevitable began in the eighteenth century.

The Old Northwest frontier became fluid in the summer of 1794. In the Battle of Fallen Timbers, near the rapids of the Maumee River on the Ohio-Indiana line, General "Mad Anthony" Wayne pinned down battalions of a half-dozen allied tribes and sent their remnants running—defeating Indians as they had not been defeated before in the West. In the Treaty of Greenville which followed, the tribes ceded their rights to the southeast corner of the Northwest Territory, setting a precedent for all the treaty-making of the following century. Pioneers began to move up the valleys of the Ohio's tributaries, and the Old Northwest frontier began to tongue out—north toward Lake Erie, west to the Mississippi. Acre by acre the settlers' front advanced into Indian lands.

Already among the Indians, however, were fur traders of British inclination—men to be reckoned with in the decades ahead. They dominated the tribes and helped to prolong the threat of border savagery. Together these entrenched traders and their native clients constituted a menace to be dealt with by the American government. Two instruments were indicated: the United States Army and the War Department's Indian agents. Soldiers were ordered into the Old Northwest to establish the American presence; government civilians followed to act as liaison between the tribes and Washington. When the citadel on the St. Peter's at last was established—to warn ambitious men in Canada as well as the Indians—its assigned task was shared by its commandant and an Indian agent. The army stronghold that became Fort Snelling was commanded by a series of officers. But one man, Lawrence Taliaferro, remained here as ambassador to the Indians for twenty years. Throughout that period Taliaferro and his Fort Snelling colleagues were pitted against unscrupulous fur traders.

Surrounded by warring tribesmen, Fort Snelling guarded the frontier when it stopped at the Mississippi. When the West moved on toward the mountains, Snelling continued as the river's most northerly sentinel. Here Zachary Taylor commanded, John Charles Frémont began to learn his trade, George Catlin and Seth Eastman recorded the savage life on canvas. But the roles of such men were minor. There were others, some heroes, some villains: Henry Leavenworth, Josiah Snelling, Kenneth Mackenzie, Ramsay Crooks, "King" Rolette, Henry Hastings Sibley, and Taliaferro perhaps most of all.

This book attempts to reconstruct the story of these early men of the West and of the fort which for some of them was the center of the wilderness. Such a focal point it was for Lawrence Taliaferro, and the story could not be told at all were it not for the journals and papers left by this singular Indian agent. He was far removed from the prototype of Indian bureau representatives in the West that followed his retirement. Even in the days when Indian agents were expected to be men of honor, he was outstanding. He was, in the simplest sense, a friend of Indians. Most of all, in the terms of this narrative, he was there—he knew more about the continuing life at Fort Snelling than anyone else. Through the legacy of his often irascible observations there is a chance to shed new light on a neglected frontier sector and on its citadel hub in the era when Louisiana Territory was newly joined to the Old Northwest. But the full story of Fort Snelling began long before the arrival of Lawrence Taliaferro and his contemporaries.

CITADEL IN THE WILDERNESS

CHAPTER ONE

——————•◦•——————

RIVER TRAVELERS

ON AUGUST 9, 1805, Lieutenant Zebulon Montgomery Pike embarked from the United States Army post near St. Louis, and on September 4 his detachment of twenty soldiers had sailed and poled their seventy-foot keelboat as far north as the Wisconsin River; there they paused at the French village of Prairie du Chien, the most northerly point of civilization in the Mississippi Valley. Seventeen days later Pike and his men had moved two hundred miles farther into the wilderness to the forty-fifth parallel and they pitched their tents on the northeast corner of the island at the mouth of the St. Peter's River.

"You will..." said the orders carried by the twenty-six-year-old lieutenant, "obtain permission from the Indians who claim the ground, for the erection of military posts and trading houses at the mouth of the river St. Pierre [the St. Peter's and later the Minnesota]... and every other critical point...." Pike had been sent north to pursue the Mississippi to its source and to notify the Sioux and Chippewas of the American determination to assume control of the newly acquired Louisiana Purchase. Not twenty-four hours after their island bivouac had been staked out, Pike and his men were doing business. On their second day, at the sound of shots, they looked up at the high promontory rising above the two rivers and saw the Sioux chief, Little Crow, and a hundred and fifty warriors firing in salute. On Monday, September 23, at high noon under a canopy of sailcloth, Pike and the Sioux leaders signed a pact which resulted—more than a dozen years later—in the erection of a great stone fortress which was to keep the Indians at bay for forty years.

17

". . . the Sioux nation," Pike's treaty read, "grants, unto the United States, for the purpose of establishment of military posts, nine miles square . . . from below the confluence of the Mississippi and St. Peters up the Mississippi to include the falls of St. Anthony . . . [and] the Sioux nation grants to the United States the full sovereignty and power over said district for ever. . . .

"The United States promise, on their part, to permit the Sioux to pass and repass, hunt, to make other use of said districts as they have formerly done without any further exception than those specified."

The future fort was intended to benefit the Sioux, Pike told his silent audience. He stressed that it was the intention of the United States to establish trading posts at which "the Indians may procure all their things at cheaper and better rate than they do now, or than your [British] traders can afford to sell them to you, as they are single men, who come far in small boats. But your [new] fathers," said Pike, "are many and strong, and will come with a strong arm, in large boats." He added that he thought "the traders who come from Canada are bad birds" because they instigated the Chippewas to fight the Sioux of the St. Peter's.

Who the first such culprit among the traders may have been is not recorded. Nor does anyone know what white man first stood on that promontory which rises where the forty-fifth parallel crosses the Upper Mississippi. Almost certainly he was a Frenchman, for in 1689 Nicolas Perrot, acting for Louis XIV, took formal possession of the Sioux country and specified the junction of the big river with that of the St. Peter's by name. A decade later one of Perrot's henchmen sailed into the entry beneath the high bluff to build a log trading post farther up the St. Peter's, and the French continued to hold sway over the Sioux and the Chippewas for two-thirds of a century. Their defeat in the French and Indian War made the Montreal fur trade British, and hence the tribes of the Upper Mississippi then pledged tacit allegiance to the English king. But the land itself—west of the river to the Rocky Mountains—was alternately claimed by Spain

18

and France until Thomas Jefferson manipulated his dramatic purchase.

Louisiana, the vast wilderness drained by the Missouri and its tributaries, had been made American without a shot fired in anger. On November 30, 1803, Spain returned to France control of the domain the Spanish government secretly had ceded to Napoleon three years before. Three weeks later, December 20, colonial officials in New Orleans transferred Lower Louisiana to the United States. And finally, early in March, 1804, the Spanish and French flags in St. Louis were hauled down in the presence of Jefferson's personal representative, Captain Meriwether Lewis. The Stars and Stripes was officially raised for the first time in the new American West, and the change was immediately announced to Indians called to council.

"Your old Fathers, the Spaniard and the Frenchman," a Spanish official told the gathered tribesmen, "grasp by the hand your new Father, the head chief of the United States. By an act of their good will, and in virtue of their last treaty, I have delivered up to them all these lands. They will keep them and defend them and protect all the white and red skins who live thereon. . . ."

What the land contained, besides redskins, was only vaguely known to Jefferson and his administration, and the President had been plotting its exploration for a long time. Every scrap of knowledge about the new domain was sought by Jefferson. In the fall of 1803 he suggested to Congressmen the possibility of expeditions to the Missouri, Mississippi and St. Peter's rivers. The following spring he sent Meriwether Lewis and William Clark up the Missouri to find a water route to the Pacific; he dispatched his accomplished scientific correspondent, William Dunbar, into the Arkansas country. And Zebulon Pike was ordered north from St. Louis.

Pike found the site he had selected for fortification still marked by hostile Chippewas and Sioux, visited seasonally by voyageurs from Montreal, by Britons who poached unchecked on the northern lands of Louisiana. In 1805—part of Jefferson's magnificent acquisition though it was—that site was English in point of occupation. Men of the Hudson's Bay and North West fur companies still spread their claim on the Indian trade westward from Lake Michigan to the Missouri and beyond. Many such traders passed the site as they plied their trade with the Sioux trappers, who were recognized by some veterans of the West as "the greatest beaver hunters."

To please the hunters at his treaty gathering in the fall of 1805, young Lieutenant Pike issued a couple of hundred dollars' worth of trade goods before the St. Peter's meeting broke up. But, according to the recollection of a veteran trader, the young American failed to charm fully at least one of the Indian delegates. The next morning, after a rainstorm had thrashed through Pike's camp, a Sioux headman named Red Whale heard a rumpus among the soldiers and went to see what it was about. "He found a man tied to a tree, ready to be scored," the trader remembered, "and the Indian was told by the American commander [Pike] that the man had lost the flag and must be flogged."

Red Whale protested, said the trader, and asserted the American banner must have been blown away by the storm through no fault of the sentry. And when Pike remained adamant, insisting the soldier must be punished, Red Whale was worked up enough to pull his knife. "I'll stick the first one that strips that soldier!" he cried. He told Pike it was really his fault, that the storm had been so black a man couldn't see the length of an arrow. Anyone might have let the flag get away, Red Whale said, and again blamed the commander: "You knew the wind was strong enough to tear it to pieces, and you should have taken it into your tent."

According to the trader, Pike gave in to Red Whale temporarily, but when the Indian left, the unlucky soldier was again tied up and a new rumpus ensued among his fellows. This brought Red Whale back shouting, "White man's blood must not stain my land," the trader recalled. "Young man!" the Indian went on, "my name is Red Whale. I know all that happens for many a day's journey around me. It was your fault, and not the soldier's, that your flag floated down the river. Now I warn you, if you hurt this man during the Winter, I will make a hole in your coat when you come back in the Spring."

Pike's own version of the affair was briefer. He wrote tersely in his journal that the sentry was duly flogged, and he made no mention of Red Whale. It was not like him to confess his own ineptitudes—nor, perhaps, to take seriously the concern of an Indian for a white soldier's welfare.

Still, the story may illustrate Pike's inability to recognize that his rapport with Indians was minimal. For, though he had received the Sioux concession of land on which to build a fort, he failed to carry out one of his most important objectives—not a single Indian chief agreed to accompany him for a council in St. Louis. Yet he convinced himself that he had been very persuasive: "If a subaltern with but 20 men, at so great a distance from the seat of his government," he said in his journal, "could effect so important a change in the minds of those savages, what might not a great and independent power effect, if, instead of blowing up the flames of discord, they exerted their influence in the sacred cause of peace?" More to the point is the fact that Pike himself—not sufficiently wary of Dickson's hold on the natives—exerted no influence. After his departure the very Indians he had visited remained loyal to their British traders and eagerly joined the English forces in the War of 1812.

Nevertheless, Pike had worked hard that winter. From the site of future Fort Snelling he had traveled north by canoe and sled to erect a stockade near Swan River, not far from present-day Little Falls, Minnesota. Having thus secured himself in what might turn out to be hostile country, he said that "had it not been for various political reasons, I would have laughed at the attack of eight hundred or a thousand savages, if my party were within." The truth was that then, as always, he had more reason to be wary of the wiles of alien white men.

A month after he settled down in his stockade Pike had been visited by two Indians who reported that a British trader, Robert Dickson, was busy prejudicing the Sioux with whom Pike had met. Dickson was said to have offered the Indians on the St. Peter's as much liquor as they wanted if they would do all their trading with him. Pike reacted to this with more vanity than sense of mission. Dickson's deed seemed to him to have "self-

interest and envy for its motives; for, by the idea of having prevented liquor from going up the St. Peter's, he gave the Indians
to understand that it was a regulation of my own, and not a law
of the United States; and by assuring them he would sell to them
on the Mississippi, he drew all the Indians from the traders on
the St. Peter's, who had adhered to the restriction of not selling
liquor, and should any of them be killed, the blame would all lie
on me. . . ."

Dickson was also said to be encouraging the feud between
Sioux and Chippewa, which Pike was duty bound to eliminate if
he could. But Dickson turned up in person a few days later and
suavely denied any animosity toward Americans. In fact Pike
wrote, "He gave me many assurances for the prosperity of my
undertaking." Somewhat naïvely, the young lieutenant was "induced to believe" Dickson's protestations of good faith—in the
same way other Americans were to be hoodwinked by this trader.
Although he was to remain a British partisan even after the end
of the War of 1812, Dickson found it easy to acquire an American trading license in 1807. He got it by persuading Frederick
Bates, then Meriwether Lewis' deputy as governor in St. Louis,
that he was a "man of honour" who could be counted on to
cooperate. "I greatly rely on Mr. Dickson," Bates wrote Lewis
in Washington. "By him we shall be correctly informed of whatever passes among the Sioux. . . . He will do whatever we may
reasonably desire of him, and return to St. Louis with intelligence when necessary. He has been our friend, uniformly, and
his deportment and professions when this singular indulgence
was conceded him, convince me that he will cooperate most
heartily in all our Indian measures." But the evidence seems
clear that Dickson for years remained consistently loyal to his
British homeland and did as much as anyone to turn the left flank
of the War of 1812 into an Indian war.

For young Lieutenant Pike, Dickson was only one of a number of Mississippi Valley traders who slyly pretended to cooperate
with him while continuing to send their furs to the North West
Company and other foreign enterprises. During his winter on the
Mississippi, Pike found the flag of Great Britain flying over the

trading post of the Nor'Wester, Cuthbert Grant, at Sandy Lake. *"I felt indignant,"* he wrote, underlining the words, *"and cannot say what my feelings would have excited me to, had he not informed me that it belonged to the Indians.* This was not much more agreeable to me."

He was moved, however, to more determined action in the future. The next time he found the Union Jack aloft, Pike shot it down even though the man in charge of the post treated him, he said, "with marked attention and hospitality." This time his host was another North West Company partner, Hugh McGillis, who gave him "a good dish of coffee, biscuit, butter, and cheese for supper." McGillis was director of his company's "Department of Fond du Lac"; he had headquarters at Leech Lake and one hundred and nine men spread out over the northern region of what is now Minnesota. The furs for which these men traded with the Chippewas were carried to Canada without passing a customshouse, a fact which caused the United States an annual loss of $26,000 in duties, according to Pike's estimate.

Still McGillis' guest, the American officer reached for his pen and wrote down the terms under which his country would permit foreigners to continue trading in U. S. territory: no more flying of the British flag, no more distribution of medals, flags, or liquor to the Indians, no more bypassing of the customshouse at Mackinac at the straits between Lakes Michigan and Huron. Tongue in cheek, McGillis agreed in writing to all conditions; he carried his pretense to the point of accompanying Pike in the search for the Mississippi's source, which the lieutenant placed in the body of water now called Cass Lake. But McGillis did not tell Pike what by then may have been known to many seasoned traders of the region—that the principal source was miles away in the wishbone-shaped pond which later was named Lake Itasca. And Pike missed an encounter with another trader who might have helped him. For, fifty years after Pike's expedition, a Canadian named William Morrison claimed that as early as 1804 he had discovered the Mississippi's source to be Itasca, "and if General Pike did not lay it down as such . . . it is because he did not happen to meet me." Morrison also maintained in his mellow old age that Pike "had been told that I knew the source," and that only his own absence on a trading expedition prevented a get-together with the American explorer.

It seems likely that the passage of time caused Morrison to remember himself as more cooperative in 1806 than he and his fellows really were. Traders from Canada were then far from ready to recognize any American territorial claims in more than token terms. McGillis and Grant went right back to their old ways as soon as Pike was out of sight. Robert Dickson, however, was wary of the implications behind the American expedition, and he followed Pike downriver to St. Louis. Just how serious was the possibility of United States control being established on the upper river? Not very, it seemed to Dickson. His Scottish partner James Aird had been licensed by the Americans to continue their trade on the Missouri. Before that summer was over, Aird was back on his old trading grounds and was being hailed by the returning Lewis and Clark as the first informed white man the explorers had seen in two years. Three weeks later Will Clark wrote in his journal that he and Lewis "were very politely received by two young Scotch men from Canada"—two *engagés* of Robert Dickson & Company, James Reed and Ramsay Crooks. The latter was then learning the trade of which he was to become a master and which would make his a formidable name at the confluence of the St. Peter's and the Mississippi rivers.

Yet in 1806, Crooks was only one of many Dickson employees whose sphere of action stretched from the Great Lakes to the Plains country and whose British loyalties irked American fur traders. In the wake of the Lewis and Clark and the Pike explorations rumors of British activities flew up and down the Mississippi and the Missouri. A year after Pike's Minnesota expedition there were reports that the British were urging the Upper Mississippi Sioux to attack St. Louis. In July of that year Colonel Thomas Hunt, commanding the Missouri garrison at Bellefontaine, was warned that tribes from the Great Lakes and the Mississippi and Missouri valleys were forming an alliance against the Americans. In Louisville William Clark, now Superintendent of Indian Affairs, heard rumors that tribesmen with whom he and Lewis had parleyed less than two years before were on the warpath.

Tensions ebbed, rose, then ebbed again. There was no reason to question the reports of unrest among the Indians—nor the fact that many tribes were supplied with British hunting weapons. Lewis, in his capacity as governor of Upper Louisiana, repeatedly asked the army's help in policing the frontier. But Jefferson was loath to resort to force. "Commerce," he said, "is the great engine by which we are to coerce them, and not war."

Lewis received even less support from Jefferson's successor James Madison, and after the explorer's tragic and mysterious death in 1809 the situation became alarming. The Indians whom Pike had left behind remained subject to the devices of Robert Dickson and his British colleagues. At the same time, the Shawnee chief, Tecumseh, and his brother who was called the Prophet continued their efforts to unite many tribes against American injustice. In these years of unrest before the War of 1812, according to one trader, "the Prophet was the instrument, and the British traders the soul."

In 1811, while Tecumseh was away enlisting the support of southern tribes, the Prophet, at Tippecanoe Creek, attacked an American punitive force organized by William Henry Harrison, then governor of Indiana Territory. Although frontiersmen exaggerated the brief battle as a great victory, the encounter served chiefly to reinforce Indian ties with the British. In the conflict to come, followers of Tecumseh and the Prophet, along with the war-loving Sioux of the Upper Mississippi, fought side by side with British troops. The official reasons for America's second war with Great Britain centered on violations of maritime rights. But on the frontier that war was welcomed as the long-delayed opportunity to restrain permanently foreign traders in United States territory. The War of 1812 did not end that effort, nor did it eliminate the need for a military post at the St. Peter's junction with the Mississippi.

CHAPTER TWO

THE NAMELESS WAR

BRITISH TRADERS like Robert Dickson also welcomed the possibility of formal conflict. Their activities were sufficiently open that Governor Harrison had long been unshakable in his suspicion of British support of Tecumseh and his brother. While Dickson and others continued to court the northern tribes, Harrison had been stabbing in many directions, trying to counteract the mounting independence among the tribes in his sprawling Indiana Territory. As early as 1806 he had been as wary of the Prophet's exhortations as he was of Tecumseh's political skill. "If he really is a prophet," Harrison had said condescendingly to the natives in 1806, "ask him to cause the sun to stand still, the moon to alter its course, the rivers to cease to flow, or the dead to rise from their graves."

The Prophet responded immediately by proclaiming that on June 16 he would cause the sun to darken. He sent out a call for a gathering of tribesmen from miles around, and on the appointed date he appeared in midmorning before an assembled multitude. He was dressed in a long, dark robe and wore a crest of outspread raven's wings upon his head. Exactly at 11:32 A.M. he pointed at the sun and asked the Great Spirit to blot its light. As he did so the moon could be seen slipping slowly across the face of the sun. The astonished Indians watched while the sky turned from gray to black and the birds went to roost and animals lay down as if at twilight. Precisely as the phenomenal moment was about to end, the Prophet called again to the Great Spirit and asked for the return of light. The awestricken audience saw his request granted, and the news of the Prophet's magic flashed like prairie fire throughout the Mississippi Valley tribes. Just as swiftly, among whites who were as convinced as Harrison of British chicanery, there spread the rumor that Canadians had given the Prophet advance word of the solar eclipse that was so important it brought Harvard scientists to the Illinois country and government observers to the Upper Mississippi. Forgetting that this scholarly activity was hardly secret, warmongers —whose sights were set on wresting all of Canada from the British—found it easy to believe that no Indian could have made use of such a natural phenomenon had not the script for the Prophet's performance been written by enemies of a frontier that was by divine right American. It was decades early for the coining of the phrase "Manifest Destiny," but the spirit had risen. As early as 1803 the *New York Evening Post* had trumpeted that the "destiny of *North America*" belonged by right to the United States: "The country is *ours,* ours is the right to the rivers and to all the sources of future opulence, power and happiness. . . ." By 1812 Henry Clay as chief of the War Hawks had made no bones of it. "The conquest of Canada is in your power," he said to Congress; and a colleague added that "the Author of Nature [had] marked our limits in the south, by the Gulf of Mexico; and on the north by the regions of eternal frost."

In that north Robert Dickson and his fellows saw things differently. Jay's Treaty of 1794 had required the abandonment of British military establishments south of the Great Lakes, but it had accepted the Canadian demand for free commerce below a border that would not be firmly fixed for years to come. Some Canadians who were less than realistic still hoped that American settlement could be forced to contain itself south of the Ohio River; more pragmatic minds supported a plan for an Indian buffer state dividing the United States and Canada yet maintaining free trade. The British fur men, like Dickson, looked askance at settlement, Canadian *or* American, and they supported the Indian claims to the land, justifying their own presence among the natives as suppliers of goods who had no intention of interfering with ancient freedoms.

Tecumseh's ceaseless efforts to confederate the tribes and the Prophet's appeal to the dormant Indian spirit of independence were in line with the designs of the northern traders. In the years before the 1811 clash near Tippecanoe Creek the brothers had traveled the Mississippi Valley, crisscrossed Wisconsin, and had sent out emissaries with blackened bodies throughout Minnesota. Tribe after tribe agreed to join in resisting the encroachment of Americans hungry for land. Worried about British domination of Mississippi headwaters, Will Clark in St. Louis was convinced that Tecumseh's influence would prevail with the Kickapoos, the Potawatomis, the Sacs and the Sioux. Worried about foreign traders, the Indian agent at Prairie du Chien requested two infantry companies and urged that Indians be encouraged to develop Mississippi Valley lead mines "to make them depend on the U. S. instead of the British and Canadians." Governor Benjamin Howard of Missouri Territory wrote the Secretary of War that the fortification of Prairie du Chien was "indispensable to hold the British traders in check."

Robert Dickson, who may well have been more accepted by the Northwest natives than any man of his time, assured Canadian authorities that they now had the means of "retaining and supporting all the Indian tribes in their present happy disposition so favourable to the interests of Britain." Six feet tall, rugged and redheaded, Dickson had spent more trading seasons in the country west of the Great Lakes than anybody then on the scene, and if there was one man who could judge the Indian disposition it was he. Arriving from Scotland in his teens, Dickson began to learn Indian dialects in Canada and around Lake Erie, and in July, 1787, he had traveled as far west as Mackinac. There for a dollar a day he served as interpreter when (in spite of the British loss of the Revolutionary War) chiefs of the Menominees, Winnebagos and five bands of Sioux from the mouth of the St. Peter's acknowledged George III as their ruler. He liked the Sioux and they liked him. He turned in his pay for trade goods and spent that winter at the junction of the Mississippi and the St. Peter's bartering for furs.

That spot became the center of Dickson's world and he widened its perimeters in ever enlarging circles. He was equally at home in a tepee on the Missouri, at council fires on the Maumee and the Wabash, with the Chippewas among the pines at the head of Lake Superior, in a governor's mansion in St. Louis, with the British army on the Aux Canards, or among the fur tycoons in the Beaver Club in Montreal. He married a sister of the Yankton chief Red Thunder and built a home on Lake Traverse. In fact, he lived like many a man on every other frontier, the difference lying in the degree of his scope. He was at various times the founder and president of Robert Dickson & Co., a partner in John Jacob Astor's South West Co., and an agent for Lord Selkirk and the Hudson's Bay Co. Traders like Dickson, said one of his contemporaries, "were then the aristocrats of the country. . . . To see gentlemen selecting wives of the nut-brown natives, and raising children of mixed blood . . . in as much luxury as the resources of the country would admit" was the way of the world of the men who knew Indians as well as Robert Dickson did.

After the American government outlawed the importation of foreign goods in 1811, Dickson and several other traders loaded their canoes in Canada with $50,000 worth of merchandise, slipped past Mackinac Island and took the Fox-Wisconsin route to Prairie du Chien where hundreds of destitute Sioux, Winnebago and Menominee Indians had gathered. The natives had been told of the new American law that banned the British goods they coveted, and they hailed Dickson's smugglers as heroes. Once more Dickson had proved himself their friend, and once more United States authorities were made to seem impotent. The American agent at Prairie du Chien reported the law-breakers to Will Clark in St. Louis, but Clark lacked the military strength to police a region so far from headquarters. Dickson stretched his muscles. He went up the Mississippi to the site of the future Fort Snelling and supplied a hundred Sioux lodges with much-needed gunpowder. A few months later, in February, 1812, he was asked by Canada's Lieutenant Governor-General Isaac Brock to formally enlist the northern tribes as allies for the coming conflict.

Congress declared war on England on June 19, 1812. Before this news had reached them these two men had met to plan strategy for Indian participation, and soon thereafter Dickson sent to Brock his first detachment of savage warriors "to take part in every engagement." He dispatched his St. Peter's expert Joseph Renville (who had served Pike as an interpreter) to round up Sioux from the prairies. At the mouth of the St. Peter's he had no trouble enlisting Chief Little Crow on the basis that $2,000 voted by Congress in payment for Pike's St. Peter's treaty had never been delivered. Then with Renville's conscriptees, and with the addition of followers of the Mississippi chief Wabasha, Dickson and Little Crow led the Sioux to Mackinac in time to surprise the commander of that American garrison before he had received notice that the United States was at war. The Americans surrendered without firing a shot.

Bloodless victory, quite naturally, was not to the liking of the Indian delegation, and the natives' howl for action was quieted only after Dickson released a herd of cattle to be chased and slaughtered. Frustrated or not by the lack of scalps, the tribes were convinced by the fall of Mackinac that they were on the winning side; and by the time the leaves began to turn in that autumn of 1812 almost fifteen hundred warriors arrived at the straits to do Dickson's bidding.

Even more consequential was the effect that the easy British conquest at Mackinac had on General William Hull, at the head of the hastily mustered U. S. forces in Detroit. Commanding Hull's Indian opponents was Tecumseh, seizing his last chance to win back the land of his people from American settlers. With him was the Sac war chief Black Hawk, who had become a Tecumseh disciple in 1808 and who had been told by Dickson, "If you do not immediately strike upon the Americans I will turn all the other Indians against you and strike you to the ground." It seems doubtful in retrospect that as dedicated an anti-settler as Black Hawk needed such a threat to cause him to act, yet no matter what his price for participation he was in the thick of things when the fighting against Hull got under way, and he was one of several who later maintained they had seen Tecumseh killed.

Black Hawk, Tecumseh and their followers were already at Detroit when Hull arrived to dawdle away two weeks instead of immediately assaulting Fort Malden on the Canadian side. The American commander was still ignoring his lieutenants' clamor for action when news arrived on July 21 that Mackinac had fallen the previous week. What little courage Hull had left vanished. He pulled back his detachments which had clashed with Indians under Tecumseh, sent an expedition to make an aborted effort to join advancing reinforcements, and stalled. When Brock, commanding the British, paraded his Indians in a continuous fashion to exaggerate their actual numbers, Hull refused to heed his subordinates' demand for battle and had a white flag run up over Fort Detroit. The gathered Northwest Indians thus brought about the only instance of a United States city surrendering abjectly to an invader.

Hull's lack of appetite for matching arms with Indians served to encourage the natives generally and to increase the number of Dickson's recruits. In the following spring of 1813, after a flying visit to the St. Peter's, he and Renville led the Sioux and allied tribes into the Ohio country to join Tecumseh in the unsuccessful sieges of Fort Meigs in May and August. To discourage more Indians from following Dickson, William Clark that summer shipped Sac, Fox and Iowa women and children by boat from the Mississippi to the Upper Missouri and marched their men west across the prairie; thus he prevented, he told the Secretary of War, "nearly 1000 warriors from joining the British party." The settlements of Missouri Territory were deeply affected by Dickson's activity and the fall of Detroit, and Governor Howard believed his frontier was exposed "not only to injury but to total overthrow." When Fort Madison on the Des Moines, the only Mississippi fort north of St. Louis, was forced in September to evacuate in the face of a Winnebago attack, Howard's conviction seemed almost proved. Even the signal October events—the victory of Harrison and the death of Tecumseh on the river Thames —failed to secure the Upper Mississippi. Dickson's Indians and the British still held Mackinac, and the cries for an American expedition up the Mississippi were increasing.

With battles going against them on the Eastern Great Lakes the British began to worry about the West. Sir George Prevost wrote Lord Bathurst that Dickson's Indians on the Mississippi were the only barrier between the Canadian fur traders and the Americans. Should that barrier be destroyed, he said, the Yankees would push up the Red River of the North and execute "their long formed project of monopolizing the whole Fur Trade into their own hands." Prevost also told Bathurst that most Indians would have been lost to the British were it not for the "judicious, resolute, and determined conduct of Mr. Dickson." Intent upon maintaining his record, Dickson got even busier in 1814.

William Clark notified the War Department that Dickson was at Prairie du Chien raising a large force against Missouri Territory. When such an attack might come, he promised, the Mississippi must be defended "from its source to its mouth," and he launched a plan to do something about it at last. He built a flotilla, the largest boat holding one hundred men in addition to the oarsmen, and in June shoved off for Prairie du Chien "to frustrate the plans of Mr. Dickson"; it was an expedition the *Missouri Gazette* termed "more important to these territories than any hitherto undertaken." To the readers of the eastern seaboard, *Niles' Weekly Register* reported: "A military expedition, of about 200 men in five barges, under the command of gov. Clark, left St. Louis on the 1st of May, for Prairie du Chien, supposed with a view of building a fort there and making a station to keep in check the Sioux, Winnebago and [Menominee] indians, lately stirred up to hostility by the infamous British agent, Dickson."

Arriving at the Prairie, Clark found that Dickson had departed three weeks ahead of him, not for St. Louis but to once more reinforce Mackinac in order to keep the Canadian fur trade open. The fur headquarters on the Wisconsin River was taken over by Clark's men, and they threw up a log structure they called Fort Shelby, left it in care of Lieutenant Joseph Perkins and sixty soldiers, and returned with the governor to St. Louis.

But within a month Dickson's authority was reestablished. Cooperating with the British commander at Mackinac, he sent a party of traders and voyageurs along the Fox-Wisconsin route, and after a three-day siege, as Perkins' ammunition and water began to fail, Fort Shelby was surrendered. The *Missouri Gazette's* boast that Clark's expedition to Prairie du Chien had "cleansed it of British spies and traitors" was short lived.

Dickson's Indians continued to control the Mississippi in spite of Will Clark's promise to the War Department to make the river American and keep it that way, even above Dickson's old stamping grounds at the junction with the St. Peter's. No sooner had Lieutenant Perkins surrendered than Black Hawk, back at his headquarters near Rock Island, ambushed a U. S. Army detachment belatedly ordered to reinforce Perkins. A month later Black Hawk, with the aid of the British, took on Zachary Taylor who had been sent to punish him; Taylor limped home to St. Louis with his gunboats perforated by British and Indian missiles. In typical frontier fashion, the war was not limited to such head-on engagements. Traders like Dickson encouraged the Indians at all kinds of mayhem and various kinds of harassment.

Dickson symbolized the British determination to maintain their hold on the fur trade country west of the Great Lakes. Fort Shelby (renamed Fort McKay), whose capture he had engineered, remained a British redoubt until May, 1815, six months after the signing of the Treaty of Ghent ended the War of 1812. Dickson, in effect, never surrendered. He lined himself up with the Earl of Selkirk, who had acquired control of the Hudson's Bay Company as a means to support a utopian colony in the Red River Valley. And he weighted his threat to American interests when he encouraged Selkirk's hope that the entire valley, which cuts deep into United States territory, could be held as a British enclave.

Official reports said that Dickson had been directed to fortify the high ground which narrowly separates the St. Peter's and the Red. He was said to be "sharpening the savage scalping knife," luring the Sioux of the St. Peter's to join in the new grab for American land. As late as 1818, army officers declared that "the military force in this country is too small to keep Dickson and his emissaries in check. . . ." They made the point that there had been too much delay in garrisoning the Upper Mississippi so as "to awe the establishment of Lord Selkirk [and others] into proper respect for our laws." Thus a new reason for the realization of a St. Peter's fort was established. For on this unprotected frontier the war that had so little justification that it never found an adequate name had so alienated Indians and their ancient traders that a prolonged armed truce seemed the best possible forecast.

CHAPTER THREE

NATURE'S RAMPART

THE TRUCE was soon stretched close to the breaking point. To protect the interests of American citizens, Congress passed the Act of 1816, which banned foreigners from trade on American soil. Within six months, however, the Hudson's Bay and North West companies not only were still operating south of Canada, but "on the headwaters of the Mississippi" a fur post supplied by John Jacob Astor was assaulted by Hudson's Bay men who imprisoned an Astor partner and two of his clerks, confiscating trade goods "amounting to the value of Several Thousand pounds." Astor, whose influence in Washington had been in ascendancy since the days of the Jefferson administration, interpreted the incident as so great an insult that he wrote to James Monroe, Secretary of State, urging that a military expedition be dispatched to seize merchandise that Hudson's Bay had brought illegally into the United States.

No action was taken on Astor's demand, for military authorities were proceeding according to earlier plans to block British use of the Mississippi and the other water routes from St. Anthony Falls to Mackinac. While troops of the Third Infantry settled in at Green Bay and Prairie du Chien, the two terminals of the decades-old Fox-Wisconsin artery, infantrymen of the Eighth Regiment moved up the Mississippi to Rock Island; Fort Dearborn was reestablished at the head of Lake Michigan. From St. Louis, Major Stephen H. Long, a veteran topographical engineer, was ordered north to assess the Fox-Wisconsin portage and the St. Peter's promontory which Pike a dozen years before had recommended for the site of a fort. On this summer journey in

1817 Long noted the blockhouses and picket palisades going up at Fort Edwards on the Des Moines River and at Fort Armstrong on the Rock. At Prairie du Chien, in the shadow of Fort Crawford, he set down his impressions of the Mississippi's most northerly white settlement:

"Exclusive of stores, workshops, and stables, the village at present contains only sixteen dwelling houses occupied by families. These are situated on a street parallel with the river, and about one half mile in length. In the rear of the village, at a distance of three quarters of a mile, are four others. Two and a half miles above are five; and at the upper end of the prairie, five miles from the village, are four dwelling houses. Besides these, there are several houses situated upon different parts of the prairie, in all not exceeding seven or eight; so that the whole number of family dwellings, now occupied, does not exceed thirty-eight. The buildings are generally of logs, plastered with mud or clay; some of them comfortable habitations, but none of them exhibit any display of elegance or taste. The inhabitants are principally of French and Indian extraction. There are very few of them that have not savage blood in their veins."

Retired voyageurs who had worked for British traders after the end of the French regime, most of these Prairie du Chien villagers (wallowing, as Long wrote, in "unconquerable slothfulness and want of enterprise"), had welcomed the arrival of an American garrison with tongue in cheek. Gallic or Indian though their blood might be, they had become English sympathizers and they would not easily give up that long-established loyalty until the strength of the new American frontier posts should be proved.

As Stephen Long described Fort Crawford while it was being erected, it was a typical western outpost. "The work," he said, "is a square of three hundred and forty feet upon each side . . . constructed entirely of wood, as are all its buildings, except the magazine, which is of stone. It will accommodate five companies of soldiers." Two blockhouses, two stories high, "with cupolas or turrets upon their tops," occupied the northwest and southeast corners of the fort, and the palisade wall rose twenty feet from the ground, "thus presenting," said Major Long, "an in-

36

surmountable barrier to an assailing enemy." Yet he had nothing but criticism for the military value of Fort Crawford's location. "No complete command of the river can be had here," he reported, and emphasized that an adjacent valley afforded such protection for attackers that an enemy could approach "completely under cover and secure from the guns of the fort." Command of the river was all-important to a military engineer like Long, and he found it when he sailed up the Mississippi and into the mouth of the St. Peter's in his six-oared skiff. Here he inspected the promontory on which Pike had met the Sioux more than ten years earlier. On this "high point of land, elevated about one hundred and twenty feet above the water," he foresaw in a prosaic phrase the architecture of the future, "a military work of considerable magnitude . . . to control the navigation of the two rivers." Six years later, when Long returned at the head of an expedition to study the Canadian boundary, that magnitude was a reality.

Meanwhile even as Long recorded on July 9, 1817, that there was "little or no danger to be apprehended from the Indians living on the Mississippi above Prairie du Chien," the need for a fort at the St. Peter's entry was underscored not only by the continuing traffic between the tribes and the British but by an increase of native warfare. As Indiana became a state in 1816 and Illinois followed two years later, more and more settlers' cabins encroached upon the hunting grounds of the Sacs and Foxes, pushing these allied tribes northward. The St. Peter's Sioux resisted these intruders, adding a second front to their age-old war with the Chippewas. A major retaliation came from the Sacs and Foxes in the summer of 1817, and they were no mean opponents, for their capital, Saukenuk, was, in Long's words, "by far the largest Indian village situated in the neighborhood of the Mississippi between St. Louis and the Falls of St. Anthony." Long emphasized Saukenuk's strength by pointing out that this single community, in which Black Hawk lived, could "furnish eight or nine hundred warriors, all of them armed with rifles or fusees [flintlocks]." Holding these combat-ready Sacs and Foxes thereafter in check became the responsibility of Fort

Armstrong and Fort Crawford; effective policing of the Sioux-Chippewa battleground made necessary the erection of a stronghold on the St. Peter's.

One other reason made the fortification of the St. Peter's entry important—the river's source lies within a mile of the Red River Valley. One of the easiest portages anywhere could be made to the St. Peter's from the Bois de Sioux River, the most southerly tributary of the Red. Thus a water route, flowing past Lord Selkirk's burgeoning colony, was something to ponder; its northern leg, the Nelson River, empties into Hudson Bay, and Selkirk had used this route to bring transatlantic immigrants to the interior. No formal military invasion seemed likely after the War of 1812, but the concern over the incursions of Red River traders like Dickson remained unabated.

Meanwhile, competition between the North West Company and Selkirk's Hudson's Bay fur men had been growing more and more intense. The situation was further complicated by the increase in the number of Selkirk colonists in one of the regions most coveted by the northern fur trade generally. A series of clashes culminated in July, 1816, when North West winterers and half-breeds killed twenty-two settlers while Selkirk himself was leading a hundred armed followers on his first trip to his new domain. Hearing the news and swearing vengeance, Selkirk took his men along the north shore of Lake Superior to attack and capture Fort William, the Nor'Westers' great rendezvous on Thunder Bay. Then he sent scouts southwest into American territory to seize William Morrison and three other traders who recently had signed contracts with Ramsay Crooks, now in charge of American Fur Company operations. The angry earl would not believe that his prisoners had severed connections with North West, and he ignored their protestations that his man had accosted them on United States soil; the boundaries, said Selkirk, had not been agreed upon. Morrison and a companion managed to escape and to make their way back to the Mississippi headwaters, but Selkirk men continued to harass American traders even after the return of their leader to London. In 1819 Morrison reported to Crooks that three Selkirkers had come south of the forty-ninth parallel to the American Fur Company post on the Red River; there they had called United States Indians to council and promised them whiskey if they would bring their furs to Hudson's Bay traders. Robert Dickson had tried to persuade Wisconsin traders to move themselves and the fur-trapping Menominee Indians to the Selkirk colony. And Dickson's wartime deputy, Duncan Graham, had done his best to lure the Indians of the St. Peter's.

Hudson's Bay had not yet licked the North West Company, and so it was not alone in its struggle with American traders. Nor'Westers had taken over Astor's interests in Oregon during the war, and in 1818 they started their move inland from the mouth of the Columbia by building Fort Nez Percé at the Walla Walla fork. Thus British fur men were encroaching on the Louisiana Territory in a pincer movement, and United States forts— as earnests of the American intent to hold the frontiers—became a matter no longer to be delayed. John C. Calhoun was the man who did something about that situation. A native frontiersman, a leader of the Congressional War Hawks who had brought about the second clash with England, he took over the War Department when James Monroe became President, and by 1818 he had a workable plan to secure the headwaters of the Mississippi and the Missouri as well. In projecting forts on each of these rivers, Calhoun had devised a two-pronged thrust at restraining restless Indians and poaching Britons, and his scheme caught the fancy of newspaper readers from St. Louis to the Atlantic. The western thrust—to the Yellowstone fork of the Missouri where Lewis and Clark had debated their views about the location of a fort—quite naturally got the loudest cheers from expansionist citizens. Chauvinistic ardor was high-pitched as the Missouri expedition under General Henry Atkinson, including a scientific party led by Stephen Long, fumbled with newfangled and exorbitantly expensive steamboat transportation. Atkinson's much-touted assault on the West bogged down for the winter of 1819–20 near Council Bluffs, then fizzled out when Major Long's scientists probed to the Colorado Rockies and dismissed the entire

Plains country as "the Great American Desert . . . uninhabitable by a people depending upon agriculture for their subsistence."

None of the opportunistic suppliers who caused this Missouri effort to cost $256,818.15 (so Congress was told by an irate member) had their hands in Calhoun's Upper Mississippi project. On February 10, 1819, the Fifth Infantry was ordered to concentrate at Detroit. Led by Lieutenant Colonel Henry Leavenworth, it was transported that spring by schooner across Lakes Huron and Michigan to Fort Howard at Green Bay where serviceable riverboats were built. On June 9, the day Major Long, in the famous *Western Engineer,* steamed up the Missouri from St. Louis ("Average running time five hours per day. Average leisure time for examining the country ten hours per day."), Lieutenant Colonel Henry Leavenworth and the nucleus of the Fifth started up the Fox-Wisconsin river route in their bateaux. Three weeks later Leavenworth's party, including two wives of officers, one of whom was in her last month of pregnancy, rowed into Prairie du Chien—roughly the same distance it would take the steamboat *Western Engineer* a dozen more days to cover. After the birth of Lieutenant Nathan Clark's daughter and a futile five-week wait for recruits from St. Louis, Leavenworth sent a detachment to garrison Fort Armstrong on the Rock River and divided the rest of his command, leaving all but ninety-eight soldiers at Fort Crawford. With the newborn infant and the two wives, he pushed up the Mississippi in two large boats, fourteen bateaux and his own barge. Along with Indian Agent Thomas Forsyth, who had preceded him by two days, he was at the mouth of the St. Peter's on August 24.

He found a country drenched with the heat and the fruits of heartland summer. Clouds here prowl the high sky in cumulus battalions, streak the horizon with cirrus tendrils; the blue air shimmers in the dog days sun. As Leavenworth landed on the bottomland of the St. Peter's right bank, the untenanted bluffs rose loaf-shaped around Pike's island at the junction of the two rivers. Across the stream, from the promontory point, he could see the St. Peter's Valley arc away as the land rolled west. On the banks of streams he could see post oaks, cottonwoods, hickories, walnut trees, lindens, sugar maples, white birches and elms; various evergreens, the American box, pine, cedar and juniper; cherry trees, prickly ashes, gnarled plums. Closer to the ground were the gooseberry, black and red raspberries, chokeberries and grape vines; and the carpet was strewn with wild parsley, rue, spikenard, red and white roses, morning glories, and flowers unfamiliar in the East. Leavenworth may well have agreed with his predecessor Long: he had come to a place that "needed no embellishments to render it romantic in the highest degree."

But the natural attractions did not deter Leavenworth from the first order of business. After a day of investigating the environs, he set the troops immediately to work "in making roads up the bank of the river, cutting down trees, etc." He had decided to make camp on the bottomland and, while the women still lived in the boats on the river, the soldiers erected a stockade and within it threw up forty-five separate quarters for the officers, their families and the ranks that had increased to more than two hundred after the belated arrival of recruits. Barracks and officers' apartments were equipped with chimneys constructed of sandstone quarried from nearby bluffs and had timbers of pine that "had been found extremely difficult to obtain." Within a couple of months—while the wilderness peace was rent by the sounds of carpentry and Chiefs Black Dog and Little Crow came to beg for food and gunpowder—the commandant was wrestling with the problem of locating a permanent bastion. "The point of land above the junction of the St. Peter's and the Mississippi and which commands both rivers," he wrote his superiors in Washington, "may easily be fortified against an Indian force. . . ." But as Long had acknowledged two years before, the site wasn't quite perfect, and this troubled Leavenworth. The confluence bluff, he reported, "is commanded by other ground within striking distance on both sides of the Mississippi—It would require great labour & expense to fortify it against an European enemy furnished with artillery."

Leavenworth, a lawyer from Delhi, New York, who had remained a soldier after the War of 1812, never really made it as an Indian fighter, and in 1819 his combat experience had been limited to bouts with British regulars at the battles of Chippewa and Niagara. With English traders still enticing American Indians to Canada for periodic handouts, his nervousness about the European enemy was understandable enough. But why he chose to billet his men on the swampy, bosky bottom that fall is something else again. The mosquitoes which had swarmed the area on their arrival seemed an insignificant menace when winter appeared and, one by one, the enlisted men succumbed to scurvy. By January Leavenworth was writing: "Our officers and their waiters and the women of the garrison have been very healthy, but the men have been quite sickly. . . ." The commander blamed "the nature of our transportation [because of which] they have been compelled to be in the water during the hottest of the summer. To this cause and the want of fresh provisions may in my opinion be imputed the sickness of our men: and hence comes the scurvy."

His view was corroborated in the 1820 Surgeon General's report. The river trip across Wisconsin and up the Mississippi, according to army medics, had obliged Leavenworth's infantrymen "to labor in the water beneath the rays of the ardent sun, sleeping in their wet clothes and exposed to a damp atmosphere impregnated with malaria . . . and in this state of predisposition to scurvy they began, late in the season, the establishment of their winter quarters. . . . They were destitute of groceries and vegetable food, except flour and corn which were more or less damaged from having been wet; and their animal food, which was principally salted, they were obliged to eat during a portion of the winter in a putrescent state. . . ." Unofficial reports blamed the condition of the meat on unscrupulous army contractors who drained the brine to lighten their loads on the upriver haul, replacing it with water to avoid detection. At any rate, no matter who was to blame—and men of Atkinson's bogged-down Missouri expedition were also dying like flies that winter—at least forty of Leavenworth's stricken soldiers were dead when spring came.

In May, after weather so severe that "the roof of our cabin blew off," one survivor remembered, "and the walls seemed about to fall in," Cantonment New Hope was vacated in favor of a summer location near a running spring on the bluff; this bivouac, with more accuracy than optimism, was christened "Camp Cold Water." Leavenworth's vacillation about where to locate his permanent fortification continued as he mulled over the possibilities of a site on the St. Peter's about two miles above the entrance into the Mississippi. He reported that the upper site "is the most accessible, and is not commanded by other [high] grounds," but unfortunately because of its distance from the confluence "the Mississippi cannot be commanded." Not until August, 1820, had he settled on a spot a couple of hundred yards from the edge of the promontory and ordered his troups to begin hauling in timber. By then he had been superseded in command by Colonel Josiah Snelling, who was en route from the Missouri garrison at Bellefontaine.

Notwithstanding his difficulties in determining a permanent location, Leavenworth had seen to it that his post—a good two hundred miles farther into wilderness country than Atkinson's—was in better straits than it had been the previous autumn. Nathan Clark, the quartermaster, had been authorized to sell to officers "such articles of subsistence as they may require at the rate of cost to the government—whiskey 50¢ gallon, Bacon 12¢ per lb., flour 50 per lb., peas 23⅓ ¢ bushel, soap 10¢ lb., candles 19¢ lb., salt 70¢ bushel." On May 13 the Commanding General of Subsistence issued a general order depriving women and boys under eighteen of a whiskey ration, but the situation at St. Peter's was by that time in most other ways improved. The commandant had his men tilling about ninety acres of bottomland and prairie which they had planted to corn, potatoes, various vegetables and fruits, marking off separate gardens for the hospital, the regiment and the few individual families. Early peas were ready in the middle of June and the first corn was eaten six weeks later. Thus, after a perilous winter, Camp Cold Water was ready for a series of visitors that began with the warm weather.

Delayed en route from St. Louis by Leavenworth's request to deal with a couple of Winnebago murderers at Prairie du

Chien, Indian agent Lawrence Taliaferro—who was to spend two decades at St. Peter's—arrived toward the end of June. It is likely that Taliaferro, who pronounced his name to rhyme with Oliver, had come upriver with Leavenworth, for whom he had waited at Fort Crawford and who we know was back at Cold Water on June 25. For on that date Stephen Watts Kearny, an emissary from General Atkinson on the Missouri, recorded in his diary that he was "most kindly & hospitably received & entertained by Col. L. & his Lady." But whether or not Taliaferro had yet arrived, the rest of Leavenworth's companions "were a little astonished at the sight of us," Kearny recorded, and added without thought of numerous itinerant traders that his party comprised "the first whites that ever crossed at such a distance from the Missouri to the Mississippi."

Kearny stayed long enough to witness the wedding, performed by Leavenworth, of a Fifth Regiment lieutenant to the daughter of one of his fellow officers and shoved off for St. Louis on June 29. On the following afternoon Leavenworth's troops saluted the explorers led by Lewis Cass, governor of Michigan Territory, who turned up after a trip across Lake Superior and an unsatisfactory try at locating the true source of the Mississippi. By this time Taliaferro had not only arrived but had been there long enough to have the Indians' nominal obeisance. While the Cass party, which included the future Chippewa agent Henry R. Schoolcraft, dined at Leavenworth's mess table and "were presented with green corn in the ear, peas, beans, cucumbers, beets, radishes, and lettuce," Taliaferro rounded up about three hundred Sioux whom Cass induced to join in a peace treaty with the Chippewa delegation which had come south with the governor. The powwow was a farce. Both tribes played their roles to please their new American "Fathers" and both believed that nothing could stop the intertribal feud that had been carried on for more generations than any of the Indians could rightly remember.

At Cass' treaty—surprisingly present and apparently welcome —was a trader who had intimate knowledge of the bitter suspicions on which the feud was based. The ineluctable Robert Dickson, in order to develop his new business arrangement with

Lord Selkirk, a few seasons earlier had delegated his brother-in-law, the Sioux chief Red Thunder, to establish a truce with the Chippewas that would encourage both tribes to trade with Hudson's Bay. Red Thunder made progress with some of the business-oriented Chippewa bands but not with that of Chief Flat Mouth, who refused to believe the Sioux were sincere; when almost immediately two of his relatives were killed in an ambush, Flat Mouth found ample support for his suspicions. Pretending to accept Red Thunder's denial of implication in the killings, the Chippewa chief agreed to meet Red Thunder for peace talk and arrived at the rendezvous with a bodyguard that outnumbered Red Thunder's two companions fifteen-to-one. The denouement was predictable. Surrounded, Red Thunder began to sing his death song. In his own notion of a good time, Flat Mouth permitted the three Sioux to try to escape, then ran them down, shot them and deprived them of their heads.

Dickson is said to have been more than usually upset by such summary treatment of his wife's brother, but he was a man whose ability at give-and-take was elastic. (In St. Louis after the War of 1812 he and Tom Forsyth were reported to have joined in uproarious laughter over Dickson's offer to pay handsomely for the delivery of Forsyth's head.) Now that the American presence was established in the St. Peter's country he was not blind to the potential of Yankee friendship. He wound up his day at Cass' treaty by writing nonchalantly to an old associate at Prairie du Chien: "I have met with every attention from the garrison at this place. I have found Col Leavenworth a most excellent man." Five days later he put the seal on the peace he had made with the Americans when he supplied Lawrence Taliaferro with his personal census of the Sioux bands which had become Taliaferro's charges. Dickson's appreciation of Leavenworth was lost on Taliaferro who, far from considering the commandant excellent, was pleased when Cass blamed Leavenworth for the dissolute behavior of the Sioux; Leavenworth's "self-conceited vanity" would not affect the Indians much longer, the Indian agent told Cass, because he was so soon to be replaced by Josiah Snelling, who was then winding up a court-martial at Fort Crawford.

45

Not long after Cass departed, however, Leavenworth proved Taliaferro's prediction optimistic. In spite of the Pike treaty, by which the Sioux had surrendered nine square miles as a site for the fort, Leavenworth saw fit to call another conclave to discuss real estate. His motivation remains obscure, but after years of dormancy some of the effects of this August treaty matured into a lengthy controversy. Leavenworth's interpreter at the meeting was Jean Baptiste Faribault, a trader he had met at Prairie du Chien the year before. The son of a French lawyer who had come to America as secretary of Montcalm's army, Faribault had served the North West Company for years before setting himself up independently to trade with the Sioux. He was in many ways an ideal choice to help the U. S. Army establish itself at the St. Peter's entry. He had been imprisoned for his American sympathies during the late war, and this fact made him a man who could be trusted with the chore of translating government policy into a language no Fifth Regiment soldier had mastered. He had had to be persuaded to leave his Prairie du Chien home, and Leavenworth apparently now wanted to reward him. The Fifth's commander called the neighboring Sioux together to tell them he would like to see Pike's island deeded to Faribault's half-Sioux wife. He also seems to have had reason to be grateful to half-breed Duncan Campbell and his sister Peggy, for the Indians were asked to assign a square mile of St. Peter's land to each of them. On August 9 the Sioux acquiesced, in return for "many acts of kindness received by said Indians from said Leavenworth . . . and such other compensation (if any) as the said Government may think proper to appropriate." Taliaferro believed that Leavenworth had exceeded his authority, and he objected on the spot, later passing his protest on to the War Department. In the meantime he took comfort in the impending change of command.

Less than a month passed before Snelling appeared at St. Peter's, but in the interim Leavenworth boiled over at what he took to be condemnation for the sluggish pace he had set for the erection of a permanent fort. Ten days or so after the departure of Cass and his party, Leavenworth exploded at the word which had been brought upriver from Snelling. Although the order naming Snelling as commander of the Fifth had been issued in June of the preceding year, although Snelling was a full colonel and Leavenworth his subaltern, although Snelling was in residence with a major part of the Fifth at Fort Crawford, Leavenworth managed to find reason to take umbrage. Acknowledging "an order by which you have assumed command of the 5th Rgt.," he could not refrain from asserting to Snelling that "candour requires me to say, that I feel injured by the *manner* in which you have done it." And he added, "I had no reason to suppose, that the Inspector General would make any report to you, or others, which would create a belief, that it was your duty to waive the usual etiquette, and assume the command before you arrived at 'head Quarters,' in order, *'to carry the intentions of the Government into effect—'* " In his reply a week later Snelling quietly denied that the Inspector General had said "any thing which implied disapprobation" of Leavenworth's conduct at St. Peter's.

But the bur was under Leavenworth's collar, and there it was to fester for three years. In June, 1823, just four days before he was to set out from Council Bluffs on his misbegotten Arickara campaign (in which he allowed the Rees to escape and sewed seeds of antagonism for Americans among the Sioux), Leavenworth found time to protest to Washington. He wrote to Quartermaster General Thomas Jessup that "Col Snelling of the 5th Regiment has for a long time been motivating my destruction. . . . you will perceive from the information I know you possess as to the Missouri and Mississippi Expeditions in 1819 that injustice has been attempted toward me. The fact is that Col Snelling is hungry for the credit done to the latter expedition in your report laid before the Congress in 1820. . . . You will perceive that the Colonel flies from the assertion as to the establishment of the *post* and takes up the cudgel to prove that I did not build what he calls Fort St. Anthony. He says that 'a temporary cantonment of unhewn logs was thrown up to shelter the troops the ensuing winter; in the spring of 1820 they were removed to a place called Camp Cold Water . . . , and a second set of huts erected.' This *temporary* cantonment not only sheltered the troops the ensuing winter but the whole garrison except one or two companies remained in it the next winter after Col Snelling arrived there. The second set of huts he mentions were Bivouacs made of poles and covered with bark, and were erected by the men without using any article which could have been required for the permanent work. They cost the government not one cent but saved many dollars in the use of tents. The troops were placed here to enable them to recover from the effects of that terrible disease (the Scurvy) with which they were affected in consequence of the badness of the provisions which we had received from the contractor.... The fact is the men did not recover from the Scurvy until the Autumn of 1820 [but] were sickly during the whole summer.... The Col is careful to ... create the opinion in the mind of a stranger that the *Inspector General* was greatly dissatisfied with my remissness in not commencing the permanent work, and that it was necessary for him to act with great promptness in relieving such an inefficient officer. ..."

Acting with great promptness was characteristic of Josiah Snelling, whatever else may be said of him; he had not been present at St. Peter's more than two weeks before he had chosen his own site for the permanent fort, infused life into Leavenworth's convalescent troopers, and, in full dress ceremony, laid the cornerstone on September 10, 1820. This son of a well-to-do Boston baker had been in the army since 1808 and had been fighting or otherwise dealing with Indians for most of twelve years. He had come west in 1809, was an officer in the Fourth Regiment when it had been trained by Zebulon Pike and as a captain had led a charge against the Prophet when the Fourth joined Harrison at Tippecanoe Creek. At Bellefontaine he had become a friend of the family of Colonel Thomas Hunt. Snelling may have learned a good deal about the West from the Hunts. The colonel's troops had saluted the return of Lewis and Clark, and his nine-year-old daughter Abigail had been among those civilians who watched the flotilla slip down the last stretch of the Missouri to St. Louis. After Snelling's first wife had died he and

Abigail renewed their friendship in 1813, in Detroit. Then fifteen, Abigail was living there with a brother and Snelling was serving with troops under Colonel Lewis Cass, who fought Tecumseh just across the river. The war managed not to interfere with the young widower's courtship of Abigail, and on August 13, three days before Hull's ignominious surrender, Snelling married his frontier inamorata. He was a vociferous prosecution witness in Hull's court-martial, an impetuous battlefield commander who was cited for gallantry and, after a year of relative civilization as a lieutenant colonel on Governor's Island, he was back in the West in 1819, there to spend the rest of his life.

Arriving at the rivers' junction, Snelling threw out Leavenworth's plan and determined to build a stone fortress on the natural rampart where the view to the left shows, a visitor wrote later, "the broad deep valley of the Mississippi, with the opposite heights descending precipitously to the water's edge; and to the right and in front, the St. Peter's, a broad stream, worthy from its size . . . to be called the Western Fork of the Great River itself. It is seen flowing through a comparative vale, with swelling hills and intermingling forest and prairie, for many miles . . . Beyond their junction, the united streams are seen gliding at the base of high cliffs into the narrowing valley below. Forests, and those of the most picturesque character, interspersed with strips of prairie, clothe a great portion of the distant view."

For Snelling this view was more than a picture postcard. He could mount guns pointing north and south on this bluff to cover the upper Mississippi, the highway patrolled by the Chippewas. South and west, he could command the St. Peter's and the movements of the Sioux—the nearby Mdewakanton bands, the Wahpekute, Wahpeton, Sisseton, the itinerant Yankton and Yanktonais from the Missouri watershed; even the Teton sometimes wandered east. Between Snelling's bluff and the southernmost detachment of his regiment at Fort Armstrong were the seething Sacs and Foxes and their fractious neighbors, the Winnebagos. Maintaining as much peace as possible between these tribes was a more realistic part of Snelling's mission than erecting a fort that would withstand a British siege, for Canada's colonial government had agreed in 1818 to recognize the forty-ninth parallel as the border. Therefore, unlike Leavenworth, Snelling was willing to risk the unlikely possibility of an artillery attack from nearby high ground in order to have command of native traffic on the waters of the two rivers.

Observing that he had to go "nearly ten miles from the garrison" to cut usable timber, the new commander decided to build his fortress of stone which was "better, and cheaper," aside from the fact—he did not refrain from noting—that "the nails and iron brought in 1819 were nearly all expended in the erection of the temporary cantonments at St. Peters and Camp Cold Water. . . ." The structure's "peculiar [diamond-shaped] form was chosen," he added, "to adapt it to the shape of the ground." He stepped off the lines, 400 feet along the St. Peter's bluff, 400 feet at an obtuse angle into the prairie, then the same distance at an acute angle to the Mississippi. Here "on the North side the hill is a perpendicular bluff," he said in 1824, "on the South the ascent is steep and a road has been cut." He sealed his diamond with a wall ten feet high and about two feet thick, with a sally port opening on the west. Bulging out from the easterly point was a semicircular battery, "the guns of which command the two rivers." Nested in the corner on the south was a three-story hectagonal tower with loopholes for musketry to "command the landing, the road, and the St. Peters," and with cannon mounted at the top. To command the prairie and the high ground behind the fort, Snelling incorporated in the wall a round tower with a twenty-two-foot-high platform for cannon; another battery in a pentagonal tower pointed north across the Mississippi.

Four years after he broke ground, Snelling was still putting finishing touches on his stronghold, but in evaluating his work one must realize that in the two thousand miles from the Mississippi to the Pacific there was not a single structure to compare with it. Not even Bent's Fort, the famous adobe castle of the Southwest, or the great American Fur Company posts of the future, were as sturdily built. All this in spite of numerous vicissitudes. "Many things have conspired to delay the completion of the buildings," Snelling wrote Jessup in 1824; "for two years the number of horses and working cattle were by no means adequate to the purposes of building and agriculture; our timber . . . has generally been procured with immense labour; it has also been my misfortune to see the corps two seasons in succession reduced to a mere skeleton by discharges."

Nevertheless he was able to tick off considerable achievement: "The Commanding Officers Quarters is a stone building containing in the first story two large rooms and two bed rooms with a spacious hall in the center; in the basement a kitchen and offices; it may be proper here to observe that all the officers quarters are one story high in front, with a basement story fronting the rear, the level of the parade being higher than the natural elevation of the hill on the south side. . . .

"The officers quarters built of wood, containing in the first story fourteen rooms with a small bedroom annexed to each and in the basement, a kitchen and pantry; six of these kitchens have cellars under the parade.

"The Commissaries and Quarter Master's store . . . is erected in a chasm of the hill . . . four stories high in front; its rear facing the interior of the garrison has the same elevation with the wall, it is a large and well finished stone building capable of containing four years supply of provisions and Quarter Masters stores."

One stone barracks, he continued, contained "ten rooms, six of them now occupied as a Hospital and divided as follows . . . kitchen, sick ward, convalescent ward, store room, stewards room and surgery; the three rooms on the right are occupied by the sutler's family and one is vacant. . . ."

Snelling's other buildings within the fort included two troop barracks of ten and sixteen rooms each, a guardhouse, a schoolhouse, a bakehouse, six workshops for blacksmiths, carpenters, wheelwrights, etc., a magazine, and the sutler's store (the nineteenth century's post exchange). Inside the walls his men had dug a well twenty-four feet through solid limestone, to a point at which the "water rushes in through a fissure in the rock in sufficient quantities to answer all the ordinary purposes of the garrison." The stables were outside and large enough for one hundred horses. Seven miles up the Mississippi at St. Anthony Falls a stone gristmill, termed by Snelling "a citadel in itself," a frame sawmill, both connected to the falls by a race, and a barracks large enough to shelter an entire company comprised a separate establishment.

Even before the construction was completed, the wilderness sanctuary was christened, in pursuit of Father Hennepin's name for the Mississippi waterfall, Fort St. Anthony—after the patron saint of the French Jesuit who may have been the first white man in the vicinity. But the work of the Fifth Regiment commander had been too formidable to let that name stand. In the early summer of 1824 General Winfield Scott came upriver to inspect the army's most flamboyant western post.

"I wish to suggest . . ." Scott wrote to the head of the army, "the propriety of calling this work *Fort Snelling*, as a just compliment to the meritorious officer under whom it has been erected. The present name is foreign to all our associations, and is, besides, incorrect, as the work stands at the junction of the Mississippi and Saint Peter's rivers. . . . Some few years since the Secretary of War directed that the work at Council Bluffs should be called Fort Atkinson in compliment to the valuable services of General Atkinson on the upper Missouri. The above proposition is made on the same principle." Thenceforward from that summer, Fort Snelling it was.

"The distant view of Fort Snelling, its flag gleaming in relief against the sky, is startlingly fine," one visitor told readers in the East. "A situation more commanding . . . can hardly be imagined."

CHAPTER FOUR

PEOPLE OF LAKES AND STREAMS

WORD OF THE military presence at St. Peter's had been swift in making its way among the tribes, and the natives' reaction was mixed; but the fact that the Indian agent and the army officers would be kept busy was clear enough. Begging or militant, or just plain curious, tribesmen turned up at the river junction from far and near. Forty-one western Sioux arrived in September, 1819, after a twenty-day march on foot, because they had heard that presents were being passed out. "They were very earnest for something and mentioned many articles—particularly guns, Powder—ketles &c—" wrote Lieutenant Josiah Vose. "They soon left us and apparently rather dissastisfied—" Arriving two weeks later, Black Dog, whose village was only a few miles upriver, was even more churlish. "He spoke in a loud tone of voice and with a haughty air, and ask'd by what right or authority we had come to this place, and further observed that the land was his, and that we had no right to it," Vose reported.

The lieutenant managed to mollify Black Dog by patiently reminding him of the treaty with Pike and of the payment in goods which Tom Forsyth had distributed the preceding month. "I further stated to him, that we did not come here with hostile intentions, that we were their friends, and that they would find it much for their interest to be peaceable and to treat us in a friendly manner—" Maybe so, said Black Dog, but Vose might do well to realize that he "had been with the British, and that the British always treated the Indians very well & give them all they wanted." Having scored this point, Black Dog departed, but only after the lieutenant had been persuaded to offer the visitors "a Small Quantity of Whiskey to drink. . . ."

The men of the Fifth Regiment never could be sure of the temper of the natives who hung around their three posts during the early days. In March, 1820, two members of the regiment were killed within a quarter-mile of Fort Armstrong because, an Indian eyewitness testified, two Winnebago braves had an urge to see if they could get away with murder. With Lieutenant Colonel Leavenworth acting as prosecutor, they were tried and sentenced to hang, then flung into an Illinois jail where they were kept all winter with no heat and without food or water for as many as three days at a time. Savage as had been their own crime, their reprehensible treatment in the guise of justice was bound to offend other tribesmen. A Winnebago chief made a formal protest so stirring that the *Illinois Intelligencer* reminded its readers that the United States boasted of itself as a Christian country. "Is this," the newspaper demanded, "the Spanish Inquisition?"

Obviously such miscarriages of justice made the job of policing the frontier more difficult, for news traveled fast up and down the rivers. With Fort Snelling equidistant between the Great Lakes and the Missouri, Lawrence Taliaferro and Josiah Snelling found themselves assigned to a nerve center. Neither had had time to be well installed at St. Peter's when they received word that death had come naturally to Manuel Lisa, bringing an end to his longtime pacifying influence over the western Sioux. Soon afterward, death did *not* come naturally to two of Lisa's *engagés;* Isador Poupin and Joseph Andrews were slain on the Missouri when they encountered a sullen band of Sissetons. Because of "the disposition then manifested" by these Sioux, Snelling wrote, "I had no hope of obtaining the murderers of our people on the Missouri. . . ." But he had the cooperation of the Indian agent, and Major Taliaferro decreed that no trader was to offer any more goods to the Sissetons until the murderers were surrendered. The prospect of facing the future without fresh supplies of tobacco, gunpowder, blankets and other necessities—plus the influence of Taliaferro's interpreter, Colin Campbell—hit the Indians where they hurt most. At a council at Big Stone Lake a brave named Ironfriend and a companion admitted the killings and agreed to deliver themselves to Snelling. In a typical Indian gesture, the aged father of Ironfriend's fellow assassin, sure that his life was nearly over anyway, substituted himself for his son.

"These unfortunate wretches," Snelling wrote, "were delivered up last evening with a great deal of ceremony, & I assure you with affecting solemnity. . . ." According to Philander Prescott, a young civilian who was present, "the Indians made a great show and parade on the delivery of the two hostages [,] firing guns [,] hooping [,] yelling [,] running to and fro with all sorts of jesticulation. a formall delivery was made of the hostages out side the fort [,] the gates all closed and the cannon all ready in case of an attack [.] the Indians said that their great father had demanded some of ther bodies. here they are [;] kill and eat if you wish [;] if not we hope you will return them safe to us again. . . ."

According to Snelling, the Indian procession was formed behind a Sisseton who carried the British flag and was led by Ironfriend and the other murderer's father, "their arms pinioned, & large splinters of wood thrust through them above the elbows, intended so I understood, to show us that they did not fear pain & were not afraid to die." Ironfriend flaunted a large British medal around his neck, and both prisoners carried offerings of such things as fur pelts while they sang their death song in chorus with their friends. In front of the guardhouse, "a fire being previously prepared, the British flag was burnt, and the medal worn by the prisoner given up," said Snelling. "The blacksmith then stepped forward & ironed him & he was conducted to the guard house." When the self-appointed martyr stretched forth his ancient wrists for the handcuffs, Snelling told the old man that "it was not our custom to punish the innocent for the guilty, that he would be detained as a hostage & kept in confinement, but that he should be well treated, & when the other murderer was taken he should be permitted to return to his land."

But the much-vaunted American justice was again mismanaged when Snelling sent Ironfriend to St. Louis under guard. Because no witness appeared against him the prisoner was released, only to be killed on his way home by a settler who just plain didn't trust Indians and felt free to shoot one who was unarmed and alone. Naturally nobody much minded Ironfriend's death, and it may be that the belief that he would fare no better caused Ironfriend's real partner in crime to stab himself to death when he was finally caught.

The truth, according to old Indian hand Josiah Snelling, lay in the fact that "our judicial code is not adapted to these people. . . ." In a note to Taliaferro he averred that Indians "should be dealt with as the Scotch say, 'by the strong hand'; on the commission of the next murder, let me be authorized to proceed to their camp, inflict summary punishment on the offenders on the spot, and we should hear no more of it."

Snelling heard more from the Sioux in short order. The Charger, better known as Wanata, got wind of the new authority setting up shop at St. Peter's and became determined to challenge it; he was, perhaps, the most recalcitrant of the English sympathizers. (Perhaps, too, the fact that he was Red Thunder's son and heir as a Yankton chief—and thereby Robert Dickson's nephew—had something to do with the determination.) A much decorated veteran of the War of 1812 whom tradition accepts as having been commissioned a British captain and given a junket to England after hostilities ceased, Wanata devised a scheme to infiltrate Snelling's temporary log fort and take over.

"The plot was well laid, and, had a less experienced officer been in command," a son of Snelling's wrote with understandable prejudice, "[it] would undoubtedly have been successful." Henry Snelling may be suspected not only for his fealty but for the fact that he was not more than three years old at the time. Nevertheless, it isn't hard to believe that Wanata's arrival at St. Peter's was at least as memorable as any occasion during his father's tenure, and that the details were drummed into the small boy's head at many a family session. In outline, Henry's version agrees with other reports; what embellishments it obviously has are harmless.

"Wanata's intentions," so the tale goes, "were to put an overwhelming body of savages in the forrest which surrounded the fort and enter with only fifty men. During the sitting of the council, and in the midst of his speech, the presentation to Col. Snelling of a wampum belt was to be the signal for the commencement of the murderous work, for which purpose each warrior had his weapons concealed under his blanket. While the greater part were to rise and dispatch the officers within, the remainder were to rush out and taking the guard by surprize were to open the gates and admit the whole savage horde, who were to have approached during the conclave, when an indiscriminate slaughter was to take place.

"On the day appointed the wiley chief, fully convinced of the success of his plan, gathered his warriors and disposed them to the very best advantage, and with the friendly wampum in one hand and the pipe of peace in the other, he presented himself before the gates; but contrary to his expectation, he found them all—except the northern one—closed and secured. This did not, however, shake his resolution, for, as he afterwards stated, he was impressed with the belief that his intentions were unknown, and that the closing of the gates was accidental, as there appeared to be no increase of sentinels, or show of extraordinary vigilence. The troops, however, were under arms. Feeling secure in his secret he entered with fifty warriors, with a proud step and lofty mein; but if surprise was great when he found the gates shut, it was doubly so when, on entering, he beheld two large bodies of men drawn up in martial array on each side of the gate within. He cast a momentary glance of inquiry upon the officer of the day, yet exhibited not the slightest sensation of fear, nor sign that he understood the nature of such a display. But when the gate was closed behind them, some of the savages not so cautious, or stoical as the rest, testified their surprise and mortification by giving way to the exclamation "Ugh!" so common among the aborigines.

"They were directed to the Council chamber, where the commandant laid aside all mystery and at once attacked Wanata with a revelation of his designs, and upbraided him in no measured terms for his intended treachery. They were then led out to the parade ground, where three large fires had been kindled; despoiled of their flags, tomahawks, knives, and every thing else that had been presented to them by the United States government, which were committed to the flames and they themselves ejected from the fort in disgrace. . . .

"There was but one way," continued Henry Snelling, "to make atonement for their want of success, and the indignities put upon them. Wanata set the example by making skewers of wood and thrusting them through the fleshy parts of his arms and legs. Some [of his men] followed in the same expiatory act, while others cut and hacked themselves with their knives."

Self-torture as an act of expiation was not infrequent among the Sioux—especially those of the western bands—and it was also practiced as a rite of thanksgiving for safe return from war or other dangers. Wanata, in fact, seems to have been a devotee. Before setting off on one trip into Chippewa territory, he made a vow to the sun that should he complete his trip in safety, he would give thanks by distributing his possessions among his people, and by abstaining from food and drink for four days while continuously performing the sun dance, a basic version of the ceremony that later became a famous Plains rite. This torturous business required that he so slash the skin of his breast and arms that ropes could be attached and run up to the top of a tall pole. For more than ninety hours he dangled and bobbed about, until the loops of skin were torn free and he collapsed in a swoon which rewarded him with some vision of future prowess.

For at least one hundred and fifty years before Wanata, Sioux chiefs had been called upon to show great prowess in persistent intertribal conflict. That warfare had found a new dimension when seventeenth-century French traders had brought firearms to the Chippewas. Themselves pushed westward by the uprooted tribes of eastern Canada and of the burgeoning American colonies, the Chippewas claimed the land around Lake Superior and they fought savagely for the proprietorship of the new hunting grounds and the right to monopolize the trade for white man's goods. Still equipped only with Stone Age weapons, the Sioux—who called themselves Dakotah (allies)—were forced to press the Cheyennes, their neighbors in western Minnesota; they also pushed south into the traditional lands of the Iowas, the Winnebagos, the Sacs and Foxes. As the westering Cheyennes met and settled near the Mandans, the advance Dakota contingent moved across the divide between Red River of the North and the St. Peter's; they became the Teton Sioux, "people who live on the prairie," when they established headquarters at Big Stone Lake. The Teton band was followed by the closely associated Yankton and Yanktonais Sioux, and later by divisions of Sissetons and Wahpetons. But others of the Sioux clung for years to their ancient homeland around the headwaters of the Mississippi.

Indian legends, like most others, have a way of becoming oversimplified in the course of time. In an effort to arrest such distortion, William Warren, son of a fur trader and a half-breed Chippewa mother, devoted himself in the mid-nineteenth century to sifting and setting down as much Indian history as he could accumulate. And he records the futile Sioux effort to hold out in the North Woods which was resolved in an imaginatively conceived Chippewa campaign against the ancient headquarters of the allies at Mille Lacs Lake. "The vanguard," according to Warren, "fell on the Dakotas at Cormorant Point early in the morning, and such was the extent of the war party that before the rear arrived the battle at this point had already ended by the almost total extermination of its inhabitants; a small remnant only retired in their canoes to the greater village located at the entry." Here, "after a brave defense with their bows and barbed arrows, the Dakotas took refuge . . . from the more deadly weapons of their enemy." With the French gift of gunpowder, the Chippewas decided to blast the Sioux out of the security of their lodges and into kingdom come. They made up packages of powder, tossed them into the smoke holes of the Sioux wickiups, thus to drop into the cooking fires below. "The bundles ignited by the fire spread death and dismay," Warren wrote, and he added: "The idea possessing their minds that their enemies were aided by spirits, [the Sioux] gave up the fight in despair and were easily dispatched."

59

The survivors abandoned their Mille Lacs homes for good, but these Sioux never gave up their claim to the hunting grounds over which they continued to feud in spite of the shadow of Fort Snelling. When the post commander and Lawrence Taliaferro established themselves at St. Peters, they found Sioux ensconced on both rivers. The village of Black Dog, "a very bad fellow," said Colin Campbell, was a couple of miles up the St. Peter's; Little Crow was at Kaposia, six miles down the Mississippi. Some miles below on the big river were the headquarters of Wabasha and the beggarly Red Wing, while along the St. Peter's were a half-dozen other villages, including the area's largest, presided over by Mr. Six, or Shakopee.

Although considered the eastern Sioux's best orator, Shakopee was generally branded a good-for-nothing whose example was apt to be the opposite of any good advice he gave. In *Dahkotah; or Life and Legends of the Sioux Around Fort Snelling*, Mary Henderson Eastman, a fastidious and not unromantic army wife, called Shakopee "decidedly ugly; but there is an expression of intelligence about his quick black eye and fine forehead, that makes him friends, notwithstanding his many troublesome qualities. . . . He never combs his hair, but wears a black silk handkerchief tied across his forehead. . . . His hands, which are small and well formed [a Sioux characteristic] are black with dirt; he does not descend to the duties of the toilet." Wabasha was a different breed—in fact, through his mother he had Chippewa blood in his veins. He had impressed Pike favorably, and Stephen Long reported that Wabasha "is considered one of the most honest and honorable of any of the Indians, and endeavors to inculcate into the minds of his people the sentiments and principles adopted by himself." Moreover, said Tom Forsyth, "This man is no beggar, nor does he drink, and perhaps I may say he is the only man of this description in the whole Sioux nation." There were some good words, too, for Pike's friend Little Crow. Henry R. Schoolcraft described the Kaposia chief as "a man below the common size, but brawny and well proportioned. . . . There is a great deal of fire in his eyes, which are black and piercing. His nose is prominent and has the aquiline curve, his forehead falling a little from the facial angle, and his whole countenance animated, and expressive of a shrewd mind."

By the time the Fifth Regiment and the Indian agent arrived at St. Peter's these most powerful of the eastern Sioux chiefs, as well as those of smaller bands, were sedentary in the sense that they did not permanently abandon their home bases. The season of village residence among these Sioux was summer rather than winter. In the fall the villagers were apt to separate into groups of two or three families and to take their tepees to the shelter of the forests, where they could be closer to the game on which they subsisted and to the fur-bearing animals whose pelts they needed for barter with the traders. Under the thick, arching branches of giant hardwood trees the Sioux women first leaned three tall poles together and tied them near their upper ends; tipped against this tripod then came nine other poles, forming a cone perhaps a dozen feet high and ten feet in circumference. Eight buffalo skins sewed together with sinews were wrapped neatly around this framework and banked with hay to keep out drafts and swirling snow. On the dirt floor within, layers of buffalo robes and other furs provided an almost luxurious insulation. "I know not why," a white Kaposia visitor once jotted in his notebook, "but there is a *home* feeling about the interior of a tepee." Lounging before a fire with the smoke rising inexorably toward the peaked aperture overhead, he was moved to remember "childish positions on the parlor rug" on winter evenings.

Summer houses reminded that visitor of American log cabins. And indeed they were built with fundamental engineering skill, with strong forked posts to support the ridgepole, upright posts imbedded in the ground at two-foot intervals and horizontal beams bound securely to square off the framework. Sections of bark, sometimes five or six feet wide, were cut from elm trees to be laced onto the walls with thongs of basswood, and other bark was lapped on the roof like shingles. "Within, a platform or divan of about five feet in width & elevated some two feet & a half from the ground, extends around three sides of the apartment leaving a quadrangle space in front of the door," Frank B. Mayer wrote at Kaposia. "At the back of the divan skins are hung & buffalo robes & other peltry cover the surface, on which the inmates repose surrounded by their arms, trinkets, women & dogs. . . . One or two men are engaged in making a pipe or a ramrod or feathering an arrow, another is humming the monotonous music of the dance, accompanying himself on a drum of native manufacture, while a woman is braiding and adorning her husband's glossy tresses. The venison is simmering in the kettle and a dog is half concealed by the cumbrus trappings of a saddle and is catching musquitos under his masters feet. In such occupations as these the Indian whiles away the year, the daily routine of sleeping, smoking & gossiping & occasional swim in the adjoining river, being varied by a deer hunt, fishing, a visit to the adjoining towns, & various dances, ball plays, & mysteries of savagedom. The houses were arranged in rows with the 'tipis' intervening here & there, pleasantly varying the angularity & ruggedness of the long succession of [bark lodges]."

Actually there was somewhat less indolence than this description conveys. At Kaposia the Indians manufactured many things —canoes, dishes, spoons, saddles, cradles, snowshoes, barrels, pottery. Hollowed from tall pine trees with ax, and primitive adz, there were "no better canoes than those made by the Dakotas," said a missionary who lived on the St. Peter's for half a century. They carved dishes, spoons and ladles from hardwood knots, and their hand-hewn cradles were "as well made as though from a cabinet-maker's shop." Until the permanent presence among them of white men, the women made yarn spun from the bark of nettles or from basswood bark that had been softened by boiling; they wove sashes and garters for their men, and gaily patterned bags for themselves. Porcupine quills, feathers, grasses, pigments, small animal and bird bones, bells, braided hair, beads and fringes of fur were used with skill in embroidery and decoration.

French and British traders had long before had their effect on the customs and the paraphernalia of the Sioux, but Taliaferro's report of his first dispensations in 1820 indicates the variety of white man's merchandise to be issued periodically at the new fort. He itemizes: axes, awl blades, tinderboxes, shotguns, flints, gunpowder, fire steels, lead, knives, scissors, garden hoes, combs, looking glasses, beads, blankets, black silk handkerchiefs, thread, ribbons, gartering, calico yard goods, calico shirts, two chief's coats, tobacco, vermilion, verdigris, and one silver breastplate. The total cost of this largess to the U.S. government, he said, was $2,135.78½. This was still a time, it must be remembered, considerably before the natives were reduced to dependence on the white man, and such gifts were made in the spirit of winning friends and influencing Indians, rather than offering them the inadequate subsistence made necessary when wholesale treaties and tidal waves of settlers deprived them of their hunting grounds completely.

As army quarriers cut limestone blocks from the St. Peter's bluffs and masons threw up the walls of Snelling's fort, the Sioux of the two adjoining rivers continued their ancient occupations. Their hunting season started in October when the villages were evacuated; lodge poles were lashed to the sides of the shaggy horses and baggage piled on their backs and on cradles laced between the ends of the poles that dragged along the ground. Leaving behind only those unable to walk, along with someone to care for the invalids, the headman led out his party of hunters, squaws, children of all ages, and barking dogs; except in the case of some untoward event no one would return from the expedition until January. Moving in stages, systematically hunting a radius of several miles before changing camps, the hunters comprised a disciplined corps bound by rules that guaranteed each man an equal chance at the day's quarry and severe penalties for those who went beyond the boundaries laid out at daily conferences. Deer were the prime target, but nobody ever avoided a chance to bring home elk or bear meat, and most Sioux were so fond of raccoon that, instead of thriftily skinning it to preserve the pelt, they often burned off the fur to indulge themselves in the crisp and grease-oozing crackling. Venison tallow was always saved and packed home to be eaten with corn or rice, and all meat not consumed on the hunt was thinly sliced and dried for preservation.

They wasted little. With spring's arrival after the hunt, the women tapped the maple sugar trees and the men went after otter and muskrats, both for furs and for food; they prowled the margins of every lake and marsh for not only ducks but turtles, and for the edible roots of water lilies and other plants which the female members of their families dug up. With hoes and other garden tools in short supply before the arrival of the Fort Snelling forces, the St. Peter's villages invested little labor in their meager corn crops. They depended upon such things as wild potatoes, turnips and onions, and bountiful sources of wild berries and other fruits which crews of pickers gathered with the efficiency of organization men.

After the garrisoning of two to three hundred white men at the forks of the Mississippi and the St. Peter's, many inevitable changes began to occur, few of which could Snelling and Taliaferro have stopped. When the not infrequent starving times came upon the Indians the tribes turned with ease to the bounty of the white man, which seemed mysteriously greater to them than that of nature. And what they couldn't beg officially, through the offices of their chiefs, they found natural ways to importune. It wasn't long then before stern orders had to be posted to forbid natives "not on official business" the freedom of the post.

Taliaferro, although little time passed before he himself acquired a tawny mistress, asserted that the troops made good behavior on the part of the Indians impossible. He noted numerous reports of Indian women leaving the garrison immediately after reveille, and made repeated protests. In his journal, after one restraining proclamation had been issued, he wrote that in spite of his "official letters" on the subject, "this order was not issued until after there had been a scene of Drunkeness—debauchery and wilful neglect of duty as it regarded the intercourse with the Garrison and Indians for some months. . . ." More explicit complaint came, understandably enough, from the missionaries who, once the fort had made the frontier safe for proselytizing, began to point occasionally to the white man's guilt. One of them said that he had never known an Indian girl, "while living among her own people," to give birth to a child before she was married. The wife of another missionary wrote her mother that she was shocked "that it was so exceedingly common for officers of the army to have two wives or more—but one, of course, legally." In her observation of Fort Snelling life "there were but two officers who were not known to have an Indian woman, if not half-Indian children. . . . Once, in my childhood's simplicity, I regarded the army and its discipline as a school for gentlemanly manners, but now it seems a sink of iniquity, a school of vice."

Outside of the uniformed ranks the rapports with natives were at least not wholly iniquitous; more than a few of these frontier liaisons were even permanent and sometimes, in the literature of the fort, there is a glimpse of cap-setting among Indian coquettes of the same kind which exists wherever women are intent upon husband-shopping. Philander Prescott, who arrived at St. Peter's as a teen-age employee of the fort's first sutler, remembered in later years that there was "a young lass courting me and I was courting another. Finally the one that was after me and wanted me to marry her sent a messenger to me one day and asked me to marry her, for she said she loved me verry much. I made an excuse saying I was to young to marry and gave a small present and the messenger went off and they never troubled me again."

Obviously Prescott wasn't too young. While still working in the sutler's store he had cast an eye at the daughter of the Man That Flies when she came around with quillwork moccasins and other handicraft to barter. The appearance and deportment of this beauty named Spirit of the Moon "attracted my attention and in fact the young woman got acqua[i]nted with all the officers ladies of the fort and she became verry much respected for all her good behaviour and decent appearance and [was] cle[a]nley far exceeding the rest of the Indn girls. . . ." Philander was, however, unhurried in his courtship. "I did not make any advances to the young woman or give her any incouragement about marying her but contin[u]ed to make [her family] little presents from time to time. . . ." In fact, he was gone in St. Louis for some months and when he returned he set himself up as a fur trader and built himself a house.

"By this time the girl I left behind me had come up to see me but she only stoped a few minuts and was off again. I began to think about getting married after the Indian man[n]er so I took ten blankets one gun and 5 gallons of whiskey and a horse and went to the old chiefs lodge and laid them down and told the old people my errant and went off home. The third day I receved word that my gift had been accepted. But the girl was bashful. . . ." Philander had to wait until her parents could do something with her. "In a few days they moved their tent up and camped near my house [but it was ten days] before I could get my wife as she was then timid. At last through much entreaty of the parents she came for to be my wife. . . . Little did I think at that time I should [live] with hur until old age."

Unlike many in other parts of the West, some of the traders around Fort Snelling lived with their Indian spouses until death, if not old age. Some of them may have done as well as the members of the garrison in turning out extracurricular children, but the native or half-breed girls whom they chose for life—and eventually married legally—were as entrenched and as secure as the average woman anywhere. Even some soldiers (Lieutenant James McClure, whose métisse daughter Nancy was to grow up a respected Minnesota pioneer, was one) took daughters of chiefs as honored wives. For the bride who achieved such status the gains were obvious; she was lifted high in the caste system. So, in another way, was the profit for those who were smuggled into barracks where each bunk slept as many as four men; these gains were as tangible, and as illusory, as those which come to girls wherever conquering soldiers appear. No chocolate bars, perhaps, no chewing gum or K-rations; but instead of a pair of nylons, a yard or two of calico, a spool of ribbon, a fistful of beads—better, certainly, than being kidnapped by Sacs as was one Sioux girl to whose rescue Taliaferro went in 1823 with interpreter Alexander Faribault.

No Indian welcomed the establishment of the fort without reservation, but what was there to be had for the asking many of the tribesmen were willing to take.

CHAPTER FIVE

———◆◆———

EDGE OF A WORLD

WITH THE walls of his fort up and the last of the other structures nearing completion, Josiah Snelling needed no sign from the heavens that he had planted the Stars and Stripes on the edge of the Old Northwest for keeps. But that, in a way, was just what he got. He was crossing the parade on the balmy night of September 20, 1822, having just left the commissary. Suddenly he was "startled by a brilliant light in the atmosphere, and looking up, saw a meteor passing. . . ." It came so close to him that the sound roared in his ears with all the intensity of "a signal rocket," and when he heard it strike somewhere below the bluff "it sound like a spent shell, though much louder." In search of corroboration, the colonel dashed over to the nearest sentry, whom he found "much agitated." Asked if he had seen "any thing extraordinary," the trembling soldier "replied that a large *ball of fire* had passed very near him." Snelling wrote that "after requesting him to mark the spot where it fell, I proceeded to the other sentries, whose accounts, as far as their stations allowed them to judge, agreed with his."

In fact, nobody disagreed, and even though no trace of the spent aerolite could be found in the alluvial soil—naturally camouflaged because it was "much broken into holes or hollows"—Snelling drafted a report for government scientists and the sign of the meteor passed into the folklore of the fort. Removed as the garrison was from civilization, every happening—put aside the phenomenal—furnished prime material for the barracks yarn-spinners to embroider around the fireplaces for the benefit of recruits. For more than likely, the average enlistees were not only new to the frontier but were European immigrants new to all things American. Winters at St. Peter's were bitter and long. At thirty degrees below zero all outdoors creaked with the sounds of frost and ever-deepening snowdrifts. Indoors, when time hung heavy, the isolation was dispelled by Indian tales sufficiently fascinating to cause more than one river traveler to set them down in his diary. A recruit needed no extra sense of chivalry to romanticize the only kind of female available to him, lice-ridden though she might be; and he was all ears when the veterans retold the stories (there was always an Indian to swear that his mother had been an eyewitness) that illustrated how devoted Indian heroines were. Everybody's favorite tale was centered around the Falls of St. Anthony, seven miles upriver from the citadel. In much the way Pike and Major Long had been moved to write it down, the fireside storyteller gripped the attention of his barracks mates as he spun out this story Long called a "tale to hallow the scenery."

The heroine, whose beauty could be imagined in the flames that licked at the stones of the barracks fireplace, was named The Dark Day. A young Sioux wife and the mother of two small children, she had lived happily while she watched the increasing reputation of her husband as a hunter and leader of men. No suspicion jarred her fidelity until her husband's admirers urged that his mounting importance was such that he must have a second wife to share the duties of hostess made necessary by all those who now came to pay him court. But The Dark Day was not even told when a new bride was selected and delivered to her man. Then one morning she watched her husband as he came through the flap of her tepee and she sensed that he was about to bring an end to her bliss.

"You know," the storytellers have him say, "I can love no one as I love you. But I see that my new importance makes you work too hard. You must see that you need a helper. Therefore you must be willing to have another woman in this lodge. This I tell you—she will always be second to you in my affections, and she will be subject to your control."

The Dark Day was stricken at the thought of sharing her love.

She pleaded that she could do the work of two women, and reminded her husband of the tenderness with which she had always ministered to his needs. But when he remained adamant, giving her no choice but compliance, she did what her love dictated. As Long put it, she was determined "not to remain a passive dupe to his hypocrisy." She took the children and went home to her parents. In the spring when the ice had left the river she painted herself and her youngsters, got into a canoe and paddled toward St. Anthony Falls. Her death song of lost love was swallowed in the plunging waters when her canoe went over the cascade and she and the children disappeared without trace. Ever after, the storytellers rarely failed to add, the Indians could hear in the sound of the falls the echo of The Dark Day singing of the inconstancy of her husband.

She wasn't the only fireside heroine to stir the blood of a callow recruit. The Sioux girl named Winona was of the stuff of which Longfellow poems are made. (That New England bard, in fact, noted that he had read a book about Fort Snelling before writing his *Song of Hiawatha*.) In real life, so goes this story, Winona was in love with a redskin Lochinvar who was, of course, *persona non grata* in her family's tepee. Stripped of its romantic prolixities, Winona's drama is classic. She would have nothing to do with the dullard her parents insisted she marry. Off she went to the top of a Mississippi precipice, crying, "You have driven from the village the only man I will ever marry. All alone he ranges the forest, with no one to spread his blanket, no one to pitch his tepee, no one to wait on him. You think doing that to him shows your love for me?" Of course not. Winona was the kind of girl who would rather die a virgin than marry a man she could not love, and to prove it she flung herself over the cliff to her death—at a site still known variously as Maiden's Rock or Lover's Leap.

A soldier in Snelling's fort could tell a story like this with the same relish for sentimentality with which he had first heard it from a wizened trader like Murdoch Cameron, who first told Winona's saga to Zebulon Pike. ("A wonderful display of sentiment in a savage," was Pike's reaction.) And the men of the

Fifth got a store of tales from the traders who were always dropping in. Often as not, the hero—villain?—was a medicine man whose shenanigans could seem purty slick to a raw recruit. Take the story a Chippewa trader—one day when the sun was baking the parade ground in 1823—allowed he'd been a party to. He had run into a medicine man who claimed, sure enough, he could pour water from an empty jug, and he told that Injun he'd give him a keg of whiskey to see the impossible done. The jug was brought forth, turned upside down, and everybody agreed it contained no water. Then Mr. Medicine Man began his incantations, raising his keg to the heavens, dancing, gesturing. When the last rite had been performed, everybody got a cool drink from the very jug which had been certified empty. That Injun didn't fool this trader. The conjuror had the jug rigged with an animal bladder filled with water and, the tale had it, with a few well-placed spikes. "Owing to the agitation communicated to it, the bladder had been burst by means of spikes driven into the keg for that purpose." The medicine man claimed his whiskey and got it, but when the trader privately let him know he was on to his chicanery the Indian made him promise not to expose the trick to the other natives.

The traders brought their tales to the fort in summer. In winter they were miles away at their own lonely posts, and Snelling's men (because of his balding, red-thatched head they called him the "Prairie Chicken," or the "Red Hen") were left to their own leisure-time resources. Alcohol, naturally—whenever they could get it. The frontier cried out to passionate men, just as it was a haven for all kinds of derelicts. "Intemperance, among both officers and men," says the report of one who arrived at the fort in 1823, "was an almost universal thing, and produced deplorable effects. I regret to say that the commandant was no exception to this rule. Usually kind and pleasant, when one of his convivial spells occurred, he would act furious. . . ." Snelling wasn't called the "Red Hen" for nothing. When his enlistees "committed a like indiscretion, he would . . . compel them to strip [and] flog them unmercifully."

Violence, whether on the part of Snelling or of his men, was curiously tempered with the gentility of theatrical performances which, of a winter's evening, had ham-fisted gunners strutting the boards in gowns borrowed from the fort's womenfolk. Thirty-odd years later one of them—Joseph R. Brown, whose career began as a fourteen-year-old fife-and-drummer—said a night at the theater caused his "mind to wander back to the winters of 1821 and 1822, when a thespian corps used to murder *Rolla* in the barracks at the mouth of the St. Peters. We were one of the performers, and in the play of Pizarro we done Elvira. From what we can recollect of our manner of representing the character, however, we are inclined to believe there was some little difference between our performance, and that of Miss Deering [a mid-nineteenth century stock company star]."

Until the slow process of constructing the citadel came to an end, little enough of duty time was devoted to soldierly pursuits. "1st at day light," so one letter home reported, "the reveille beats for about 15 minutes, all the drums and fifes marching the whole circuit of the barracks to awaken the whole, who must all turn out, except sick, on parade." (Few were sick, and after that bout of scurvy that hit Leavenworth's camp, army medics repeatedly stressed the healthy aspect of the climate.) "The next call beats at 20 minutes before 7 o'clock. . . . At 7 o'clock is breakfast call which is finished in ½ hour. . . . Retreat beats at sun down which is here as late [in midsummer] as 8 o'clock, it being twilight until nearly 10 o'clock. Tatoo is at 9 o'clock when our band of which we have a very good one plays a number of favorite tunes, and all retire to their beds except the officers who sit up as late as they please." The same letter home said, "The officers are very agreeable altho too much addicted to cards, which is the prevailing vice where men are shut out [except for theatricals] from amusements during the long & severe winters." Escorting forty recruits from Jefferson Barracks to the St. Peter's in 1828, Lieutenant Philip St. George Cooke made note of the enthusiasm expressed by his fellow officers; "—an arrival, a new face, at such an outpost of civilization as this, is a bright link in that nearly severed chain which connects it with the world. . . ."

In all ways a commission in the army brought with it less

reason for grumbling than did the lot of an enlistee. While the men in the barracks did well enough on the produce of Snelling's "public gardens," on the salt meat hauled upriver by boat or fresh beef and pork from the fort's own livestock, officers lived on the fat of the land. Maybe Fort Snelling was, as Captain Nathan Jarvis described it in an overworked phrase of the period, the "ultima thule of the U. States." But it was also, he said, a place where the "epicure can enjoy almost everything he can desire. Game in abundance of every description; our mess table is sup-ply'd every day with the finest woodcock, and in the fall we will live on grouse and ducks and deer and wild Geese &c. . . ."

In another letter home Jarvis mentioned the immense flocks of game birds, of which more were killed than consumed. "The ducks," he said, "are the finest I have ever eaten."

Fort Snelling may well have had more than its share of fame as a gastronome's way station. ". . . let me give an account of our messing," Lieutenant Cooke wrote of the provisions supplied him on his departure from the garrison. "There is an abundant store of cold boiled ham, of the true Virginia flavor—of corned beef, and of chickens: and the buffalo tongue should not be for-gotten. Our coffee—not used with the stinting hand of a frugal *housekeeper*—was made after the most approved method, and with extreme care and attention; it was drawn with boiling water, like tea, and not suffered to boil afterwards. But who shall do justice to the venison, roasted in bits on a stick, with alternate pieces of salt port? . . . 'O, let me die eating ortolans, to the sound of soft music.' Bah!"

Not so indulged were the enlisted men. *General Regulations for the Army* ordered that "meats will generally be *boiled,* with a view to soup; sometimes roasted or baked, but never *fried. . . .*" The provident way for a mess sergeant to make soup called for two and a half quarts of water to a pound of meat; "apply a quick heat, to make it boil promptly; skim off the foam, and then moderate the fire. . . . Add the vegetables of the season one or two hours, and sliced bread some minutes before the simmering is ended. When the broth is sensibly reduced in quantity, that is, after five or six hours' cooking, the process will be complete."

Bread, said the regulations in sturdy army syntax, "ought not to be burnt, but baked to an equal brown colour." Bakers were cautioned to be sure the crust was not "detached from the crum. On opening it, when fresh, one ought to smell a sweet and balsamic odour." Tricky business for the tender of a frontier oven. "The troops ought not to be allowed to eat soft bread fresh from the oven, without first toasting it." As a matter of fact, toasting was highly recommended because a slice was thus made "nearly as wholesome and nutritious as stale bread." Yet even with such specifics to guide them, Fort Snelling mess sergeants were sometimes no more attentive to the edibility of the fodder they turned out than some of their twentieth-century successors. In 1823, after the fort's gristmill was manufacturing flour from homegrown wheat, bread baked in Snelling's ovens was on one occasion so "wretched, black and bitter tasting" that the men broke away from mess and flung the whole batch onto the parade ground.

Long spells without the semblance of military action told on the soldiers. Most of them preferred what the wife of Captain Seth Eastman called "the excitement, the charm of garrison life. ... How," asked that romantic army spouse, "should a soldier be employed but in active service? besides, what a capital chance to desert!" It might have spoiled her pretty tale of Fort Snelling life had she added that a deserter, by the very nature of his venture, traveled alone and therefore seldom made it out of Indian country alive. But, as she does point out, the average soldier lusted for action—"If trouble won't come, why he will bring it by quarrelling with the first rascally Indian he meets." Before such opportunities, however, an infantryman had to equip himself for the march, and Mrs. Eastman shows him adding to his arms such diverse items as tin reflectors for baking bread in the sun and "India rubber cloaks" for unpredictable rains. "Rations are put up for the men;—hams, buffalo tongues, pies and cake for the officers. The battalion marches out to the sound of the drum and fife;—they are soon down the hill—they enter their boats; handkerchiefs are waved from the fort, caps are raised and flourished over the water—" If there is an operetta quality to the

73

lady's prose it is not because she is inaccurate; more likely, her tone is due to the fact that she could not imagine how Snelling's paladins must have felt.

"Look at Fort Snelling as it now stands," the inspector general wrote in 1826, "be told that it was erected in six years by the soldiers themselves, who at the same time were tillers of the soil to the extent of many hundred acres, and you will feel disposed to give them credit if they have preserved even the proper *feelings* of the *soldier.* . . ." Such proper feelings were not always maintained by the officers. On charges of insubordination, Snelling once kept a young West Pointer languishing in the guardhouse for months. On the other hand, complaints against Snelling himself were made to Washington by his quartermaster, and one old sergeant pressed charges, eventually dismissed, accusing his colonel of "having ruined him." Again, an officer's charge against Snelling brought with it a challenge to duel, an invitation declined by the commandant but accepted by his nineteen-year-old son who recently had been expelled from West Point for breach of conduct.

The officers' offspring, with the exception of William Joseph Snelling, were small children in the early years of the fort. Some of them, indeed, in those days of high infant mortality, did not survive the rigors of the frontier; a thirteen-month-old half sister of Joe Snelling was buried soon after the family settled in, and Lieutenant Platt Green's baby followed. For those who had a chance to grow up, the world around the citadel was Huck Finn's paradise. In addition to the rivers, the fort was surrounded by a chain of lakes where young Henry Snelling went for perch, sunfish, bass, pickerel, pike and catfish that were "ravenous after the bait." For the winter sport, another officer's son had brought his skates, "and even the oldest and most stolid warriors would watch my gyrations with unbounded admiration and astonishment." At one early headcount there were four Snelling youngsters, two Garlands and two Clarks, all of ambulatory age in this wilderness environment, in addition to a growing crop of infants.

At nearby Lake Calhoun, named politicly enough for the Secretary of War, Platt Green as early as 1823 had built a leisure-time hideout known as Green's Villa. This was soon a mecca for officers and their wives bent on picnicking or a few days shooting game. In spite of all the privations, the spotty early records of fort life make it clear that every effort was made to live as much of the time as possible like country gentry, the ladies attended not only by their husbands but by any available unattached officer. Horseback rides to St. Anthony Falls were a ritual; so were boat trips to a couple of caves on the Mississippi within one of which "can be heard a waterfall which we were unable to approach on account of the darkness." Young Abigail Snelling, as at home in the saddle as such frontier matrons should be, even went on solo excursions, and once brought home a sick Indian to nurse back to health. "Many of these ladies," said the Selkirk girl who came to work for Abigail in 1823, "would have shone in any circle. Their households in the garrison were attractive places, and showed evidences of wealth and good taste." Wealth is relative, perhaps especially in Indian country, but no matter, "the society of the Fort at that period was of the most select and aristocratic."

It got really aristocratic that spring when the first steamboat ever to push that far north nudged into the oozing ground at the foot of the bluff. On board the *Virginia,* in addition to Lawrence Taliaferro who had spent the winter in the East, was Count Giacomo Constantino Beltrami, swan-necked, small-faced, dark-eyed, excitable, Italian. No more aristocratic-looking than the sternly handsome, Virginia-born Taliaferro, Count Beltrami was a fighting patriot who, with the wars at home going against him, had decided to join the ranks of Mississippi-source explorers. He had met Taliaferro in a Pittsburgh hotel, dragooned the Indian agent into escorting him to the Far West, and now, May 10, 1823, he stood before the Snellings, letters from their St. Louis relatives and friends in his slim-fingered fist. He spoke little English, but his French, like the rest of his charm, was fluent, and he soon discovered that he and Abigail, who had lived in the Gallic Missouri community, had a language in common.

The colonel graciously made him a house guest, and Beltrami settled into rounds of repartee with his hostess, buffalo hunts on the prairie, and the acquisition of, as young Henry Snelling saw it, "curiosities with which to enrich the museums of his native country." In the frontispiece of the book he wrote after leaving the fort, Beltrami is depicted alfresco, armed with a bow and a quiver full of arrows while Indians in the background have at it with clubs and tomahawks. He had arrived bursting with desire to witness an Indian battle, and he awaited such an opportunity impatiently.

Meanwhile, Taliaferro had sent out a call for the tribes to come in for council. Joe Snelling had been up at the head of the St. Peter's and had returned with Wanata, pride of the Yanktons. Beltrami appears to have been impressed enough with the chief himself, but like all good importunists he could not get his mind off Wanata's most prized possession once he saw it. The bear claw collar which Wanata wore as a badge of prowess clearly belonged, in Beltrami's scheme of things, in an Italian museum. He tried money, baubles, every ruse he could conceive without in any way tempting Wanata to part with his carcanet. At last Beltrami asked Abigail Snelling to help him, in the hope that the proud Sioux might be vulnerable to a feminine approach. Wanata offered her a fair deal. If she would cut off her hair ("very silkey," said her son, "fine and long, reaching nearly to the ground as she stood") and braid it to be worn in place of the bear claws, Wanata would be glad to accommodate Beltrami. One more defeat for Italy.

Within a few days Beltrami was frustrated again. More Sioux had trailed in after Wanata, and Chippewa bands had come downriver from the North Woods. With Snelling and his officers present, Taliaferro harangued them with peace talk and explained his plan for a mass conference at Prairie du Chien as soon as things could be arranged. As Beltrami described the scene, "The council-hall is, as it ought to be, a great room built of trunks of trees. The flag of the United States waves in the centre, surrounded by English colours . . . presented by the Indians to the *Father*, the agent, as proof that they abjure all cabal and alliance with the English. Pipes, or calumets, and other little Indian presents, offered by the various tribes as pledges of their friendship, decorate the walls and give a remarkable and characteristic air to the room. . . . The *séance* opens with a speech of the chief, who rises and addresses the agent." But no trouble, and that disappointed the Italian witness. He had to wait until Flat Mouth, chief of the Pillager Chippewas, showed up two days late. When Flat Mouth slipped into the shadow of the fort at the head of a flotilla of nineteen warrior-packed canoes, he refused to take the proffered hand of a Sioux chief who was amiably playing at peace as he had been urged. The Sioux knew an insult when they saw one, and things began to look up for Beltrami. While the Sioux raised a war party and danced all night, the battle-happy Chippewas hid their women and children behind the abandoned log structures of Cantonment New Hope. Snelling and the agent parleyed. After daybreak Taliaferro marched up to the two-hundred-pound Flat Mouth and thundered that four other Chippewa chiefs had just smoked the calumet with the Sioux and no bad blood on Flat Mouth's part was going to put an end to this peace. Unless the Pillager buried the hatchet immediately, Snelling's men "would bring out a few pieces of artillery and drive off the whole party." Flat Mouth backed down.

Beltrami moaned. "Everything conspired against my poor notes," he wrote. "I had already perched myself on an eminence for the purpose of enriching them with an Indian battle, and behold I have nothing to write. . . . I almost suspected that the savages were in a league with the gentlemen of the fort to disappoint me." Another sentence is at least as revealing: "I had half a mind to ask them to be so obliging as to fight in jest, [inasmuch] as they would not fight in earnest." The cast of Buffalo Bill's Wild West show might have understood such sentiments, but the Sioux-Chippewa feud was holy war; having already lasted longer than Europe's Hundred Years' War, it was never a jesting matter. When the Chippewas started up the Mississippi toward home, some Sioux disregarded Taliaferro's threat and tailed the enemy. Snelling detached one of his companies and sent it striding after them. Once again Taliaferro's tenuous peace was preserved when the men of the Fifth headed off the altercation before it had a chance to begin.

Beltrami accepted the fort's hospitality for another month. He apparently shared with Snelling the report that Major Stephen Long was due once again at St. Peter's; this time the visitor of 1817 was at the head of a scientific expedition to examine the valleys of the St. Peter's and the Red rivers and to proceed to the forty-ninth parallel, now agreed upon as the western Canadian border. Hitchhiking with such a party as Long was heading was just what Beltrami had hoped for as a way to get up into the Mississippi headwaters. Snelling had sent Lieutenant Martin Scott to Fort Crawford to provide Long with an escort, and Beltrami bided his time.

Taliaferro was later to boast that during this period he maintained "peace for two years and six months, lacking 15 days. . . . Colonel Robert Dickson remarked to me that such a thing had never occurred before, even when he headed these tribes. . . ." Peace was a generous word that summer of 1823. The Sioux and Chippewa failed to provide Beltrami with a pitched battle, but Snelling's detachments holding down the forts at Prairie du Chien and Rock Island were being harried—even as Taliaferro lectured his gathering—by Sac and Fox reports that the Sioux were readying an invasion of their country. Taliaferro's interpreter, Colin Campbell, had gone west, and he was with a party of Sioux who were in another aggressive mood—helping to make Leavenworth look foolish in his aborted effort to punish the Arickara. Indians of all the tribes were still visiting the British at Malden, but that summer it was the Sioux who were everybody's villains. The British agent openly told Sac and Fox visitors that the tribes were entirely justified in killing Sioux intruders. And to what must have been Taliaferro's disgust, the Englishman added that the Indians shouldn't blame American agents for being less than generous because, after all, the real father of the natives was the king, not the President.

Coming up the Mississippi, Major Long and his party got wind of the Sioux-Chippewa unrest when he stopped to parley with Wabasha, whom he had learned to admire six years before. But

Long failed to encounter anyone who was bloodthirsty, and Martin Scott, one of the best soldiers on the frontier, had no problems as escort. The major's mission was anything but military. He had with him astronomist James Calhoun, nephew of the Secretary of War; Samuel Seymour, the artist who had gone west with Long to the Rockies; William Keating, a young geologist on the frontier for the first time; and the great Thomas Say, entomologist, conchologist and zoologist. (Like that of Lewis and Clark, the party included a Negro, Andrew Allison.) Some in boats and some traveling by land, Long's men paused on July 2 to call on Little Crow, and found the whole village off on a summer hunt. Then in sultry darkness the scientists turned into the St. Peter's entry "too late to approach the works" on the promontory. Refusing to share with Jean Baptiste Faribault "and his Indian family the shelter of a hovel," they bedded down outdoors, not far from Leavenworth's Cantonment New Hope. Faribault was not on Pike's island, for the establishment he had made there had been flooded out, and he had been notified by Snelling that the claims made in Leavenworth's treaty were illegal.

In the morning, the Long party climbed the steep road Snelling's men had built from the St. Peter's bottomlands to the top of the bluff; there, to the surprise of William Keating, the expedition's chronicler, they found "at an immense distance from civilization, many of the comforts of life." Abigail Snelling's home was "even elegant," and Long's weary party, having been on the march for two months, stopped for a week of what they considered to be a much needed respite. Keating fails to give us details of how they were entertained by the garrison, but we have it on the authority of the Snelling youngsters' nurse that when the fort had a visitor "there was great striving to do him honor." Certainly they celebrated the Fourth of July; and on the sixth they took the jaunt that was *de rigeur*—to the Falls of St. Anthony—where "we recruited our strength," Keating said, "by a copious and palatable meal, prepared for us by the [mill detachment's] old sergeant; whether from the exercise of the day, or from its intrinsic merit, we know not, but the black bass . . . appeared to us excellent." (Keating wasn't always so restrained about the remarkable qualities of the local fish, for he made note of a catfish "caught at the falls weighing one hundred and forty-two pounds.")

The Long party was more interested in picking up all possible information about the country that lay ahead of them, and there were enough traders around to give them an earful. The astute Joseph Renville, who had interpreted for Pike, was signed on as guide, and the travelers explored the history of the various Sioux with Robert Dickson's half-breed son William. They were given a hint of what they could expect from the Yanktons by Charles Hess, a former Hudson's Bay trader who was then a patient in the fort hospital. Hess told Thomas Say that food that year was so scarce at Selkirk's Red River settlement, where he had been living, that people were starving. With his two half-Chippewa daughters and a couple of companions, Hess had gone out on the prairie to scare up some buffalo, at one point going off alone to chase a couple of bulls. When he returned, "he saw one of companions feathered with arrows, scalped, and his feet separated from his legs. A little further lay his daughter, murdered, and with a knife still lodged in her breast. . . ." Some distance away he found his other fellow hunter slain by Yankton arrows, but there was no trace of his second girl. Days later at the nearby post at Pembina he got word that she was alive in a Yankton village. Hess went after her. "You know me as Standing Buffalo," he told the Yankton headman. "You know you have killed one of my daughters and taken the other prisoner." The Yankton stepped back and pulled an arrow against his bowstring. Hess whipped out his gun and stood him off. But even though the Indian was now willing to dicker, he wasn't easily persuaded to release the daughter. He asked, and finally got, four yards of scarlet cloth, two white blankets, four yards of strouding, a chief's coat, a tin kettle, two guns, one pair of pistols, a framed looking glass, two knives, six double handfuls of gunpowder, two hundred bullets and a pile of blue beads. To top it all off, Hess confessed he never was rightly sure the girl really wanted to leave her abductor.

Hess' story was typical of what Long's expedition might run

into, one way or another, considering how the roving bands of Sioux had been behaving that summer. And, although Snelling asked Long to let Beltrami travel with the party, he would take no chances on the possibility of Indians accommodating the Italian with a serious assault on the government scientists. He told Martin Scott to make an express trip downriver, returning the Fort Crawford detachment to Prairie du Chien, then to catch up with Long before the travelers reached the country of itinerant predators. Meanwhile he put St. Clair Denny in temporary command of eighteen picked soldiers, and agreed to let his son Joe join up as assistant interpreter. Taliaferro lent Beltrami his horse Cadmus, and the expedition got underway, half by land and half in boats well stocked with provisions from the fort.

They met only friendly Indians the first two weeks out. At Lake Traverse Wanata, still bedecked with sixty grizzly bear claws strung around his throat, feasted them on dog and buffalo meat and presided over performances that included a song by the suspected abductor of Charles Hess' daughter. A few days later they ran into trouble. It might have been serious trouble had it not been for Major Long's cool command and the steady nerves of one of Snelling's enlisted men. While Lieutenant Scott and other sharpshooters were off in search of game, a band of close to a hundred Wahpekutes turned up, shouting insults and eyeing the expedition's horses. With Joe Snelling doing the interpreting, Long rejected their demand that his party detour to pay tribute to the Wahpekute chief. He passed out some tobacco and moved the expedition on, but the Indians trailed behind and, after no one had traveled more than a quarter-mile, a dozen of the redskins ran up ahead, firing across the expedition's path; they formed a crescent in front of the procession and leveled their guns. "Their intentions," says Keating, "could not be misunderstood . . . it was evident that the first gun fired would be the signal for an attack, which must end in the total destruction of our party. . . ." But a soldier named George Bunker was willing to risk it. When an Indian grabbed the reins of the lead horse and cocked his gun, Bunker looked him in the eye and brought up his own weapon. Thus faced with the realization that he couldn't buffalo Bunker, the Wahpekute dropped the reins and stalled. Long came galloping up to the head of the line and led his men out. The would-be Indian raiders, not quite willing to bring Fort Snelling's full might into the field, skulked off.

The escort from the fort remained with Long after the expedition left Sioux territory and proceeded through Lake of the Woods and the Rainy River country toward Lake Superior and Mackinac. But the explorers saw few Chippewas and those they did encounter were properly respectful. One whom they met was not quite what he seemed, but they had heard of him at various places—undoubtedly at the fort—and were prepared therefore to be interested. He was a Chippewa, not by birth but with credentials almost as good as if he had been born into the tribe. To his Indian friends and relatives he was known as the Falcon, but he had been christened John Tanner in Kentucky, had been kidnapped by Shawnees, traded to Chippewas and raised by a stouthearted, whiskey-drinking squaw who virtually was chief of her band. Long's people ran into the Falcon at the Hudson's Bay Rainy Lake post then run by Dr. John McLaughlin (who in ten years would be in charge of almost everything in Oregon). McLaughlin was one of several white men who had aided the Falcon in his effort to reestablish his civilized status. Another was Lord Selkirk, who had brought about a reunion with the white Indian's Kentucky family. As a result the Falcon had taken some of his half-breed children to the United States and was now en route to Mackinac with two teen-age daughters. Unhappily, the girls' mother did not approve of their removal and had paid an Indian to shoot the father. The Falcon was winding up his convalescence at McLaughlin's post when Long pulled in and offered to let the girls and their father join his party. Keating wrote that "the poor man's heart was light and happy at the idea of resuming his journey in such company as secured him against apprehensions of an attack, when his happiness met with a terrible and unexpected check." The Falcon's daughters disappeared. Unable to find any immediate trace of them and assured by McLaughlin that Hudson's Bay would swing all its weight to rescue them, the Falcon started out with Long but was forced to turn back when his wound proved to be too painful for travel. Keating told the story of Chippewa John Tanner in his narrative of the Long expedition, and the avid public which followed the published accounts of frontier experience got a second chance to wonder over the effects of Indian life on the former Kentucky youngster. For a half-dozen years earlier, Selkirk had written a pamphlet about the Falcon, and the latter had become something of a hero because of the story of his exploits in the Hudson's Bay-North West Company struggle. He himself also related the events of his extraordinary life in a book edited by Edwin James. However, there proved to be too much Indian in him when he tried to settled down in Mackinac. Although he worked for a while as an interpreter and married a white girl, his wilderness etiquette displeased his bride, who soon left him. We do not know what tales about him were brought back to the fort by Lieutenants Scott and Denny, but there is no doubt that the Falcon evoked as much interest at St. Peter's as did that other unofficial member of the Long expedition, Beltrami.

The fanciful Italian had decamped at Pembina and on his own had struck through the forest for the Mississippi. Returning to the fort, and after a brief reunion with his hosts, Beltrami left for New Orleans. Although he claimed to have stood at the source of the big river, his report was not only ridiculously romantic but meaningless. Long's men, protected and supplied by Snelling, provided a study of Indian anthropology, geological data and international trade relations that still stands up today. In some degree Long made up for his dismissal of the plains as an American desert; on this trip he had had scientists with him, the first to be commissioned by the government, and the data they collected was not to be outdated by even such successors as Louis Agassiz.

Important in quite another way that summer of 1823 was the fact that Long, with Fifth Regiment aid, had accomplished his mission without bloodshed in hostile country. Snelling and Taliaferro went through those sweaty months on tenterhooks. Most of the river Sioux, on the nearby stretches of the Mississippi and the St. Peter's, saw in the limestone walls of Snelling's citadel an admonition for reasonable, if not impeccable, behavior. It was the Indian away from the rivers and from the fort's high profile who could forget that the Americans had come to make him a peaceful citizen. With no Fifth Regiment soldier in sight, a roving warrior figured his chances against a traditional enemy were as good as ever. As if to prove the point, there was trouble in the Iowa country. Before Scott and Denny brought back their escort detail in the fall, a party of Sac and Fox buffalo hunters attacked a war party of Sioux and killed six, at the cost of seven dead of their own and eighteen wounded. In a stern mood, Taliaferro went down and retrieved the Sioux girl who had been captured, but after talk with Forsyth, the Sac-Fox agent, he was more than ever convinced it would take something besides the presence of soldiers to guarantee peace.

The twenty-eight-year-old Taliaferro—arrogant, cocksure, but sincerely interested in the welfare of any Indian—had been saying all along that what was needed was a rational effort to impress the tribes with American strength. He had been writing letters to Calhoun and Will Clark in St. Louis since his arrival at St. Peter's. He wanted that mammoth council of all the Upper Mississippi tribes in Prairie du Chien. But first he asked Clark to let him take a delegation of chiefs to Washington. It was an old ploy—Lewis and Clark had wanted to bring back some Sioux chiefs who would "become convinced, themselves, and on their return, convince their nations" of U.S. power; failing Sioux cooperation in 1806, the explorers had settled for the Mandan chief Big White. Will Clark saw another opportunity and he set a date for June, 1824, when he himself would escort Sac and Fox headmen in company with Taliaferro's Sioux and Chippewa.

After another confab with the tribes in September, Taliaferro and Snelling faced the winter of 1823–24 with the hope that the problems of the immediate future would be fewer. With characteristic optimism, Snelling in the spring had asked the president of Harvard to select a graduating student who would be willing to come west to tutor the fort's small fry. John Marsh, Harvard diploma in hand, arrived from Boston on October 8, along with two hundred and three recruits to fill out the Fifth's five companies garrisoned above the St. Peter's. We shall hear more of Marsh; a biographer was to label him "a trail blazer on six frontiers." On October 23 the orders of the day announced that "noncoms and soldiers will have the privilege of attending an evening school by paying a small compensation. . . . The school will be kept three evenings a week, tuition $1 per month." Needless to point out, the new civilization within the fort had little effect on its commandant and his major problems.

In spite of the satisfaction that Sac and Fox leaders saw in their coming trip to Washington, in spite of the presence of Snelling's detachments at Forts Crawford and Armstrong, nobody could keep the tribes' war parties in check. The militants waited through the winter for the return of good weather. In May, Tom Forsyth reported that a Sac-Fox posse of two hundred braves was out combing the prairie for Sioux and had refused to return. That month Taliaferro was getting reports that Sioux in the Red River Valley had been assaulting settlers who abandoned Selkirk's colony and were bound for Snelling's fort. In June the colonel confirmed the fact that Sioux had killed David Tully, his wife and infant, had scalped one of his small sons alive and abducted the boy with his brother. Snelling sent a party to pick up the boys from the traders who had ransomed them. A few days later he heard that the Sac-Fox vigilantes had captured and executed four Sioux on the Upper St. Peter's.

Taliaferro by this time was en route to Washington with a delegation that included Chippewas, Menominees, the Sioux chiefs Little Crow, Wabasha and Wanata, and their interpreter William Dickson. At Prairie du Chien he ran into mild trouble when some traders slyly worked on Wabasha and Wanata, persuading them to turn back toward home if they didn't want to get sick and die—perhaps like Big White. But Little Crow proved himself a trooper, according to Taliaferro. He sailed into Wabasha and Wanata for permitting their "ears to be pulled about by evil counsels. . . . Rise, let us be off to join the 'Red Head Parshasha' [Clark]." The two malcontents relaxed and Taliaferro's trip east with Clark went smoothly enough.

For Snelling things did not go smoothly. Taliaferro and his

troop were barely out of earshot when a Chippewa named Little Broth started down the St. Croix River with twenty-nine armed friends. They were looking for scalps. About halfway between the garrison on the St. Peter's and Fort Crawford they came upon a trader and three voyageurs who had stopped for breakfast on the Mississippi shore. Against the instincts of some of his fellows who thought it undiplomatic to kill white men, Little Broth could not resist a shot at the breakfast party. The ease with which one white man was thus dispatched brought up the weapons of other Indians. In seconds Little Broth's mobsters had collected four scalps and were hightailing it for the forests. By the time the news reached Fort Crawford and Snelling the culprits had vanished and the settlers at Prairie du Chien were in a state of near panic. Troops were called out and the Indians' upriver trail picked up, but a man as savvy as Snelling knew that foot soldiers chasing natives who were forest experts could do little more than serve as a show of force. Word was broadcast through the North Woods traders that delivery of the guilty Chippewas was expected. The Astor partisan William Holliday rounded up Little Broth, and after much intratribal debate three other murderers were turned over to another American Fur Company man, Truman Warren. In the absence of Taliaferro (who was already on record as no admirer of Astor's scofflaw traders) the four Indians were taken to Mackinac.

In the meantime the agent's trip to Washington had been a success. Taliaferro and his Indian embassy had what he called "a speedy interview with the President and the Secretary of War," and the chiefs marched down unpaved Pennsylvania Avenue and were taken on a tour of the capital. By the time they returned to the St. Peter's they had seen New York and all the burgeoning towns growing up in the wake of Ohio River steamboat traffic. Chances were, the agent thought, that the old awe and respect for the British might have been tempered by the sight of so many Americans; crowds besieged them wherever they went. Little Crow and his fellows now looked forward to the great conclave of tribesmen scheduled for August, 1825. As Snelling put it after he had welcomed the delegation home, the effect of the trip had been "wonderful; since their return, the power, wealth, and numbers of the American people have been their constant themes. . . ." And he added that "many of their stories approach so near the marvelous as to be discredited, such for example is the account of casting a cannon which they witnessed, and the magnitude of our ships."

Since 1805 Indians of the Louisiana Territory had been visiting the East, on the theory advanced by Jefferson that they might see for themselves the advantages of living in friendship with their white neighbors. "My children, we are strong," the President had said then, "we are as numerous as the Stars in the Heavens, and we are all gunmen, yet we live in peace and friendship with all Nations." Guns as big as cannons, and oceangoing vessels that seemed to make toys of dugouts and canoes were psychological tools for waging peace—or so thought Taliaferro and Snelling. Yet for every chief who brought home tales of wonder there were at least a hundred stay-at-home Indians who had not been astonished by the size of the eastern cities and who took their elders' stories with a grain of salt. Dealing with Indians was never as simple as it sometimes seemed.

CHAPTER SIX

THEME OF CONQUEST

AFTER SPENDING the winter of 1824–25 in St. Louis, Taliaferro was back at the fort in April, and his mood was dark. Gossip in the garrison had it that his courtship of one of the daughters of fur baron General Bernard Pratte had foundered. He had been a welcome guest in the Pratte mansion, according to one story, until a Chouteau girl—a cousin of the object of Taliaferro's attentions—had discovered the existence of the agent's half-breed daughter Mary. The suggestion that the fathering of a *bois brûlé* should have affected his social rating makes this a dubious tale, for Emilie Pratte, another of the general's handsome daughters, had accepted a man in similar straits. On March 10 she had been married to squaw man Ramsay Crooks. This event must have doubled Taliaferro's feeling of rejection, for Crooks was not only the father of a half-Chippewa child, he had become by this time Taliaferro's most militant adversary in Astor's American Fur Company. To see Crooks succeed where he himself failed was to chafe the St. Peter's agent again and again in the years ahead, and to see him now cementing his business connections with marital ties was galling indeed.

Yet in April, 1825, Taliaferro found even more abrasive news waiting for him at the fort. The preceding year he had managed to have his younger brother, Muscoe, appointed as his assistant, and he had left him in charge during his absence. Now, finding that Muscoe had quit and gone home, Taliaferro read the letter of explanation which had been left for him and exploded.

The younger Taliaferro's message to his brother accused John Marsh, the fort's educator, of beating him with a stick to the verge of insensibility. The fact, according to Colonel Snelling, that "Muscoe was so decidedly in the wrong that I am sure your liberality of feeling will prevent you from harboring any prejudice," tempered the agent's wrath not at all. The evidence that Muscoe had struck the first blow was thrown out by Taliaferro. There were extenuating circumstances. Snelling's naming of Marsh to succeed Muscoe had been tacitly approved by Taliaferro while he was still in St. Louis and not privy to his brother's version; but now, armed with Muscoe's accusations and his plea for retribution, the agent would not listen to reason. He found Marsh ensconced in the council house with a half-French, half-Wahpekute girl named Marguerite Decouteaux, and he lined out the charges against the man from Harvard: Marsh had assumed the assistant agent's duties under false pretenses—he had taken on concurrently the job of mail carrier and had been "absent some *thirty* or forty days" while hauling letters to and from Prairie du Chien. What's more, said the furious Taliaferro, he had accepted from trader Daniel Whitney "an Invoice of Merchandise to be disposed of, on Commission or *Salary* and stored the same, in the Agency house"; he had bartered these goods not only with soldiers and citizens but with Indians with whom a government agent was enjoined to have only non-profit relations.

"Now, Sir," Taliaferro added in his complaint to the Secretary of War, "to show that he is not entitled to either attention or Notice, independently of what has already been stated, Mr. Marsh did clandestinely take a letter of mine [accepting Snelling's appointment of Marsh] off the *file* in the Office of the *Commanding Officer*. . . ." Marsh, the agent pointed out, had been paid seventy-five dollars for his winter's work in the schoolhouse, and forty dollars for delivering the mail, in addition to whatever profits had resulted from his trading venture. Therefore Taliaferro had offered fifty dollars and not one cent more in payment of the time Marsh had devoted to the agent's duties.

In spite of John Marsh's gentle upbringing, his Harvard degree, his expressed ambition to return to Cambridge and medical school, his further career leaves some reason for suspicion. Nevertheless, and young as he was, he was not the kind to be pushed around, and he determined to plead his own case in Washington, maintaining that the stipulated salary due for six months' service as sub-agent was two hundred and fifty dollars (the amount suggested by Snelling and not protested by Taliaferro when Marsh had gone to work the preceding fall). Neither Snelling, about to take his family to Detroit on an extensive official leave, nor Taliaferro, busy with plans for that summer's grand gathering of the tribes, concerned themselves unduly as Marsh made ready to set off with his Marguerite for Prairie du Chien.

Taliaferro's hauteur in dealing with the erstwhile schoolteacher was typical of his reaction to any incident which challenged his own self-righteousness. His family had been in Virginia for one hundred and fifty odd years and he owed his station to an appointment made personally by James Monroe, a family friend. He did not doubt that he had been born a gentleman, and he looked the role. Patrician nose, firm and angular jaw, and high cheekbones are aristocratic symbols in a Taliaferro portrait painted during his prime years; the eyes are cool and widely set, and the mouth full and determined. He was not a large man, but he carried himself with military erectness. For he had come to St. Peter's with almost as much army experience as had the average Fifth Regiment officer. He had served at Bellefontaine, at Detroit and, he liked to point out, as a lieutenant had superintended the reconstruction of Fort Dearborn after it had been sacked by Indians during the War of 1812. By his own admission he had been an officer "noted for his proficiency in military tactics." For all his airs, however, he was liked and respected at the garrison, and throughout his life he treasured a statement signed by a dozen of Snelling's subalterns which expressed "entire approval of his conduct and deportment."

He wrote in later life that he liked his own days in uniform so much that he had left the ranks with real reluctance. "But President Monroe, having selected me from the line of the army, proposed the station upon me in a manner so kind . . . that I was forced to yield." The fact that his "pay was more than doubled" also clearly had something to do with his submission, for it was a period when the army had been reduced to six thousand men and the chance of promotion was consequently minimal, even for dedicated officers. So with the consolation that he "would have more command of my time" and "could return to the army at some future day," he accepted a challenge of the kind that corrupted lesser men. Five years later he congratulated himself. His work at St. Peter's had been "marked by but *few errors*," he crowed, and added, "[I] really find more System & impartiality than I could reasonably have believed myself capable of in the multiplicity of Various and perplexing duties. . . ."

Those duties were of the sort that led other Indian agents to take advantage of the natives' frequent naïveté, to side with traders in dishonest bartering, or to spend as little time actually on the job as possible. Taliaferro's sense of mission was such that he became quickly persuaded that his Indians might not survive were he not present to shepherd their interests. They discovered the meaning of his Italian surname and, as a result, spoke of him in their own tongues as Iron Cutter. Because of his impartiality, he said, they sometimes called him Four Hearts. He deemed it an agent's "imperative duty," an officer's son recalled, "to see that every Indian under his charge had the enjoyment of all his rights, and never seemed to realize his opportunities for arranging with contractors for the supply of inferior goods and dividing the profits." As far as Washington was concerned, his job was to keep the tribes satisfied with as little cost to the government as possible. He distributed gifts on discretion, food in times of extremity; he provided the services of a blacksmith and an armorer to repair traps and guns; he instituted a vaccination program and tried to keep his Sioux and Chippewas healthy.

But that self-righteousness restricted his admirers almost entirely to members of the garrison and the natives themselves, and the spring of 1825 saw the real beginning of his long conflict, in which Snelling shared, with Crooks and the traders of the American Fur Company. On April 10, eight days after his return from St. Louis on the steamboat *Rufus Putnam*, a week after his first confrontation with Marsh, Taliaferro issued a circular letter to all traders, pursuant to a new law which instructed Indian agents "to designate, from time to time, certain convenient &

suitable places for carrying on trade . . . and to require all traders to trade at the place thus designated and at no other place." The object of the law was to help such men as Taliaferro and Snelling to supervise fur entrepreneurs intent upon whiskey peddling and other abuses of Indian well-being. Taliaferro's circular assigning trade locations for his vast area resulted at once in an explosive meeting at Prairie du Chien of fur men who protested that the sites named showed the agent's ignorance of the terrain and of the basic need for easy accessibility to such necessities as wood and hunting grounds. Taliaferro's haughty complacency, it was intimated, had kept him from consulting experts in the field. Worse, he and Snelling were accused of using the location laws to favor the small trading outfits which were Astor's competitors. Naturally such accusations left the St. Peter's agent unruffled, though he did make some adjustments at the suggestion of Superintendent Clark. He was convinced, he wrote later in his journal, that the Astor men in his region were "men of *mean* principles and low origin—consequently are jealous—evil disposed & great Vagabonds—and it is really amusing to Witness—see or hear of their rascality."

Yet he was less amused at the moment than he was in retrospect. That spring, after he had sent out the call for the tribes to gather for the excursion to Prairie du Chien, he was as intolerant as ever when his plans went awry. He blamed Astor's North Woods traders for prejudicing the Chippewas against participation in the council. He believed, first, that the American Fur Company held a firmer grip on the Chippewas because of the tribe's fear of hostile Sioux; and second that Astor's men were deliberately trying to sabotage any possibility of permanent peace that might come from the powwow. Unscrupulous in their use of liquor to beguile Indian trappers, such traders, he felt, would stop at nothing. And Snelling agreed with him, the colonel reporting from Detroit on practices he had observed along his route which were unrestrained "by any moral rules."

By midsummer, because of this unfettered influence of traders antagonistic to governmental regulation, Taliaferro had been able to round up only twenty-six Minnesota Chippewas. (Although

Flat Mouth begged off sick, the distinguished Curly Head, along with Strong Ground and Hole-in-the-Day, were in the van.) The agent also had three hundred and fifty-nine Sioux gathered at the fort. In a great armada of canoes, the Fort Snelling delegation slipped down the Mississippi between towering bluffs and pulled in at a point known as Painted Rock for the traditional pause to adorn themselves in costumery and paint. Then, said Taliaferro, "the grand entry was made with drums beating, many flags flying, with incessant discharges of small arms. All Prairie du Chien was drawn out, with other delegations already arrived, to witness the display and landing of this ferocious looking body of true savages." With skins of skunks attached to their heads as symbols that they never ran, the Sioux chiefs viewed the Indian lodges lining the Mississippi banks for miles above and below the white settlement. Henry Schoolcraft was there with one hundred and thirty-two Saulteur Chippewas, and there were Winnebagos, Ottawas, Menominees and Potawatomis on hand. Taliaferro reported to Lewis Cass, Clark's co-commissioner for the negotiations, and found John Marsh.

Still governor of Michigan Territory, Cass had been at work for months gathering anthropological data about the natives under his jurisdiction. Marsh saw in this project an opportunity; when he heard that the governor was en route to Prairie du Chien, he had taken off up the Fox-Wisconsin trail and had introduced himself to Cass at Green Bay. Already on record as an admirer of top American Fur Company traders, Cass apparently had listened attentively to Marsh's complaints about Lawrence Taliaferro. At Green Bay he had been struck immediately by the thought of a Harvard graduate who in so brief a time on the frontier had mastered a serviceable grasp of the Sioux language; that in itself recommended the ambitious Marsh as a collaborator in Cass' Indian studies. But obviously the chunky schoolmaster also had admitted that, under the aegis of Edward Purcell, the Fort Snelling surgeon, he had been studying medicine—another attribute not to be underestimated in gaining the confidence of natives. Marsh's qualifications seemed too unusual to ignore and Cass had offered to have him appointed sub-agent at Prairie du

Chien; for the immediate present Cass had promised to pay his young Harvard discovery out of his own pocket to assist in the Indian project. Faced with so considerable a coup on Marsh's part, Taliaferro bided his time, but he wasn't going to let off his brother's manhandler too easily—not if he had any influence in the Indian department.

For the present it behooved him to maintain his influence at the conference about to begin. As Tom Forsyth, on August 4, brought in the Sacs, Foxes and Iowas, the tribes passed and repassed the treaty grounds in their canoes, then hit the beach in battle formation, armed with spears, clubs, guns, and knives, glaring defiance at the Sioux. Taliaferro suavely held his Dakota chiefs in check. Wabasha, Little Crow, Wanata and Sleepy Eyes (who had been installed as head of the lower Sissetons in Washington the year before) stood steady, while Keokuk, Tiamah and the Sac-Fox delegation, heads shaved except for the red-daubed scalplocks, bearing flags of feathers, beating drums, and whooping ear-shattering cries, advanced menacingly on the council area. Schoolcraft, whom Taliaferro scorned as a pretentious literateur, was impressed by this "wild, native pride of man, in the savage state . . . confident in the strength of his arm." Yet Taliaferro was not chiefly concerned about the easy use of words; he saw Schoolcraft as a tool of American Fur Company policies —policies that were to have a direct effect upon the St. Peter's agent soon after the council began.

August heat baked the rolling Wisconsin landscape, and Cass, Clark, the agents, and the tribal headmen gathered under a canopy of leaves. Nearby sat more than a thousand natives, their skins bared to the weather, along with men of the Fifth Infantry sweating in white pants, tight blue jackets, crisscrossed breast belts and high shako caps. The conclave had been called because, said Clark, "Your great father has heard of your war songs, and of your war parties, [and] they do not please him." The establishment of boundaries to which each tribe would adhere was prescribed as the means to prevent hostilities.

But the hostile feelings had not been left behind when the tribes had set out for the council. Taliaferro was soon called to account on the charge that a Sioux brave had brandished his war club at a Chippewa in the very shadow of the Fort Crawford gate; to prevent bloodshed, Cass told the St. Peter's agent he had better send his Chippewas to join their fellow tribesmen in School-craft's area of the camp grounds. Taliaferro saw this as a ruse on the part of Astor's friends to concentrate all the Chippewas in the hands of an agent they could control. Throughout the treaty (he wrote later in his third-person autobiography) he had felt "the inveterate hostility of the American Fur Company's traders from the North and elsewhere. The Chippewas . . . who had known their friend [Taliaferro] from 1820, yearly visiting the post at Fort Snelling, kept the agent constantly informed of the secret councils called to detach them from his camp . . . but all in vain —they would not be detached." Taliaferro added that Astor's "drunken Scotchman," John Holiday, had been delegated to "bully" him, and he accused Schoolcraft of maneuvering to in-fringe on what was properly Fort Snelling jurisdiction. However, the commissioners "on reflection," he said, "found the Sioux agent too well booked up on Indian affairs," and the showdown over the Chippewas was set aside.

Even with the presence of Will Clark, highly respected by most red men for his explorations twenty years before, the In-dians were slow to accept the idea of hard-and-fast boundaries. Clark told the chiefs they could discuss the proposition among themselves, but he and Cass went easy in dispensing whiskey. The Indians were enjoined to get the work done before celebrat-ing. They, in turn, called this edict downright stingy. To prove that it wasn't a matter of saving the drinks for the white men present, Clark shocked the Indians by filling kettles with liquor only to pour it out on the ground. The natives "loved the whiskey better than the joke," Schoolcraft said wryly. But in spite of the fact that Keokuk treated the Sioux as if he wanted only a chance "to make their blood flow like water," the several tribes managed to come to reluctant agreement on whose territory was whose. Then they feasted, and the whiskey flowed. Liquor failed to end this rally of tribes on a happy note—it never did with Indians. In Josiah Snelling's words, written from Detroit while Taliaferro was escorting his delegation back to the fort, "herds of Indians are drawn together by the fascinations of whiskey, and they exhibit the most degraded picture of human nature I ever witnessed."

On the homeward trail Taliaferro's Sioux showed more than signs of degradation—they began to die. Lack of sanitation in the steaming council bivouacs, the white man's diet of beans and salt meat, and the government alcohol exacted their toll. Curly Head of the Chippewas succumbed at Lake Pepin after passing his chieftainship on to the brothers Hole-in-the-Day and Strong Ground; Hole-in-the-Day's wife died. Some survivors blamed the epidemic on the government mixture of sugar and alcohol. Others were blunt—the booze had been poisoned. Taliaferro found fifteen victims abandoned by their escorts and insisted they be carried by those who were still ambulatory. At the fort two Sioux died, and several others were admitted to the hospital to convalesce. Never ecstatic about the conference their agent had arranged, the Sioux became more and more incensed, and Taliaferro had two hundred and fifty dollars' worth of goods distributed to show the government's goodwill. To console them for the loss of relatives, he gave out more than one hundred gallons of whiskey without which, a native had assured Snelling once, they were unable to cry—it took spirits to produce a good flow of tears.

The winter that followed was brutal. Snow came early, piled high, and lasted into April. When the game vanished, many Indian families were snowbound and starved to death. One episode foreshadowed the Donner party experience twenty years later. Their lodges buried in drifts, some Sioux resorted to cannibalism; a handsome squaw who was rescued and brought into the fort had eaten her dead infant and sampled the flesh of her father before she lost all sanity; later, slipping away from Taliaferro's care, she jumped from the bluff and died in the river. At Selkirk's colony some of the immigrant settlers froze to death, and others were reduced to eating their horses, dogs, and—that classic of extremity on every winter frontier—boiling shoe leather for what was euphemistically known as soup. That last snowstorm hit Fort Snelling on April 5, the sky flashing with lightning, and thunder reverberating over the prairie; and five days later the thermometer had crept up to five degrees below zero. Although within ninety-six hours it was warm enough to rain and the ice in the St. Peter's began to break, the frozen Mississippi held firm until April 21. Then came the "Great Flood," the worst of that era. Taliaferro recorded in his journal, April 23, that the flood level was twenty feet above the low-water mark. "High water and ice take all houses on the St. Peters and Mississippi near this Post—except at Land's End Factory." At Prairie du Chien, low-lying Fort Crawford was flooded and the settlers were driven to the hills. With them went Winnebago agent Nicholas Boilvin, who was in charge of John Marsh's Marguerite and the infant son who had been born in a February blizzard; Marsh had gone east where, with Cass' help, he had persuaded Calhoun's successor as Secretary of War to put him on the government payroll.

Taliaferro maintained his hauteur. "Observed a communication," he told his diary laconically, "in the St. Louis or Missouri Republican of March 23, 1826, containing some ill natured remarks in relation to myself. The author being a man of ill fame —consequently shall not notice his gross and palpable misrepresentations and speculations. *Strange but true.*" True to his creed he held himself above calumniation; and even though Marsh had persuaded the Indian department to pay him the sub-agent's salary which Taliaferro had refused him, the St. Peter's agent was unconcerned so long as Marsh was working for someone else. With the rampageous flood subsiding, life at the entry, for the moment, posed few problems. The steamboat *Lawrence* pulled in from St. Louis, and Captain Reeder on May 3, wrote Taliaferro, "invited all Ladies and Gentlemen of the Fort to take a trip of pleasure to the Falls by water accompanied by Band of music. . . . There was dancing &c on board."

That complacency soon ended. On the Upper Mississippi and all its tributaries there appeared signs that the Indian boundaries established the year before were being ignored. If one tribesman killed another on Indian territory, there was little to be done unless the lives of whites were threatened. The treaty could demand peace, Taliaferro could preach peace, but neither he nor Snelling had authority to mete out punishment for breaches of the 1825 tribal covenant. They had to wait until crimes were committed against American citizens. Even before the flood had struck, a Prairie du Chien farmer and his family had been slain, but it was weeks before the news reached the authorities. Unknown assailants had shot a man named Methode, his wife and five children, while they were tapping sugar trees near Painted Rock. No clue existed except a scrap of red cloth clenched in the teeth of the family's dog which was also killed. Then as spring came on, Boilvin encountered a Winnebago whose red leggings had been ripped. Little theorizing was required to fit the pieces together, but the accomplices in the murders had vanished and the settlers who were scattered around Fort Crawford lived in terror that these killers on the loose might strike again.

Lieutenant Colonel Willoughby Morgan, commanding the detachments of the Fifth stationed at Crawford, seized two Winnebago chiefs as hostages with the predictable result—fellow tribesmen rounded up the murderers and they were locked in the Crawford guardhouse. But the Winnebagos, generally, continued to be uncooperative. White men were moving in on their lead mines and otherwise disregarding their rights. Now was as good a time as any, it seemed to the Indians, to make a stand. They filled the hot summer with threats. Willoughby Morgan relayed to Colonel Snelling their demands for the release of the prisoners at Fort Crawford, and both officers stood firm. Winnebago ambassadors then parleyed with Wabasha, and there were rampant rumors that Wabasha was willing to league himself with the Winnebagos if the Sioux villages on the St. Peter's would support an uprising. Snelling, in close touch with Taliaferro, acted. He sent Companies A, B, and I downriver to back up Morgan. "I have no serious apprehensions for the safety of Fort Crawford," he wrote the agent, who was then with the Sissetons on the St. Peter's headwaters, "but the reports afloat were of such imposing character that I thought it my duty to reinforce [Morgan]." Still more complacent than he might have been, he added that if Crawford had fallen "for want of aid, I should have lost my

Capt. Seth Eastman, who several times commanded at Snelling, painted this view of the fort as seen from the southeast, probably from sketches he made on Pike's island. After his retirement from active service he was commissioned to paint a series of pictures to hang in the office of the House Committee on Military Affairs. His "Fort Snelling," is one of them.

"We sailed with our violens [*sic*] and other music playing," wrote young Lt. Zebulon Pike of the 1805–06 journey during which he persuaded the Sioux to cede the site of the future citadel. But there were moments on his Mississippi trip that were less felicitous, for he had little luck controlling British traders.

Army engineer Stephen Long traveled in a six-oared skiff presented to him by Lewis' partner William Clark when he inspected the high ground above the St. Peter's and recommended "a military work of considerable magnitude." Six years later when he paid a second visit in 1823 he found the site as strongly fortified as he had imagined.

Lt. Col. Henry Leavenworth led the first troops to the confluence of the Mississippi and the St. Peter's but was superseded by Josiah Snelling, a full colonel. Leavenworth fixed his place in history after he was transferred to duty on the Missouri, and the fort he established there provided frontier protection for the community that still bears his name.

Abigail Hunt Snelling had just entered her twenties when she came to the St. Peter's to reign at cotillions in the wilderness and to raise a covey of children. She had been a child herself, living at a fort near St. Louis, when Lewis and Clark made their triumphal return from the Pacific.

Josiah Snelling was a Boston baker's son who fought the Shawnees at Tippecanoe Creek under William Henry Harrison and distinguished himself in the War of 1812. His thinning red hair inspired his men to refer to him as "the prairie chicken."

The first troops spent a miserable winter in 1819–20 in a log stockade on the bottomland just across the St. Peter's from the future fort. This rough sketch, drawn from imagination, does little more than suggest the isolation and the primitive facilities with which the Fifth Regiment had to cope while dealing with Sioux and Chippewa Indians:

Undoubtedly idealized to some extent, this portrait of Lawrence Taliaferro nonetheless suggests the man as he was—perhaps more aware than absolutely necessary of his aristocratic lineage, yet fair-minded and sympathetic to the problems of his Indian charges whose life in the Fort Snelling vicinity is shown obscurely in the background.

This portrait of Count Beltrami is the frontispiece of the Italian's account of his visit to the American West. The background terrain is interesting but it does not immediately convey either the prairie or the forests through which this romantic traveler moved during his Minnesota excursion.

MINNESOTA HISTORICAL SOCIETY, FROM AN ORIGINAL
IN THE HILL REFERENCE LIBRARY, ST. PAUL

Eastman in this watercolor shows the Sioux use of the travois to haul their worldly goods behind a horse. A white man's kettle obtained through trade can be seen near the center of the load, and next to it an infant in a papoose. The beast of burden at the right is likely to be the child's mother.

Joseph Nicollet found traders generally cooperative when he explored the Mississippi headwaters in the 1830's. In this modern mural, painted for the courthouse in Brainerd, Minn., he is shown, second from left, entering the Morrison trading post at the mouth of the Crow Wing River. The tableau may seem a bit stiff, the Chippewas somewhat romanticized, but the atmosphere generally reflects the fur trade as it was policed by Snelling.

MINNESOTA HISTORICAL SOCIETY

Captain Eastman tried to police whiskey peddlers who pandered to Fort Snelling Indians, but a native tippler was much too good a subject for the painter to ignore. Tongue in cheek, he called this oil "Good Medicine." His wife, whose books Eastman illustrated, had her own title, "The Lonely Indian." The Sioux elbow-bender, she wrote, "is in mourning having obtained a bottle of fire water (whiskey) to drown his sorrow . . . The dress is that of the Indians living near the headwaters of the St. Peter's."

Far from accurate, this map is as colorful as the man who drew it, Lawrence Taliaferro. He shows Cloud Man's village at the top, the public gardens which provisioned the garrison, the agency compound, the Indian council house, and the American Fur Co. establishment in 1835.

This miniature of Ramsay Crooks was done in 1825 when his differences with Josiah Snelling and Lawrence Taliaferro were an important influence on life at the citadel.

Henry Hastings Sibley was painted in his middle years by an unknown artist and the portrait now hangs in the restored Sibley house. He became the first elected governor of Minnesota before he was fifty, an occasion that may be commemorated here.

Samuel Pond and his brother Gideon came to Fort Snelling in their twenties and spent the rest of their lives in the vicinity as missionaries to the Indians and ministers to early settlers.

Fort Snelling commanded the land of the long horizon and Captain Eastman often painted such sweeping vistas as this. The above engraving, made from Eastman's oil, is one of his many illustrations for the treatise on U.S. tribes of which Henry Schoolcraft was the editor. This is the Santee Sioux country as it was in the heyday of the citadel.

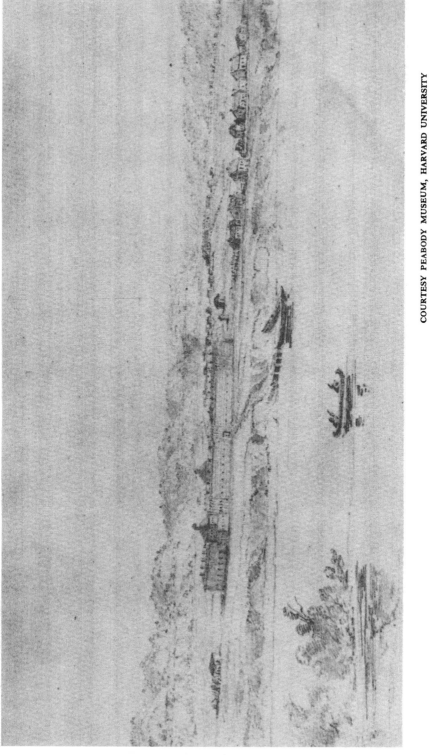

The nearest settlement to Fort Snelling was some two hundred miles downriver at Prairie du Chien, shown in this Eastman pencil sketch made in 1829. The wooden Fort Crawford stockade appears in the foreground along with a half dozen voyageur homes. Stretching out behind the stockade can be seen other houses of settlers and traders, some of

Taliaferro helped George Catlin find models among both the Sioux and the Chippewas. This sketch shows He Who Stands on Both Sides, who warranted the year's most valuable player award for his prowess as a Sioux lacrosse player.

Unlike Seth Eastman and J. C. Wild, Capt. Nathan Jarvis must be considered an amateur draftsman. During his tenure as the fort's medical officer he penned many illustrated letters home, including this one, offering an "idea of the position of the Fort at least better than I can describe it." He said he drew this view from the opposite bank of the St. Peter's.

BY LAWRENCE TALIAFERRO,

AGENT OF INDIAN AFFAIRS AT ST. PETERS—TO ALL WHOM IT MAY CONCERN.

Whereas, Henry H. Sibley, Agent of the Am. Fur Company _____ having applied for a

LICENSE to trade for *one* year at the *Entry of the River St. Peters near Fort Snelling*

the place designated for carrying on Trade with the *Medawakanton, and other Sioux* _____ Nations, or Tribes of Indians,

and at no other place; *he* _____ having furnished an Invoice of Merchandize, intended for Trade, and *has* given bond, according to law,

for the due observance of all such regulations as now are, or hereafter may be established for the government of Trade and Intercourse with the Indian

Tribes—LICENSE for *one* _____ year is hereby granted to the said *Henry H. Sibley, Agent of the Am. Fur Company*

to trade with the said Indians, according to the regulations aforesaid; who *is* hereby authorised to take with *him Antoine Martell*,

Jean B. Henery, Adolph Stonefleurance Eugene Lancliot and Charles McMellay & Not

John Muller, Oliver Racicot, Charles Morreau, Joseph Buison, Joseph Robinson, Louis Provencalle _____

Citizens of the United States, to assist in trading at the said place for carrying on trade, for the term aforesaid, unless this permission be sooner revoked, and

the said *Henry H Sibley and his heirs* _____ recalled.

IN TESTIMONY WHEREOF, I have hereunto affixed the Seal of this Office. GIVEN UNDER MY HAND, at

Office of Indian Agency St Peters the *thirtieth* day of *September* in the year of our Lord

one thousand eight hundred and thirty *five* _____ and of the Independence of the United States of America the

sixtieth _____

Law Taliaferro
Indian Agent
at St Peters

MINNESOTA HISTORICAL SOCIETY

As Indian agent it was Taliaferro's job to screen the applications of all who sought to trade with the Fort Snelling Indians. Those who qualified were issued licenses like this one given in 1835 to Henry Sibley as agent of the American Fur Company. Ten of Sibley's "hands" are included by name in the license.

Painter J. O. Lewis drew this conception of the 1825 treaty at Prairie du Chien, to which Taliaferro brought his Fort Snelling Indians. The two figures standing in the center should be Lewis Cass and William Clark, who were joint commissioners.

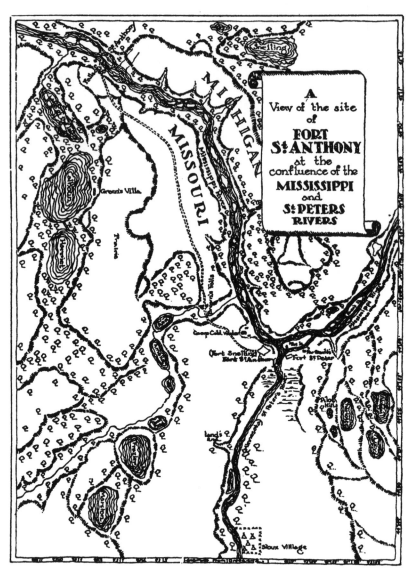

FROM MEMOIRS OF A BOYHOOD AT FORT SNELLING, BY H. H. SNELLING

Accurate views of the Fort Snelling area were mapped by two of the garrison's engineers and are combined in this drawing by Dorothy K. Phelps. The serpentine St. Peter's here flows almost straight north past Cantonment New Hope, which the younger Snelling called Fort St. Peter.

reputation forever." The Sacs and Foxes from Rock River, after all, were even then sending a delegation with a peace pipe to the Sioux. The possibility of an end of the ancient conflict among those tribes, he must have reasoned, should cause the Winnebagos to calm down.

He was proved right for the time being, but wrong in the end. No Sioux joined up with the Winnebagos, but neither did they meet with the Sac-Fox peace delegation. They remained quiet until the spring of 1827. When the summer of 1826 had passed without a Winnebago assault, the War Department looked at the situation optimistically and ordered Snelling to evacuate Fort Crawford, which had been enough damaged by floodwaters to warrant rebuilding. In October Morgan cleared out his garrison and marched, with the imprisoned Winnebagos, to Fort Snelling. In November John Marsh, no longer beholden to either Taliaferro or Snelling, warned his mentor, Cass, that unless Crawford was reactivated in the spring it seemed probable Prairie du Chien "will be nearly deserted." He thought the contention between the Winnebagos and the Americans over the lead mines at Fever River might necessitate "some interference on the part of the government." For their part, like the Sioux on the St. Peter's, the Winnebagos remained relatively quiet until the following spring.

On May 24 Taliaferro returned from St. Louis with instructions to have no more to do with the Chippewas; John Quincy Adams' Secretary of War ("a new hand," Taliaferro said pithily) had been induced to assign the responsibility for the Upper Mississippi bands of the northern tribe to Henry Schoolcraft. The St. Peter's agent was livid. He had spent seven years "gaining the friendship & confidence of the Sioux & Chippewas to a degree almost without parallel in any age or Country." He had told Clark that "every Chippeway on the Mississippi prefers me to any other man known to them." And he scored a direct hit on Schoolcraft, whose reputation as an author of works on Indians was burgeoning, by adding: "I am no *writer of books* nor do I expect to add to my fame or fortune in that way—but move on and do my country's service without such aid to give a more lovely and glowing colour to my humble operations."

Taliaferro's ire aside, the reassignment of the Chippewas was futile, and soon proved dangerous. "You might as well," a St. Peter's trader said, "try to Stop the Water in the Mississippi from going to St. Louis, as to attempt to keep the Chippeway Indians from St. Peters." Taliaferro was no sooner off the boat than he found Flat Mouth pulling up with a party of Chippewas, including Hole-in-the-Day and Strong Ground, their canoes laden with maple sugar for trade with the garrison. The agent called them to council, told them the government expected them henceforward to deal with Schoolcraft's agency, and listened to Flat Mouth reply that he felt like a dog driven away from the door. "I am ashamed of this," the big Chippewa told Taliaferro, "but I know you are doing this not by your wish." Obviously the lack of welcome at St. Peter's was not Flat Mouth's wish; for he had avoided the Prairie du Chien council, he had not signed the boundary agreement, and he felt no obligation to stay out of Sioux territory. The additional fact that he had refused to shake hands with the Sioux three summers before may have been even more accountable for what was about to happen.

Soon after his arrival, some curious Sioux showed up at the agency and, in a surprisingly friendly mood, Flat Mouth and his eight warriors invited the callers to feast with them in a Chippewa lodge. Twenty-three-year-old Joe Snelling, who was to become the first American to write about the Sioux, and who was then a fur trader, said that the Chippewas smoked the peace pipe with their guests and "no one could have suspected any sinister purpose." But for reasons unexplained the Sioux, in departing, turned on their hosts. "The eight foremost halted outside the door, while the last held it aside with his foot, and all discharged their guns into the lodge, excepting one who missed fire," the colonel's son wrote. "The assassins gave the Indian *cri de joi*, and fled like deer."

In his quarters above on the bluff, Taliaferro heard the shots and noted the hour: 9 P.M. Investigating, he found eight wounded Chippewas ("3 supposed mortal 4 very severely and one slightly") and had them carried into the council house, where the fort's surgeon worked to save their lives. Meanwhile Taliaferro sent runners to the nearby Sioux chiefs to tell them that the flag had been insulted and that satisfaction was due the Chippewas from the cowardly killers. Speaking for the victims, Strong Ground stood up before Colonel Snelling and said, "You know that two summers ago we attended a great council at Prairie du Chien, when by the advice of our white friends we made peace with the Sioux. We were told then that the Americans would guarantee our safety under their flags. We have come here under that assurance. But Father, look at your floor; it is stained with the blood of our people shed while under your walls. If you are great and powerful why do you not protect us? If *not,* what use are your soldiers?"

Snelling put his men to use the next morning when he sent Major John Fowle out with two companies to deal with about three hundred and fifty Sioux who had appeared on the prairie west of the fort. Seeing the marching ranks, the Indians turned tail, but Fowle pursued and rounded up more than a score, nine of whom Snelling delivered to the Chippewas for interrogation and summary punishment. Identifying two as among those guilty of the massacre the night before, Flat Mouth's delegation got Snelling's permission to execute them immediately. The two Sioux were told to run and were cut down by Chippewa fire. The usual prairie mayhem followed. Women and children hacked the bodies with tomahawks and knives, drank blood, sang and danced in frenzy. Two days later two others of the slayers were given up by the Sioux, and the gantlet justice repeated.

Meanwhile, the Sioux were being harassed on another front. Tom Forsyth wrote Taliaferro that the aging Black Hawk (who, like Flat Mouth, had not participated at Prairie du Chien) had been threatening for two weeks to mount an expedition against Taliaferro's charges. The Sac chief had scorned a bribe of three horses and other temptations and had laughed at Forsyth's threat to put him and his war party in irons and send them to lifetime jail sentences in St. Louis. A second offer of seven horses also failed to impress Black Hawk, and the recalcitrant Sac bolstered his threat by enlisting the war party of another non-signer of the 1825 treaty. Then, for reasons Forsyth couldn't explain, the old partner of Tecumseh cooled down.

To the north of the Sacs word spread among the tribes that the Fort Snelling reservation was one place where it didn't pay to breach the peace, but the facts seem to have gotten garbled by the time the news reached the Winnebagos. One of their better known characters, the heretofore friendly Red Bird, accepted the rumor that the Indians who died at the fort were not Sioux but the Winnebago prisoners from Prairie du Chien, who had yet to be brought to trial. In the prevailing Winnebago mood, Red Bird was uninterested in checking the facts and he began plotting reprisal. In less than a month the situation was sufficiently tense for John Marsh to surmount his recent differences with the St. Peter's agent. He warned Taliaferro that he had reason to believe that "a party of Sioux from the lower band and about thirty Winnebagos are going to St. Peter's to kill *you* and any American that they can find at a distance from the Fort." He told Snelling that a scheme was afoot to loot and burn Prairie du Chien, including the abandoned Fort Crawford structures. He had double-checked the reports and was convinced that "they deserve more credit than common Indian stories. It is said and believed by the Sioux and Winnebagoes that the two Winnebago prisoners have been given up to the Chippewas and killed by them—this, though I cannot believe it, has all the effect of truth with the Indians."

Red Bird, who did believe it, set his reprisal plan in motion even before Marsh's warning had been received at St. Peters. With three other Winnebagos, among whom was a headman called the Sun, he got his hands on some forbidden liquor and primed himself and his companions for big deeds. He and his malcontents skulked around the village, threatened the wife of a trader, then headed across the prairie to McNair's coulee. Not far away was the farm of Registre Gagnier, a mulatto half-breed. In the farmhouse kitchen, Red Bird's desperadoes found Gagnier and his wife and infant, and Solomon Lipcap, a discharged Fort Snelling soldier who a year or two earlier had saved Henry Snelling from drowning. Mrs. Gagnier confidently looked up from the washing she was doing and offered to serve the visitors some fish and a drink of milk. Gagnier, normally sympathetic to Indians because of his blood relationship, sensed that this was an occasion for precaution. He took his rifle from the wall, and as he did so Mrs. Gagnier, at the stove, heard a gun go off, swung around, and saw her husband dying on the floor. At that moment one of Red Bird's companions shot and killed Lipcap. Mrs. Gagnier rushed toward the door where the Sun hovered, surprised him, wrestled away his gun and chased him outside. But emotion overpowered her and she was unable to shoot. She ran to the village for help and when she had returned with some armed neighbors the killers had disappeared, leaving the eleven-month-old baby alive but scalped.

The drunken Indians turned up shortly on the Mississippi just as one of two keelboats, both returning to St. Louis from Fort Snelling, was pulling into shore for a respite. Supported now by other Winnebagos, Red Bird and his friends fired at the boat, shattering the leg of a Negro crewman. Another man on board was killed in the second volley. Thus began a battle that lasted until nightfall, when the boatmen managed to slip away to Prairie du Chien. Joe Snelling, on board the second vessel, reported that the crew "fought like bull dogs," losing two dead while they finished off seven Winnebagos. Their arrival in the settlement increased the fear caused by the events at the Gagnier farm, and Marsh and other village leaders herded as many settlers as they could round up into the shelter of Fort Crawford. Riders were sent in various directions, and Colonel Snelling rushed down from St. Peter's with four companies of the Fifth. Taliaferro wrote Will Clark that he had strong hopes of keeping the Sioux peaceful, but assured his boss that "nothing short of a force of one thousand men well equipt for the service, can restore anything like tranquility to this bleeding frontier." There was, he urged, no time to be lost.

As Snelling was regarrisoning Fort Crawford, Henry Dodge—a man who had thrashed several jurors who were tempted to indict him as a henchman of Aaron Burr—rode in at the head of a hundred and thirty mounted volunteers from the lead mines. Governor Cass came down from Green Bay, and Major John Whistler marched his command out from Fort Howard. At the head of more than five hundred men, General Henry Atkinson came upriver from St. Louis. When Atkinson's combined forces moved up the Fox-Wisconsin route, the swift massing of so many troops cowed the Winnebagos. On the general's arrival at Crawford, Snelling had returned upriver to insure the maximum effectiveness of his own fort, but he dispatched John Fowle and four other Fort Snelling companies to be based henceforward at Crawford. These men of the Fifth joined the expedition that brought the Winnebagos to heel on September 9. Red Bird had come into the American camp bearing a white flag and had delivered up himself and his three accomplices. He seemed to Thomas L. McKenney, head of the Indian bureau, a savage prince. "His face was painted, one side red, the other intermixed with green and white," McKenney said. "There he stood. Not a muscle moved. . . . He appeared to be conscious that, according to Indian law, and measuring the deed he had committed by the injustices and wrongs and cruelties of the white man, he had done no wrong. . . . As to death, he had been taught to despise it. . . ." His law, McKenney added, was the Biblical law of an eye for eye, but in the interest of his tribe and with the new realization that the Winnebagos could not win against a superior military force, he bound himself over to White man's justice. With Red Bird's surrender, the threat of "a general Indian war" of which Taliaferro had warned Clark in midsummer vanished, for a time at least. But another phase of Northwest troubles was just approaching a climax. On September 12 a bargeload of trade goods was drawn up at the St. Peter's landing, and Lawrence Taliaferro learned that Ramsay Crooks and the American Fur Company had taken over the last of the independent companies outside of the mountain trade.

CHAPTER SEVEN

THE HINGE OF THE FUTURE

THE SUMMER OF 1827 was a season of big changes in the fur trade, and the arrival at Fort Snelling of Kenneth Mackenzie and his bargeload of goods was part of a scheme that would affect traders and trappers from Detroit to the Rockies, from the Rainy River country to the Sante Fe trail. Ramsay Crooks, Astor's director of operations, after long plotting had brought into the American Fur Company the men and the organizations whose competition in the region between the Mississippi and the Missouri most deprived him of full success; their cooperation now was to help make the company a virtual nationwide trust. But there were changes other than those for which Crooks was responsible.

Soon after Snelling and Taliaferro had settled in at the St. Peter's entry, a revolution in the fur trade had been started by William Ashley, lieutenant governor of the new state of Missouri. Instead of clinging (as had such experts as Manuel Lisa and Robert Dickson) to the ancient pattern of fixed trading posts to which Indians brought their pelts for barter, Ashley and his partner Andrew Henry had initiated the system of roving brigades of white trappers who were supplied annually at wilderness rendezvous. These were the restless discoverers of the West who became famous as the mountain men; they traveled in small parties wherever the search for beaver took them, coming together in the summer at a designated place to which their supplier brought the year's goods. Ashley, having made himself rich in five years, did not appear in person at Rendezvous 1827, but there in his place were his successors, Jedediah Smith, David Jackson and Bill Sublette.

The success of this new partnership—which became apparent that summer at the Bear Lake rendezvous on the Utah-Idaho border—reinforced Crooks' determination to extend American Fur operations into the mountains. He had been working in this direction for months, and in the previous December he had hammered out a coalition with Pierre Chouteau, Jr., which made Bernard Pratte & Company the Western Department of the Astor trust. In the same period Crooks had been gunning for Kenneth Mackenzie, a dominating force in the fur region over which Fort Snelling stood guard. He had tried first to plow Mackenzie and his partners under, and failing that, at last had managed to close a deal that removed from the St. Peter's one of the few traders with whom Snelling and Taliaferro had found they could cooperate.

The Crooks campaign had begun soon after Taliaferro, exercising an agent's prerogative, in 1822 had issued to Mackenzie and Robert Dickson the passports needed by foreigners to proceed from Indian country to Washington, D.C. Mackenzie, like others, had come to the entry by way of Selkirk's Red River settlements. Drought, grasshoppers, bitter winters and starving times had eroded the Scottish earl's utopia. Each year since 1821, colonists imported by Selkirk had found the going too rough in British America and had headed down the Red River trail to seek shelter at Fort Snelling or at points farther south. Indians had seen to it that some, like the family of those boys John and Andrew Tully, never made the distance. But others, like the orphaned youngsters themselves, had found homes at the fort. John Tully had been taken in by Abigail Snelling, and Andrew by the wife of Captain Nathan Clark. Other squatter families lived for a time in the old Camp Cold Water log barracks, then began to farm and to sell their produce to the garrison. Snelling was permitting to develop on government property a settlement that was to cause trouble in the future. And ironically he was giving shelter to refugees from a colony whose charter claimed territory which was part of the United States. The immigrants from Red River were not all colonists, however. At least as responsible for the current exodus as the settlers' troubles was the merger in 1821 of the Hudson's Bay and North West companies, which threw hundreds of fur trade employees out of jobs. Kenneth Mackenzie was among those affected by the merger, but the reasons for his departure were not as simple as the Selkirkers' search for a more beneficent environment. His entrance into the St. Peter's trade was due, in a large measure, to the schemes of that sometimes enigmatic half-breed, Joe Renville.

Born about 1779 of a Sioux mother in Little Crow's village at Kaposia, Renville had followed his French father's trade and went to work for Robert Dickson a few years before the Britisher had taken Ramsay Crooks into his employ. Allied off and on with Dickson through the rest of the veteran trader's life, Renville had led detachments of Sioux during the War of 1812 and again had joined Dickson in the Red River country after the conflict was over. By birthright Renville knew the Sioux, their country and their combustible relationship with the Chippewas better than any man who ever lived among them. More than that, he had a quality rare among *bois brûlés,* the ability to lead. Indeed, his penchant for command was to make his relationship with Kenneth Mackenzie a frustrating experiment. In the restless years after the war of 1812, Renville developed a plan for an independent organization that would wedge itself into territory not yet dominated by either Hudson's Bay or American Fur. At the Red River Settlements he had sized up a number of young Scots who had been Nor'Westers or, like himself, had worked for Hudson's Bay. One of these was Daniel Lamont, and another was William Laidlaw who had been manager of the Red River model farm (and who had passed Camp Cold Water in 1820 with cattle and seed he was conveying from Prairie du Chien to Selkirk's destitute settlers).

While Renville and the Britishers huddled, discussing plans for a new outfit to be called the Columbia Fur Company, Mackenzie began to kibitz. There seems no doubt that Mackenzie was, by instinct, a take-charge type. He had immigrated about 1818 and joined the North West Company. After the merger he was at the Red River Settlements in a capacity that is today unknown; all that is certain is that while there he became the father of a son and a daughter of mixed blood, whom he was to abandon. He never did care much for amenities. In Renville's fledgling organization he saw an opportunity ripe for exploitation. He and Lamont and Laidlaw were soon friends, and Mackenzie became one of the founders of Renville's company. But though all three Scots were educated, as Renville was not, they were equally lacking in the formality of U.S. citizenship, which was necessary to obtain a license to trade below the border. Circumvention was simple enough. The trio made a trip to St. Louis in search of credit and of some full-fledged American who would be willing to serve as front. Such cooperation was offered by William P. Tilton, a man who remains obscure in the literature; and thus during their absence, in the same season in which Ashley began the mountain trade, Joe Renville was able to stake out (under the official disguise of Tilton & Co.) the first Columbia Fur Company posts.

Dan Lamont was established at Land's End, a mile or so upriver from Snelling's then half-finished citadel, and that same year, 1822, a second headquarters took root at Lake Traverse, to which post in the following summer Renville led the Long expedition for a halt of several days. By 1823, Columbia's Fort Tilton had been built near the Mandan villages and soon the new company was in the thick of Prairie Sioux and Cheyenne trade at the confluence of the Missouri and the Bad rivers. Almost immediately this activity became a subject of interest at Fort Snelling. On May 29, 1823, while his Indians were coming in for the perennial peace talks, Taliaferro duly noted in his journal the arrival "at 12 oclock this morning [of] Mr. McKenzee, Lamont, Rainville with a return of Furs & Peltries &c." Philander Prescott had signed on with the outfit and remembered the first season's haul as "rising of 400 packs of furs and robes. This made the American Fur Company look with big eyes when they saw this large lot of furs taken from their pockets." The eyes of Ramsay Crooks may have dilated, but he himself refused to be rocked. Though he took special note of the bustling activity of

Kenneth Mackenzie, Crooks dismissed him for the moment as an untested newcomer.

More than most, Crooks could afford to await developments. Having been schooled first by Robert Dickson, having heard of the Pacific from the lips of Meriwether Lewis and Will Clark, he had joined Astor's American Fur Company and at twenty-two was with the famous expedition led by Wilson Hunt which headed into the Rockies in 1810. Like Renville's partners, he was a Scot; in fact, Crooks had come as a teen-ager from Greenock, Lamont's birthplace. And though he was not a Highlander from Rosshire, as was Mackenzie, Crooks had the same clannish proclivities which had helped to knit the Scots together to control the British fur trade. But fellow countryman or no, until he had the real measure of the Columbia partners he would fight them as American Fur fought all opposition. From the beginning Astor had argued that the government should grant his company a monopoly on the patently self-seeking theory that cutthroat competition was the cause of trouble among the Indians. He did not get that for the asking, but step by step, under Crooks' generalship, Astor interests brought an end to old regulations and lobbied new laws into passage. One of the first Crooks targets was the factory system under which the government operated its own trading establishments, offering the natives merchandise in return for furs at a stipulated rate of exchange. Minor though this kind of competition proved to be, Crooks and his colleagues wanted nothing to inhibit profits. Even before the plan to establish one of these government trading houses at Fort Snelling had been carried out, the whole system was torpedoed when Senator Thomas Hart Benton, who had been Astor's lawyer, took up the cause of American Fur. Crooks then set his sights on post commanders and agents sufficiently stiff-spined to resist blandishments.

If Snelling was such a man, Taliaferro was even more so. "I am sensible," he once wrote, "of the wiles & artifices of my enemies & therefore keep a *Journal*." Convinced as he was that little but enmity could exist between himself and Crooks' agents, he had laid himself open to charges of prejudice from the start. And it had not been long after Renville had brought Mackenzie and friends to the St. Peter's before Astor men in the field had begun to protest, as did Joe Rolette, that Snelling and Taliaferro "do all they can to injure our traders and favour the Col Fur Co."

That Taliaferro preferred to see his Indian charges deal with Columbia seems clear enough, but his reasons remain obscure. Perhaps he simply found the partners of the small company more compatible human beings. Equally likely is the possibility that his penchant for siding with underdogs inclined him toward the new outfit. In a sense, he may have thought, the Columbia traders had joined him in his crusade against the government-manipulating Astor interests. Certainly Taliaferro saw his mission as an obligation to protect Indians from profiteers, and he must have been persuaded, however unfairly, that Columbia as an organization was less opposed to his altruistic policy than were Astor's field commanders.

Although Crooks was the guiding spirit in the Astor opposition to all things Taliaferro considered to be his duty, it was Rolette who was most often termed by the St. Peter's agent as the first of all his enemies. He characterized him as "that worst of all Citizens *Jos Rolette*," and added, "When will my reports of the *Malefick practice* of this *beast* of the Creation have the effect of curtailing his intercourse in the country?" The answer was never. Rolette was far too wily. As we have seen, he was a British sympathizer during the War of 1812 and his loyalty was such that he continued to be known as "the Englishman." Perhaps at least as telling, he was addressed as King Rolette by many traders. And because of the speed and unpredictability with which he moved about the wilderness, the Indians called him *zika*, the partridge. Another alumnus of the Robert Dickson school, he had a long-time hold on the St. Peter's trade; he was already deeply entrenched, in fact, when Pike encountered him at the Rolette headquarters in Prairie du Chien. There he earned his title, king. He had married trader Henry Fisher's thirteen-year-old daughter Jane, whose portrait indicates that even in later life she had storybook beauty. Most of his life he got whatever he wanted, in the fur trade and out. He had a gristmill operating

110

as early as 1808. He sold food and other supplies as far away as the Selkirk colony. At various times the Fort Snelling commissary bought beef, wheat and candles from him. And his negotiations with the American Fur Company were no less successful. When Crooks had tried to lure him into the burgeoning monopoly, King Rolette held out for autonomy. He was willing to accept Astor as a supplier of merchandise, but he insisted on a vast district in which he was to trade at his own risk. That district included much of the Upper Mississippi and the whole of the St. Peter's. With his talent for circumventing legalities, it brought him into conflict with Snelling and Taliaferro—and in simple terms of competition into a head-on struggle with Kenneth Mackenzie. Even to the point of sobriquets. While the aggressive Mackenzie steadily pushed his way into Renville's shoes as Columbia's president, the Rosshire Scot was building the reputation that made him in the next decade "King (some said Emperor) of the Upper Missouri."

The sweeping changes in the fur trade in 1827 grew out of this rivalry. Rolette was leagued with Astor's top brass in the effort which at first was aimed at crushing Mackenzie and his partners. The King of Prairie du Chien was amply supported as he deployed his traders, sending them on the heels of the Columbia partners to set up next-door posts with instructions to undersell. When this standard method of dealing with competition failed to plow Columbia under, Astor bought out the St. Louis supplier with whom Mackenzie had established credit. Now indisputably the partners' shrewdest member, Mackenzie quickly made a new deal and continued through Lamont's Land's End post to bring profitable hauls out of what had once been almost exclusively Rolette's St. Peter's country; with Renville and Laidlaw working west from Lake Traverse, Columbia was doing equally well on the Missouri.

Meanwhile, various American Fur voices were spreading the word that Columbia was an illegal outfit. Everybody knew that Mackenzie, Laidlaw and Lamont were not yet citizens, no matter that they had entered their applications. The fact, wrote Robert Stuart, the Astoria veteran, that they were "entering

111

themselves on the Licenses as boatmen is too shallow and contemptible a farce, to be played off anywhere. . . ." They were passing themselves off as mere employees when it was obvious that they, and nobody else, ran things at "Tilton & Co." Taliaferro—even William Clark—seemed intent upon looking the other way. When a St. Louis newspaper accused the company of having as its head "a subject of his Britainic Majesty's," the agent responded from Fort Snelling that it was "believed heretofore to be under the direction of Wm. P. Tilton, Esq."

Such an answer, though legally accurate, could not possibly satisfy the irate Astor forces who were so frustrated by the competition. Stuart wrote the Columbia supplier in St. Louis: "Mr. Rolette informs me that previous to his leaving the Prairie, he sent two affidavits to Genl Clark, setting forth that McKenzie, Laidlaw &c were at the head of Columbia Fur Outfits, altho foreigners &c. What has the Genl done? . . . *you* must be aware of the fact of their heading that Co. . . . and far less should I think that a man of vigilance and sagacity of Genl Clark would permit it for a moment, if the proper representations were made to him. . . ." Stuart asked the supplier to make Rolette privy to the Columbia accounts, thus to acquire enough evidence against the Scots "to convict them." And he added an admonishment for Rolette "to be on his guard, that none of his own people commit any transgressions."

By 1826 Rolette's own voice was loud and clear. In June he wrote Clark, "Mr. McKenzie himself and a man by the name of Jeffreys [at Lake Traverse] have been in that country for two or three years travelling and trading from the Saint Peters to the Missouri. They might have held permissions to that effect from the Indian Agent at St. Peters, but I would ask you, does not the Law say that no Foreigner shall be allowed to Trade &c." In November he asserted to Governor Cass that he could prove that Taliaferro had allowed Laidlaw "to distribute liquor belonging to the Agency to the Indians—which act you will know was to give influence to that Company. . . ." He added that Snelling, in addition to following the same line, "seems to throw every obstacle in our way; unfortunately his situation as commanding

officer gives him a chance to exercise his Tyranical disposition—
but it is to be hoped for the happiness of mankind he may soon
be removed from that station."

There were no legal steps that either Cass or Clark could
take, and neither intervened officially. Snelling and Rolette ex-
changed hot words by letter. Taliaferro summed up his attitude
toward Columbia in his journal: "I hear no complaints uttered
against any agent or individual of any other Cpy—by them. A
la[r]ge majority of them being gentlemen—I suppose is the cause
of the difference." John Jacob Astor was sufficiently disturbed
by the situation to write personally to Secretary of War Barbour,
arguing that the "feelings" of Snelling and Taliaferro "are hostile
and it appears to me . . . that every advantage will be given Tilton
& Co. where it can be done to save appearances."

Astor was writing defensively. He knew that Snelling had
complained of the unrestrained distribution of alcohol by Astor
traders in the Great Lakes area; he was smarting under the ac-
cusation that his agents persuaded local authorities not to interfere with this kind of lawbreaking. He also knew that Snelling
had stressed the unfairness to the competition whose supply
loads were dutifully searched at St. Peter's, suffering the lawful
confiscation of all liquor found. None of this bothered him as
long as his traders could maintain their advantages. What galled
him was the admission by William Clark that detachments from
Fort Snelling had been ordered to search American Fur posts in
the Mississippi headwaters and to seize alcohol illegally imported
through the Great Lakes. High-handed as he ever had been during the administration of his friend Monroe, Astor indicated to
James Barbour that continuation of such seizures might bring
more legal action; in 1822, he reminded the secretary, a court
had levied a five-thousand-dollar fine against a Fort Crawford
officer for destroying a cargo of alcohol found on board an American Fur Company vessel. The inference that Snelling could be
similarly harassed was clear.

Nor was Taliaferro neglected as a target. Lobbying in Washington for the company was Robert Stuart. He was there trying

to push the passage of a bill to abolish the control exercised by
Indian agents over the location of trading posts. But he and
Crooks for the moment were also determined to have Taliaferro
removed from his job, and, finding Will Clark in town, Stuart
pressed the charges that a government official who favored one
trading company against another was unfit to discharge his responsibilities to the Indians. Clark countered by pointing to
Taliaferro's unanswerable charges against Astor traders who
used liquor to take advantage of Indian trappers. Stuart lost all
rounds. Congress, for reasons best known to itself, declined to
change the location law. Officials of the Adams administration,
generally, were less approachable than those under Monroe had
been, and the fact that Adams' opponent in the election of 1824,
Andrew Jackson, had been supported by such Astor partisans as
Lewis Cass and Thomas Hart Benton did not help matters.

Taliaferro, meanwhile, for personal reasons seemed to be offering the company an end to his persistent attacks against it. The
agent, a great worrier about his own health, had decided that
the record-breaking cold of the winter of 1825–26 was too much
to risk again and he applied for transfer to an agency in a gentler
climate. And there were the usual rumors that the Fifth Regiment
and its commander, having served so long in the remote Northwest, might be shifted to another post. Crooks and Stuart brought
their campaign against these enemies to a halt. The attrition of
the Columbia Fur Company was becoming increasingly serious,
and the Astor men recognized that the situation now required a
new approach. "The opposition of the McKinzie Co.," Stuart
wrote to Astor in July, 1926, "is becoming very formidable, and
we must in my opinion make up our minds, either to come to
some arrangement with them, or lose money for 2 or 3 years to
put them down. . . ." Crooks estimated that Columbia cost his
own company ten thousand dollars a year in profits, and while
Stuart sought to influence Astor, Crooks went to St. Louis to dig
into the problem at close range.

Stuart suggested three ways to bring the Columbia partners
into line. The first was to persuade the St. Louis firm dominated

by Crooks' father-in-law Bernard Pratte "to give them part of the Missouri & we some part of the St. Peters" in an agreement that would set up geographical boundaries and eliminate direct competition. The second was to get "the French Co. [i.e., Pratte and his partner Pierre Chouteau Jr.,] to engage two of them on a Salary for some years," thus buying the talents of Mackenzie and probably Laidlaw. Admitting a deal of any kind with Bernard Pratte & Company might not be likely, Stuart's third proposal called for an arrangement to share in the Columbia Fur Company profits by supplying it with half the required amount of goods for trade on the Missouri. Crooks wanted more than such an arrangement implied, but nothing came easily. His first attempts to form a working partnership with Pratte and Chouteau were inconclusive. At the end of July he joined Mackenzie on a steamboat that was hauling Columbia goods up the Mississippi and found himself still dickering when they pulled in at Prairie du Chien. Here Dan Lamont joined the discussions, but ten days later no agreement had been reached, and the two Columbia partners left for Land's End. Crooks sent a letter after them suggesting they meet again in the spring, either at the Prairie or at Fort Snelling. Then he went to New York and was followed by Pierre Chouteau.

At last the first of the big changes of 1827 was effected. The two men signed the contract that committed the American Fur Company and Bernard Pratte & Co. to begin sharing on July 1 all the profits and losses of trade on the Mississippi below Prairie du Chien and along the entire Missouri. Now all that was necessary to complete American Fur domination of the trade—and to equip it to eliminate the competition of the mountain men—was a deal with Kenneth Mackenzie. Crooks and Stuart began a second series of talks with the Columbia partners at Land's End in April, tried again at the Prairie, and finally in September sealed the bargain that brought Laidlaw and Lamont into the Astor company, made Mackenzie boss of American Fur's Upper Missouri outfit, and set up Joe Renville as semi-independent, trading at Lac Qui Parle through King Rolette's Upper Mississippi outfit. Taliaferro made a pointed comment in his journal. The men Crooks and Stuart had signed on, he said, were confined *"exclusively* to the *Naturalized* Scotchmen, whom they have vilafied and abused ever since they entered the Indian Country." But his indignation was balanced by the knowledge that the hounding of Snelling and himself had come to an end, just as had the Columbia Fur Company. Reporting to the War Department on the charges that had been leveled against him, the agent wrote, "I will do Mr. Stewart the justice to say that his groundless exceptions were formed from the report of Joseph Rolette [whose character and principles were still as lacking as ever] and *policy* alone compels the Company to continue him as their agent—for he could destroy all their prospects of gain in this country if discharged—of this fact there is no doubt." Clark backed up his man at St. Peter's, telling Barbour that "no evidence has been produced by the company in support of their charges or Statements, and it is believed they do not wish to go into further investigation." For a while, that is. Rolette would be slugging away at Taliaferro ten years later. So would Crooks.

Rolette's war with Kenneth Mackenzie wasn't over either. At Crooks' behest he sent his man Alexis Bailly to meet Mackenzie when the latter came upriver with that bargeload of goods in September. Together Bailly and Mackenzie went over the inventory at Lamont's post near Fort Snelling, then checked the other posts along the St. Peter's. Mackenzie failed to produce invoices for the Columbia merchandise, and the total evaluation of $12,409.75 for the trade goods on hand was recognizably so inflated that both Rolette and Crooks admonished Bailly for submitting to Mackenzie's imperious disregard of impeccable bookkeeping. Less than a year later Rolette was writing to Stuart that in spite of the agreement "not to interfere or entice away any part of the Indians who were in the habit of trading at Lake Traverse and St. Peters . . . McKenzie & Co have an outfit in charge of William Dickson on the River Jacques, 2 days march from Lake Traverse. . . . last winter [they had] Colin Campbell and a man named [Pierre] Parrant at the head of the Des

Moines." Pierre Chouteau had directed Mackenzie *"écraser toute opposition."* With destruction as an assignment, the identity of the opposition was sometimes a moot point. But Mackenzie was now on his way to the Rockies, and for the next few years he would leave the St. Peter's without his particular brand of war.

CHAPTER EIGHT

———— •• ————

VALLEY OF VIOLENCE

MACKENZIE had not yet reached the Missouri on his ride west from the St. Peter's when Josiah Snelling received the orders that called him to the army's western headquarters at Jefferson Barracks. Major General Edmund P. Gaines had been at the St. Peter's fort on a tour of inspection, and he, the departing colonel, Abigail, and the three youngest of the Snelling children boarded the steamboat *Josephine* and on October 2 headed downriver. In the diary Snelling had kept that summer there is no sign of a literary man, and any emotion he may have had in leaving the frontier landmark which had been given his name can only be guessed at. Had he not shot a farewell look at the walls rising above the bluffs he would have been less given to human foibles than all the evidence indicates; and he may also have been understandably relieved to be abandoning fur trade problems to Taliaferro and his successors. Major Josiah Vose, the veteran of Cantonment New Hope, had been transferred from Fort Armstrong to command the citadel during the coming winter, and John Fowle was still in charge at Fort Crawford. Arriving there in two days, Snelling paused only for the most cursory look around, and the *Josephine* carried his party on to St. Louis, where he arrived the morning of October 9.

John Marsh was in St. Louis too, but he does not say in a letter he wrote that day that he bumped into Snelling. Marsh was concerned with reporting to Will Clark in the place of Boilvin (who had died during that summer's Winnebago fracas) and was consoling himself for not having succeeded to his boss' title. For in spite of Cass' recommendation of Marsh, the job as Indian

118

agent at Prairie du Chien had gone to an Illinois militia officer named Joseph Street. When the river sumac had reddened and the leaves of the sugar trees turned scarlet, Street had settled in at the Prairie, choosing instead of Marsh's suggested trip to Fort Snelling to begin a protracted correspondence with Taliaferro. Street's initial reaction to Marsh, generous if less perceptive than Taliaferro's own, was gratification (he wrote Taliaferro) "to find a man of collegiate education and possessed of an active, discriminating mind." Nevertheless, Marsh soon found Street consistently demanding and no more appreciative of his work than the St. Peter's agent had been in 1824.

"Writing freely, and perhaps not wisely," Street told Taliaferro in January that he had sent his Harvard-bred sub-agent on a hundred-mile round trip through a snowstorm to investigate Winnebago complaints of white infringements in the lead regions. The chief offender named by the Indians was the same Henry Dodge whose mounted volunteers had helped to restrain the Winnebagos the previous summer. Dodge was still militant and with two hundred or so armed men had already mined and smelted an estimated half-million pounds of lead. Arguing, because the boundaries established by the 1825 treaty had not been actually surveyed, that there was no proof he was on Winnebago land, Dodge stood firm. Marsh reported that the mine operator said he would get out "as soon as he conveniently could"—obviously not until he had made himself rich. When Street threatened to have the Fifth Regiment take care of the situation, Dodge was even more outspoken. "Let them march Sir," he said; "with my Miners, I can whip all the old Sore Shined Regulars that are stationed at Prairie du Chien." The blustering stance of acquisitive white men in dealing with Indian agents was old stuff to Taliaferro. When one of Astor's North Woods traders had heard of Taliaferro's campaign against whiskey smugglers, the trader had promised to arm his Chippewa clients against the agent. Later the same man, Taliaferro wrote Washington, went further in ridiculing U.S. authority. "The Medals and Flags which you received at St. Peters," the trader was quoted as telling some Chippewa chiefs, "are nothing more than pewter and dish rags";

119

and he stressed his scorn of Taliaferro's relative youth by adding that the trophies "were given to you by a boy, and with a boys paw."

Agents could protest such vituperation, as Taliaferro frequently did. They could call on the army, as Street had appealed to Major Fowle at Crawford for action against Dodge. But the national mood was anti-Indian and thereby unsympathetic to those who spoke or tried to act in the natives' interest. Fowle answered Street's request by pointing out that he was outnumbered; he had only one hundred and forty-seven men of whom only one hundred and thirty were fit for duty. He had taken Dodge's measure in the late Winnebago campaign, and it may well have seemed apparent to him that action against the miners would serve chiefly to embarrass the War Department. More than likely, he also knew that Governor Ninian Edwards of Illinois was leading a campaign to get all Indians moved west of the Mississippi. In any event, Dodge's successful defiance of Marsh and Street, and his scorn for Fowle's regulars, helped to encourage the settlers flowing into Illinois in the belief that Indian rights could be ignored.

As usual, Indians—as individuals—broke the white man's law which most of them failed to understand. Dozens of chiefs had put their marks to the 1825 pact which defined the territories of each of the Mississippi tribes, yet the government had done nothing to make the boundaries recognizable. Indian hunters were conditioned to follow the game, and when the trails took them into hostile country, tradition made them duty-bound to fight —for their lives frequently enough, but also for that old glory of the wilderness, the bringing home of scalps or hostages as evidence of honorable retaliation. In primitive justice the excuses for reprisal were infinite. Young warriors who had not been present when their leaders had been feted at Prairie du Chien were reluctant to accept restrictions imposed in their absence.

As we have seen, the same spirit was evinced by chiefs who had boycotted the treaty. The Fox half-breed known as Morgan, who had leagued himself with Black Hawk during the 1827 threats against the Sioux, in the summer of 1828 quarreled with other chiefs about the disposition of lead region rights. In a head-strong effort to establish himself as boss, he announced that he would provoke the Sioux into an all-out war that would settle everything. Perhaps the departure of Josiah Snelling and the ensuing shifts of personnel at Crawford, and at Armstrong in his own bailiwick, encouraged Morgan in his bravado. He had seen, late in May, the entire Fifth Regiment moved out of the Upper Mississippi Valley, on orders to garrison the Great Lakes posts at Mackinac, Green Bay, Detroit and Chicago. In its place Colonel John McNeil marched in the First Infantry, with four companies assigned to rebuild Crawford, while Lieutenant Colonel Zachary Taylor brought other First Infantrymen upriver to Fort Snelling and Major John Bliss took command at Armstrong. Not yet having earned his sobriquet as "Old Rough and Ready," Taylor took a dim view of the situation, and within five weeks after moving into the stone fortress he protested to the adjutant general that Snelling's fort was undermanned. In the face of the threatened renewal of Sac-Fox hostilities with the Sioux, he stressed that "there are nominally here three companies, but only in effect two, & what with keeping a command at the public mills eight miles distant, [at St. Anthony Falls] & a party constantly with the cattle belonging to the commissaryes dept. . . . I shall be barely able . . . to mount a guard."

Wary of ventures like Morgan's, Taylor also pointed out that at least half of his command was "frequently at the mercy of Indians were they disposed to commence hostilities." And he added, "I cannot for a moment believe that the situation of this post is properly understood by those making the disposition of troops, or it certainly would not have been left with its present garrison." Not long after Taylor dropped this letter in the mailbag, the half-breed Fox took a tentative step toward instrumenting his threat of war. Morgan led his followers up through Iowa to the St. Peter's drainage and fell upon a small hunting party of Wahpekutes and killed a squaw, then took prisoner another woman and a child. First word of the attack reached Street at Prairie du Chien, and because no whites had been killed he relayed the news to Taliaferro, then sent Marsh out on Morgan's trail. It took six weeks to find him. But mutual respect having been established previously between the half-breed and the sub-agent, Marsh talked Morgan back to the Prairie, where Street accepted return of the captives and amiably let the Fox war chief go. Street figured that the sooner he got the captive female and her boy back to her village on the Cannon River the less chance there was of the full-scale hostilities Morgan seemed bent on provoking. Besides, the girl was so pregnant she couldn't walk. In less than twenty-four hours, in spite of the rigors of the December search for Morgan, Street equipped Marsh with a horse on which to transport the squaw and her child but failed to provide one for his subagent. Nevertheless, the durable Harvard man plowed through the January snow, delivered the young mother before her accouchement, then followed the Blue Earth into the St. Peter's valley and reported to Taliaferro on February 5. Always the courtly Virginian and sometimes a man to believe that he could let bygones be bygones, Taliaferro sent Street a letter of fulsome praise for Marsh, and after a decent interval dispatched the sub-agent back downriver.

At the fort on the bluff, Zachary Taylor inspected the barracks and reported them large enough to accommodate eight companies, and bemoaned the fact that he commanded so few soldiers it was difficult to post sentinels "at hailing distance around this extensive work. . . ." As he awaited the spring of 1829 he was on the alert for the trouble which soon after his arrival he had predicted would come this year. But he had orders to do nothing except maintain peace. In his frustration, he found the fort's environs "a most miserable & uninteresting country," and grumbled that "the Buffalo have entirely disappeared . . . bear and dear are now very scarce," although the Snelling gardens were planted in "tolerable" soil and produced "vegitables common to those latitudes in great perfection, particularly potatoes." Another good thing was the climate, in which his wife's delicate health improved; and in the St. Peter's ambience his seventeen-year-old daughter Ann was being successfully courted by Robert C. Wood, assistant surgeon. While he fumed, Taylor shared Taliaferro's downriver news and reports from Major Stephen

Watts Kearny, who had assumed the Crawford command during Colonel McNeil's absence.

Marsh, in spite of his bright beginning with Street and the ringing tribute paid to him by Taliaferro, had managed to get himself into an irreconcilable spot. After leaving Fort Snelling he had picked up a rumor that the Chippewas were about to challenge the Sioux, and had told his Marguerite to warn her people. Street learned of the incident and accused Marsh of "enlisting his feelings with the Sioux and becoming a partisan. . . ." A government agent must never take sides, and Street said the cause for the indiscretion lay in his assistant's relationship with Marguerite. "The unfortunate connection . . . has biased his mind and made him an apologist for [his squaw's friends and] their cause." On top of this, Street found a story in the *Miner's Journal* in which Marsh had predicted that four thousand Sioux would be up in arms come spring. Confronted by Street, Marsh disowned the article, but wrote a letter to the editor in which, although he stressed Sioux friendship for the whites, he admitted "my belief that if a general war should take place the Sioux would send a body of 3,000 or 4,000" against the Sacs and Foxes. He asserted also that Marguerite's tribesmen were "entirely tranquil," an opinion not shared by traders who were getting few furs because the tribes were too restless to trap. King Rolette was quoted as protesting that unless more troops were ordered in to enforce the peace he would be driven out of business.

Street was convinced that Marsh had a deal with the Sioux which "induced him to make this publication to scare the Foxes." He rejected the idea that Morgan or any other war hawk would believe the Sioux could get together as many as four thousand men, but he concluded that sufficient damage had been done to warrant Marsh's dismissal and he filed a brief against his subagent. "The man is absolutely mad," he said, "or his ideas have been deranged. . . ." No doubt Marsh was partial to the Sioux; yet he had no more reason than had Taliaferro for exercising prejudice—for involvement with a Sioux female was obviously no excuse for an Indian agent either to pick one tribe against another or to risk war. Aside from this sort of extravagance,

Street's charges marshaled numerous citations of conduct unbecoming for a government officer, including proof that Marsh had accepted payment for the loss of his horse while on an agency errand and had kept the money when the animal was later returned to him. The Street indictment went through channels to John H. Eaton, Jackson's Secretary of War, who already was under attack for his affair and eventual marriage with Peggy O'Neale. That summer Marsh lost his job. So, in a few months, did Eaton—both surrounded by scandal that involved their wives.

Marsh stayed on at the Prairie, operating a general store, and he was there in midsummer when Zachary Taylor left Fort Snelling in charge of Captain John Gale and himself took command at Crawford. Gale and Taliaferro had become fast friends, the captain later writing the agent, though he declared himself too proud to flatter any man, that he wanted to congratulate Taliaferro: "The whole army on this frontier," said Gale, "unite in the belief that the government has for once an honest, efficient agent for Indian affairs." Certainly during the two years Gale commanded the Snelling garrison he and Taliaferro kept things quiet on the St. Peter's front. And the troops at Prairie du Chien had few problems while Taylor supervised the erection of the new stone fort. A young lieutenant named Jefferson Davis had joined the Crawford staff, but far more interesting at the moment was the arrival of Surgeon William Beaumont from Fort Howard. Beaumont had brought with him Alexis St. Martin, a former American Fur Company voyageur who had managed, while fooling around with a musket in Robert Stuart's Mackinac store, to shoot himself in the stomach. Stuart had sent a man up the hill to Fort Mackinac where Beaumont was then stationed and had helped the army medic dig out pellets of buckshot and pieces of St. Martin's shirt from the gaping hole.

Under Beaumont's care, the voyageur thrived except for the fact that an aperture two-and-a-half inches in circumference failed to close. Beaumont quickly realized that the opening offered the chance—at a time when there existed no X-ray or any other internal exploratory methods—to observe the human digestive process. Although St. Martin was frequently so bored that he ran away, Beaumont pursued a series of experiments which he was to finish at Ford Crawford. Here the doctor paid his human guinea pig three hundred dollars a year to work around his quarters, in order to keep St. Martin available. In this early study of the action of digestive juices, bits of food were lowered on strings through the orifice, and Beaumont's meticulous findings caused a great stir in the medical world when his report was published in 1833.

In the interim the immediate stir on the Mississippi was becoming more formidable. Black Hawk would not be persuaded that the Sacs had signed away their rights to their village at Saukenuk. When the tribesmen returned from the winter hunts in the spring of 1829 they found many of their Saukenuk lodges destroyed or damaged and their best cornfields barred to them by white men's fences. Finding his field plowed up, one Sac brave had the audacity to protest and was beaten with a bean pole by the white squatter. Another interloper threatened to shoot a young Sac who objected when the settler struck the boy's mother. "It appears hard to me," Tom Forsyth wrote, "that the Indian property should be stolen, their huts torn and burned down, and their persons insulted by Strangers . . . who are now quarreling and fighting with each other about the corn fields." The whites had been told that the natives finally had agreed to give up the land in the treaty of 1816 and consequently they, in their turn, protested to Forsyth and the commandant at Fort Armstrong. The First Regiment, however, had no orders to evict the Indians. The situation deteriorated steadily, and Robert Stuart, writing to Washington, predicted a general war which would "cost the United States, at least, the trouble & expenditures of a Treaty, and a great loss in the Fur Trade, beside the effusion of human blood &c." Astor's son William blamed Clark for the effect of the strained relationships on the firm's newly welded trust, and urged Pierre Chouteau, Jr., in St. Louis to go after the Superintendent of Indian Affairs: "As our Mr. Crooks says, 'give him no peace day or night.'"

At last Clark was sent instructions from Secretary of War Eaton to put the Saukenuk land up for sale in October, 1829.

The die was cast. In his annual message at the end of the year Andrew Jackson, well established as a scorner of Indians, declared Indian presence within state boundaries to be a violation of states' rights. Where would the natives go? Why, there was plenty of room in the uninhabitable "Great American Desert" where no state government, obviously, would ever cause conflict. Congress backed up the President and voted a half-million dollars to move Indians west across the Mississippi to land not part of any state or territory. Keokuk, Black Hawk's long-time rival, reluctantly accepted the verdict. But the recalcitrant Black Hawk insisted his home could not be taken from him. So anti-American since his days of glory with Tecumseh that his followers were called "the British band," the aging chief made a trip to Malden and was told by the Canadians that if he personally had not signed away his rights he would not be dispossessed. He returned home more determined than ever.

Meanwhile John Marsh had added fuel to the fire that many in the valley feared would become a holocaust. Learning that a party of Foxes was en route to a powwow with Street, Marsh tipped off some Sioux friends who promptly enlisted a few Menominee allies, waylaid the Foxes, and wiped out all but one of the party of eighteen. The next day in Prairie du Chien the hit-and-run victors staged a savage parade so bloody with scalps and other souvenirs of the slaughter that Taylor promptly described the scene to Taliaferro and got busy on plans for a peace conference. Clark submitted to Sac-Fox demands for money to "cover" the dead victims, and set July 7 for the gathering of all the restless tribes. Before that date, Taylor's long-awaited furlough was scheduled, and he had gone south when Taliaferro arrived at the Prairie with a Sioux delegation. But Taylor had left a letter for Taliaferro that went beyond the general accusations against Marsh for the latest massacre of Foxes. "Take the American Fur Company, in the aggregate," Taylor told the agent, "and they are the greatest scoundrels the world ever knew." A new treaty might postpone the triggering of all-out war by Marsh's act, but Taylor adamantly believed that deeper trouble would result if Astor's men were allowed to manipulate any money disbursed to the tribes. It was a well-known fact that the year before, as a result of the government purchase of the Winnebago homeland, Rolette and several other traders had split $23,532.28—an amount arrived at with questionable arithmetic to cancel old tribal debts for merchandise.

Under the wary eyes of Astor-baiter Taliaferro and four companies of the First Regiment, Clark called to order the 1830 meeting of Sacs, Foxes, Sioux, Winnebagos, Iowas, Menominees, Otos, and Omahas. Nine days later the tribes had sold a forty-mile strip of land from the Mississippi to the Missouri to be used as a buffer between quarreling bands and to provide a new home for the Winnebagos. The Sacs and Foxes had offered to sell their mineral deposits, but the price was high. The troubled Indians had been learning a little, and they asked an annual payment of $32,000 for fifty years, in addition to allotments of salt and tobacco and the settlement of the $50,000 claim against them by the Rock Island American Fur traders, Russell Farnham and George Davenport. Even though the chiefs agreed to the amount, even though Clark knocked $10,000 off the traders' claim, the treaty commissioners balked at a deal that involved so much money, and the mineral-rights sale—and therefore the potential Farnham-Davenport profit—was tabled.

Although there is no record that Taliaferro had any direct influence on the commissioners' decision, he continued to feel persecuted by the Astor forces (as he would for years to come). In the following March he wrote in his journal: "I find that there is something of a combination of Persons—at work day after day to *pick* at my *actions* both *public* & private . . . by means of the *Am Fur Cpy*." Not content with the continuing friction between settlers and the Sacs and Foxes, according to Taliaferro, Rolette's man Alexis Bailly was spreading the rumor that the whites intended to extend their campaign against Black Hawk and his friends to include the Sioux. Taliaferro recorded in his journal that Bailly warned that such hostility would begin at St. Peters, the idea seeming to be that Sioux loyalty to Astor traders would insure them protection from the encroachment of settlers. This was ridiculous, and the agent told the Indians so. Then he

127

learned that General Gaines had taken over at Fort Armstrong because Black Hawk had again defied the order not to return to Saukenuk. Perhaps to emphasize that Sioux interests were best served by cooperating with the government, he offered the St. Peter's hands a chance to fight their Sac and Fox enemies alongside Gaines by volunteering two hundred and fifty warriors. (In spite of the fact that he had been relieved of responsibility for the Chippewas he lined up an equal number from that tribe. Schoolcraft, he wrote, "has not seen the Chippeways on the Upper Mississippi . . . [and] they feel this neglect.") But his eager volunteers were denied the action they craved, because Gaines was determined to handle Black Hawk without bloodshed.

For their part, individual Sacs and Foxes had no such compunctions. Frustrated when Black Hawk again was forced to accept white occupation of Saukenuk, they shunned war in the presence of massed troops. But one hundred of the combined tribes determined on reprisal for the Sioux-Menominee massacre the year before. On an island near Fort Crawford, they stole up on a party of forty Menominees and slew twenty-five braves who were sleeping off a drunk. Another Sac-Fox brigade invaded Sioux hunting grounds and killed two of Taliaferro's charges. He managed to head off immediate retaliation, but he passed word downriver that if the murderers were not punished by October the Sioux promised to carry the war club to the Sacs and Foxes. Lewis Cass, who had succeeded Eaton at the head of the War Department, ordered speedy action, and Major Bliss called a council at Fort Armstrong. Keokuk and other leaders hedged, asserting that the murderers would have to surrender themselves, which they would probably do when they returned from the distant hunts in which they were then engaged. By the following March no culprit had surrendered, and Bliss reported that the situation was so tense that an outbreak was imminent. Yet not until April 8 was the First Regiment backed up by six companies of the Sixth which General Atkinson led from Jefferson Barracks to Armstrong. Zachary Taylor's considered judgment was that reinforcements could have navigated the river as soon as it was free of ice in late March—in which case, he said, "there would have been no Indian war."

By the time Atkinson appeared, however, the Black Hawk War was on. The Indians who had slaughtered the twenty-five Menominees had split with their conservative leaders by refusing to give themselves up and had joined the British Band. In spite of remonstrance by Keokuk, resentment of the settlers continued to smolder through the winter of 1831–32, and Black Hawk's partisans increased rapidly. A Winnebago soothsayer who called himself the Prophet told the Sac chief that in addition to the help of Chippewas, Potawatomies and Ottawas the British in Canada had promised to supply arms and provisions; if Black Hawk should be defeated he would find a welcome near the Red River Settlements. Unlikely as was open British interference in American affairs, Black Hawk believed the report and proceeded with his plans. On April 6 he crossed the Mississippi into his tribe's old territory, and defied the emissaries sent by Atkinson after the general's arrival at Armstrong.

Wild reports began to drift upriver. Zachary Taylor was in Kentucky on sick leave, but Captain William R. Jouett was in command at Snelling and Captain Gustavus Loomis at Crawford. Atkinson, moving cautiously, made generous estimates of the strength of Black Hawk's forces and arrived at Prairie du Chien to assess the northern frontier. The general ordered Loomis to block Sioux and Menominee river travel with a line of five or six boats across the Mississippi, and asked Street and Taliaferro to increase their vigil of tribal activity. Then, with as many of the First Regiment as could be spared at Fort Crawford, Atkinson returned to Black Hawk's theater of operations. On June 3, Taliaferro wrote in his journal: "Our express returned this evening from Prairie du Chien. Bad news—our first movement against the hostile Sacs—has proven abortive and our loss has been 60 killed & missing."

In view of the tales of terror that were circulating throughout the Mississippi Valley, Taliaferro's version of the Sac victory at Stillman's Run was understandably exaggerated. Three weeks earlier, after moving for forty days up the Rock River, Black

Hawk had bogged down, finally disabused of the reports of British help and unable to find a friendly tribe willing to supply his people with food. When scouts brought him word that three or four hundred whites were following him within a couple of miles, he decided to surrender; his women and children were on the verge of starvation, but at least as important were the reports that Atkinson was supported by four hundred and fifty regulars and more than fifteen hundred volunteers. Black Hawk sent three warriors with a white flag to lead the white detachment to his camp; and apprehensive of the reception his messengers might get from undisciplined frontiersmen he dispatched five other braves to observe at a distance.

The braves saw the three messengers with the white flag surrounded by militiamen under Major Isaiah Stillman. Suddenly chaos broke out. Mounted whites, thirsty for blood, ignored the restraint of their officers and streamed at full gallop toward the five observers. The warriors turned to flee, and shots rang out. Two Indians fell. Firing broke out in Stillman's bivouac and two of Black Hawk's peace emissaries escaped as their partner was killed. The old war chief heard the news as soon as the survivors reached his camp and he moved swiftly, secreting forty or so warriors behind foliage before the torrent of disorganized American horsemen bore down on him. His braves waited until the leading whites were within a few feet of the ambush and then they struck. The bloodthirsty frontiersmen were panic-stricken. On rearing horses they tried to flee and as they turned tail they raced straight through what was left of Stillman's camp and on to the settlements, where they spread terror. Not for three days were all the frightened militiamen accounted for; then it became clear that the rumor that fifty to sixty were dead was false. The total was eleven killed.

Zachary Taylor, who arrived on the Black Hawk front in time to witness the wild retreat, said later that Atkinson ought to have prevented "that disgraceful affair. . . . That attack made on the indians brought on the war. . . . Had the regular troops overtaken [Black Hawk's forces] . . . before any blood had been shed, they would have been removed to the West side of the

Mississippi, without there being a gun fired. . . ." Taliaferro reacted to the news with that complacency which rarely failed him.
"So much for throwing a small force 36 miles in advance of the
main army," he wrote in his journal of June 3. "Indians so war-
like—confident and well equipt as the confederated Sacs & Foxes
& Winnebagos—are not to be trifled with, and as I predicted in
a letter long since addressed to the Suprt of Ind Affairs—matters
have unfortunately occurred." And he took no chances on the
Sioux getting any ideas about taking on Fort Snelling while
Black Hawk demanded the attention of hundreds of armed Americans. He called the neighboring bands to council on the sixth
and quoted himself as telling them: "We did not wish to draw
Blood but the Sacs & Foxes have forced us to flog them—and
you may be assured that it will be well done. We are not like
you. When we begin to fight we continue at war until our enemies
are no more."

About this time Atkinson decided that the way to handle the
Sioux and their friends the Menominees was to offer them action.
He wrote that he wanted sent to him as many warriors as could
be collected so that he could "employ them in conjunction with
the troops." Having met John Marsh on his spring trip to Prairie
du Chien, the general apparently had made note of the former
sub-agent's close connections with the Sioux, and he specified
that Marsh accompany the Indian volunteers. Equipped with the
promise that his recruits would be paid and their families provided for, Marsh lined up more than two hundred braves, with
Wabasha the most prominent chief. Temporarily, at least, Marsh
was no longer in disfavor. Street said his ex-employee "appears
to have devoted his whole soul to the cause and gives by his
example great spirit to the Indians, who seem impatient to meet
the foe."

In spite of Street's enthusiasm, Marsh's forces funked when
they reached the front. They arrived on the Pecatonica River
shortly after Henry Dodge's armed miners had annihilated a
small party from the British Band. They fell on the corpses and
hacked them to pieces. Shortly afterwards, when they approached
Black Hawk's rear guard, the Indians led into Prairie du Chien

with such spirit suddenly lost their interest in tomahawks and abandoned Marsh as they hightailed it for home. Street was chagrined when he found them back at the Prairie, and he laced them out in a lecture duly noted in an Illinois paper. These Sioux had proved to be cowards, he wrote Taliaferro; they were afraid to avenge themselves on their enemies and were fit for little but hoeing corn.

Wabasha's Indians were no more capricious than some of the white volunteers, a good many of whom bolted at the smell of battle. Others, convinced that the entire campaign against Black Hawk was a failure, departed for their homes when the period for which they had enlisted was over. Among those thus disenchanted were Illinois' new governor, John Reynolds, and young Abe Lincoln, who later made political capital by ridiculing the part played by himself and other volunteers. Line officers like Atkinson and Taylor had no means to control the untrained individualists whose morale was continually subjected to accounts of wanton massacre, some true, most not. Newspapers published little that was not distorted and aimed at inflaming the country. Marsh warned his brother in the East that reports he had read "in the public papers are mostly exaggerations. . . . The Indians were first attacked by the whites, but the whites were defeated with considerable loss. The Indians up to this day [July 18] have been generally victorious although the number of the hostile [Black Hawk] party does not exceed five hundred, and the whites in the field against them are between three and four thousand." The old Indian fighter in the White House failed to see why, in three months, Black Hawk had not been brought to heel, and he ordered the War Department to reprimand Atkinson for insufficient action and the inadequacy of the commander's reports.

Advised that Atkinson was stalled in the process of organizing a second conscription of Militia, Jackson ordered General Winfield Scott into the field. With eight hundred regulars, six ranger companies, and as many militia as he might require, Scott was to proceed through the Great Lakes and trap the British Band between his own forces and those of Atkinson. Scott's expedition turned out to be a total loss when a cholera epidemic broke out among his men before they reached Chicago. By this time Atkinson was so depressed that he told Scott the campaign would probably extend into winter, and he said that so long as Black Hawk's people could "subsist on roots and fish taken from the swamps and lakes" they might elude capture forever.

Indeed, Black Hawk was then well into present Wisconsin, but communications among American elements were generally poor and between the Upper Mississippi forts almost nonexistent. Henry Schoolcraft—on the expedition during which he named the Mississippi source Lake Itasca—arrived at Fort Snelling July 24 to find that Captain Jouett had had no word from Crawford for more than two weeks. Taliaferro was on sick leave, ill enough that Will Clark considered his life in doubt. The latest news about the Black Hawk campaign was that Felix St. Vrain, Forsyth's successor as Sac-Fox agent, was dead. The brother of Ceran St. Vrain, who was then helping to build Bent's Fort on the Colorado plains, had been waylaid while making his way upriver with a message from Atkinson. Undoubtedly Jouett and his men relayed the story that thirty of Black Hawk's Winnebago allies had ambushed St. Vrain and six other whites; they had capped the massacre by cutting out and eating the agent's heart to invest themselves with St. Vrain's courage.

Even with Taliaferro absent, Jouett had had no threats from the local natives, but he did have trouble with traders. Earlier in the month Hazen Mooers, one of Rolette's men, had started up the Mississippi—in spite of the new law prohibiting the use of liquor even by white men in Indian country—with a boatload of high wine. Jouett sent Lieutenant Jefferson Vail to intercept Mooers at Lake Pepin. The ensuing altercation stopped just short of gunfire and resulted in fifteen days of imprisonment in the fort for Mooers and his *engagés*. It also resulted in an American Fur Company suit against Jouett for false arrest that was to drag on for years. But that summer other Astor traders found time to abet rather than defy the military. Pierre Pacquette came upon some Winnebagos who knew Black Hawk's whereabouts and he passed on to Colonel Dodge the fact that the remnant of the

British Band was camped in southern Wisconsin. With Pacquette as a guide, Dodge and Colonel James Henry led six hundred men to find the wily chief's trail. They caught the Indians at a place called Wisconsin Heights, near the present state capital. They struck at sunset, and before darkness closed in the Americans had lost one man and had killed almost seventy of Black Hawk's warriors. But Dodge and Henry let the enemy escape, and in the morning, instead of pursuing Black Hawk across the Wisconsin River, they spent the day recuperating. His mission accomplished, Pacquette left them, and that night the Americans had no interpreter to translate the offer of surrender made by a Black Hawk emissary shouting across the river.

John Marsh, meanwhile, was relaying messages between Prairie du Chien and Atkinson who, with Zachary Taylor and General Hugh Brady, had brought up his headquarters to join Dodge and Henry, sixty-five miles east of Fort Crawford. The day after the Wisconsin Heights battle Dodge had asked Captain Loomis to seal the mouth of the Wisconsin River with artillery and thereby cut off Black Hawk's easiest avenue of escape. Loomis had gone further by marching the Crawford garrison out and spreading the men along the riverbanks. He had also called in Marsh and sent him to round up Wabasha, giving the Sioux a second chance to take an active part in finishing off their Sac-Fox enemies. Joseph Street lined up Menominees and friendly Winnebagos. Loomis wheeled out First Regiment cannons and armed the steamboats *Warrior* and *Enterprise* to patrol the Mississippi north of the Wisconsin. At Wabasha's riverside village the *Warrior* took on board Marsh and one hundred and fifty painted Sioux whom General Atkinson delegated to round up Sacs and Foxes wherever they could be found.

Black Hawk had left the Wisconsin and moved cross-country to the Mississippi, where the small stream known as Bad Axe River falls in from the east. There, while contriving makeshift rafts and trying desperately to get his women and children across the Mississippi, Black Hawk was caught; first raked by canister from the *Warrior,* then by merciless small arms fire from regulars and militia under Atkinson, Taylor, Brady, Dodge and Henry.

With probably no more than three hundred survivors Black Hawk made the west bank where Wabasha's Sioux gave chase. Only a few women and children of the British Band were spared —bloody evidence of the extent of the tribal enmity. Black Hawk himself escaped the Sioux mayhem and moved north to brief shelter among friends of the Winnebago Prophet. Other Winnebagos, inspired by the proffered reward of $100 and twenty ponies, trailed him to the lake country east of Fort Snelling and surprised him while he slept. They brought him in to Street's agency, and he was imprisoned for a short time in Fort Crawford. Lieutenant Jefferson Davis escorted him to Jefferson Barracks, and after a trip to Washington to face Andrew Jackson and to spend the winter in Fort Monroe, Black Hawk and other participants in the senseless war were brought back west through the Great Lakes and the Fox-Wisconsin route by the Fort Snelling officer, Major John Garland. To his humiliation, the leader of the Saukenuk rebels was turned over to Keokuk who was designated by Jackson as the indisputable head of the Sacs.

Not much time elapsed before nineteenth-century writers began to romanticize the Black Hawk War as well as the rebellious chief. He was made to seem the peer of Pontiac and Tecumseh—which he was not. Certainly there had been reasons to protest the insulting treatment of the natives by Illinois settlers. Yet Black Hawk's reactions had been emotional, for he possessed no political skill. Had the behavior of the whites been less reprehensible the removal of the tribes would have been insufficient cause for creating a Sac-Fox hero. And had Atkinson acted with less circumspection there would have been, as Zachary Taylor pointed out, no war—such as it was.

Peace came to the upper valley, but it was almost immediately marred for the First Regiment's commander, who at long last had been made a full colonel. Taylor was at odds with Jeff Davis almost as soon as the young West Point officer returned from his delivery of Black Hawk to Jefferson Barracks. Taylor's eldest daughter, Ann, was now a garrison wife at Fort Snelling, married to Dr. Wood and the mother of two of the fort's small fry. But her eighteen-year-old sister, Sarah Knox Taylor, had come up from school in the South to join her parents, and Knox's immediate interest in Lieutenant Davis was at the root of the commandant's displeasure. "I will be damned if another daughter of mine shall marry into the Army," Taylor blustered to Major Stephen Watts Kearny. "I know enough of the family life of officers. I scarcely know my children or they me. I have no personal objections to Lieutenant Davis."

Nevertheless Davis was barred from the commanding officer's quarters, and the attractive Knox had to use subterfuge in order to meet her suitor. During that winter after the crushing of the Sacs and Foxes, Joseph Street's daughter Mary frequently entertained Jeff Davis in her father's house—where by connivance on such occasions Knox Taylor invariably was present. Nor was Knox above camouflaging her commitment to the handsome southerner, especially after Davis was transferred to Fort Gibson in Oklahoma. She was as popular at Fort Snelling as at Crawford. "She was here last spring on a visit," Captain Nathan Jarvis wrote his brother, "and was considered a great belle as well as something of a coquette and has had some time or another made conquest of the heart of every unmarried officer of the Regt. . . ." Jefferson Davis knew better. Even then the lovers had a clear understanding, and Davis was writing Knox that she was "the last from whom I would expect desertion. . . . I approve entirely of a preference to a meeting elsewhere than at Prairie du Chien, and your desire to avoid any embarrassments that might widen the breach. . . ." Yet the breach did not close. In the early summer of 1835 Sarah Knox Taylor—who was to sicken and die within three months of her imminent marriage to Davis, and who had been denied, as she wrote, "the sanction of her parents" —left the First Regiment for the last time.

Another who already had left was Joseph Street's and Lawrence Taliaferro's erstwhile assistant, John Marsh. A warrant had been issued for his arrest on the charge of unlicensed selling of guns to Sioux friends. He tacitly admitted his guilt by escaping downriver in a canoe, leaving behind him a small son whose mother, Marguerite, recently had died in childbirth. He was thereafter variously reported as having turned up at Kenneth

Mackenzie's Fort Cass, on the Yellowstone, as a storekeeper in Independence, Missouri, as a prisoner of Comanches, and as a man who made it rich in the California ranch country. There, twenty years later, he was killed by one of his hands. "Very competent," one of Marsh's Fort Snelling school pupils said of him, "but a violent tempered man. . . ." Marsh was of a different breed than the next highly educated young adventurer who was to dominate life at the St. Peter's entry.

CHAPTER NINE

---•---

THE NEW TRAVELERS

RESTLESS in the study of law, seventeen-year-old Henry Hastings Sibley had abandoned the snug privileges inherent in his father's success and headed north from Detroit. Son of Solomon Sibley, who had been successively United States District Attorney, territorial delegate to Congress and justice of the Michigan Supreme Court, the tall and athletic young man in June, 1828, crossed Lake Michigan to the Mackinac Strait. From there he followed the canoe route through Huron and the St. Mary's River to Sault Ste. Marie, where Fort Brady was garrisoned by four companies of the regiment commanded by Josiah Snelling (who that summer died of a stroke in Washington). At Brady, Sibley worked as a clerk for the post sutler, and in the fall was hired by Mrs. John Johnston, the Chippewa widow of a former American Fur partner who had taken over her husband's trade. As a first step toward a career in the wilderness the move had compensations, for there were three educated Johnston daughters, and the literarily inclined Henry Schoolcraft was married to one of them. Aside from their appreciation of these métisse girls, young Sibley and Schoolcraft had in common a flair for writing, and their accounts of frontier life were to be widely read in the years ahead.

But unlike Schoolcraft, Sibley did not tarry long in the Johnston hospitality. He had made a friend of Robert Stuart, Astor's resident manager at Mackinac, and was hired by him as a clerk in the spring of 1829. Sibley had found his milieu. He not only mastered the fur trade, but before he was twenty-one had been made justice of the peace for Mackinac county. In 1832 he was named American Fur's purchasing agent with headquarters in

Cleveland. Two years later, when John Jacob Astor—anticipating the inevitable decline of the trade—sold out to Ramsay Crooks and associates, Sibley was offered a partnership on shares. With King Rolette and a rising business genius named Hercules Dousman he took charge of the company's Sioux Outfit: headquarters, Fort Snelling.

After final conferences with Rolette and Dousman at Prairie du Chien, Sibley, Alexis Bailly and a handful of voyageurs mounted their horses in October, 1834, and forded the Mississippi. Through the dense vegetation that covered the western bluff, they followed Indian trails to Augustin Rocque's trading post at Wabasha's village. The stop made here was to linger in Sibley's memory for fifty years as a day's idyll during which they slept in real beds, ate wild honey and venison, and dallied appreciatively with a comely French-Sioux lass. Here almost certainly Sibley also met for the first time the girl's cousin, Jack Frazer, half-breed son of James Frazer (who was the great explorer Simon Fraser's brother and a witness to Zebulon Pike's Fort Snelling treaty). Jack Frazer soon thereafter became one of Sibley's closest companions. Now in the crisp fall of 1834, however, Jack was a twenty-eight-scalp-carrying Indian whose only major distinction was that he had made some effort to prevent the slaughter of Black Hawk's women and children.

Continuing the journey with Bailly, Sibley reached his destination on October 28. When he rode up to "the brink of the hill overlooking the surrounding country," he said, he halted to take in "the picturesque beauty of the scene." Below him, near the abandoned site of Cantonment New Hope, lay the traders' hamlet called St. Peters. ". . . when I descended into the amphitheatre, where the hamlet was situated, I was disappointed to find only a group of log huts, the most pretentious of which" belonged to Bailly, with whom he was to spend the winter. But Fort Snelling was "perched on a high and commanding point," and the new man rode down to the river, crossed it and went up the bluff road to deliver the letters of introduction with which he was armed. There he found in command Major Bliss, up from Armstrong, and a complement of youthful bachelor officers leagued together in a garrison clan inexplicably referred to as the "bote screw." Fur trader or not, the young patrician from Detroit was soon a member.

Sibley came to the fort representing a new breed, but there were other newcomers and another breed. Arriving from Connecticut six months earlier, Samuel and Gideon Pond stepped off the *Warrior* at St. Peter's landing intent upon devoting their lives to the Indians. Hearing the news, Bliss sent for the strangers, demanding passports or other authority for entering the Indian country. They had none—nothing except a latent illumination that had touched them after a revival back home. "When I was brought out of that gloomy darkness into the light of the Sun of righteousness," Samuel wrote, "I felt constrained by the love of Christ . . . and we looked westward for a field of labor." Samuel set out first, got as far as the Mississippi lead regions and began to hear about how unwashed the Sioux were. Waiting only until Gideon caught up with him, Samuel booked passage for St. Peter's and was given a letter to Bliss by an Illinois preacher. Although that was not a substitute for the authority from Washington required by the law, the utter sincerity of the two young men persuaded the commandant to put them to work. Little Crow's village had been given a plow and a team of oxen, but none of the able-bodied Indians would admit that he could figure out how to use them. The Ponds therefore got the job.

Unordained though they were, the Ponds were the forerunners of the missionaries who soon arrived at the fort to bring the white man's Book of Heaven to the Sioux. As early as 1831 a small delegation of Flathead and Nez Percé Indians had trudged, sick and starving, into Will Clark's St. Louis office to ask that missionaries be sent among their tribesmen. No St. Peter's native had issued any such invitation. But the story of the mountain savages' request for "the book containing directions how to conduct themselves"—about which they had heard from a white visitor—was published two years later in the *Christian Advocate and Journal*. Soon churchmen of all persuasions were awake to the challenge. Revivalism was widespread in the 1830's, and missionary zeal was being assiduously whetted by many and various religious organs. When the Reverend Jason Lee crossed the Rockies in his signal journey to Oregon in 1834, his sponsor, the American Board of Commissioners for Foreign Missions, already had dedicated emissaries among Upper Mississippi Indians. Watching the *Warrior* pull up on May 6, 1834, with the high-headed Pond brothers aboard, was the Reverend William Boutwell, who had been with the northern Chippewas since 1831. Boutwell had gone to the Mississippi source with Schoolcraft and, indeed, was responsible for the name Itasca. When Schoolcraft had asked for a word to signify true source, Boutwell suggested the Latin *veritas caput,* and the two explorers linked two syllables of the first word with one of the other. A graduate of Dartmouth, Boutwell linked himself, a few weeks before the arrival of Sibley, to Ramsay Crooks' half-Chippewa daughter, Hester, then took his bride to a mission station on Leech Lake. Crooks' son-in-law had been "rejoiced" to welcome the Ponds, wrote Samuel, and Boutwell remarked in his own diary of his pleasure that the brothers, unlike such zealots as himself and Jason Lee, had not needed the urging of the American Board to join the crusade.

Like some Northwest missionaries, Lee had been aided and encouraged by men of the fur trade. Bostonian Nathaniel Wyeth, still hoping to survive in the cutthroat competition provided by American Fur, had brought Lee to the 1834 Rendezvous at Ham's Fork, Wyoming. There things did not go as scheduled for either man (and there was in what happened to Lee a clue to the missionary future on the St. Peter's). What happened to Wyeth was simple. The year before, he had forced Kenneth Mackenzie, the greatest menace to his survival, temporarily out of the trade by reporting that the King of the Missouri was running a still in Indian country. Now in the summer of 1834, while cooperating with the Rocky Mountain Fur Company in the deadly opposition, Wyeth was double-crossed. RMF sold out to American Fur and broke its contract to buy the goods Wyeth had rushed from St. Louis to Ham's Fork.

If there were few complications in this deal which brought Wyeth close to bankruptcy, there were some then unexplainable factors in Jason Lee's experience which were akin to those that would tantalize missionaries on the St. Peter's for a quarter-century. For at Ham's Fork, Lee met the Indians who for three years had been waiting for the Book of Heaven. The reason for ignoring these Flatheads (which Lee did in spite of the fact that his mission was to them and no other tribe) has been persuasively argued by Bernard De Voto. The Flatheads were natives to a region which then was written off as non-arable. The prevailing belief was that a nomadic people had to be led into the ways of civilization before it could be Christianized. Because the Flathead homeland could not be converted (everyone said) to agriculture and self-sustenance, Lee went on to the lush Columbia Valley, where he saw the prospect of forcing other Indians into a sedentary life which would condition them for acceptance of the Book. This method was the common one, but it cannot be described as successful. In De Voto's words: "That it could succeed only by means of the greatest cruelty men can inflict on other men, only by breaking down the culture that made them men—this mattered not at all, it was the end in view." To this end the preachers who came to the St. Peter's were failures. After he had spent more than two decades with the Sioux, Samuel Pond said that he could name "very few" of them who "gave decicive evidence of piety."

But in 1834 the mood was optimistic. The same fervent winds that blew Jason Lee across the mountains brought a Fort Snelling reconnaissance in the person of Thomas S. Williamson, a young Ohio physician who had deserted his small-town practice for the missionary life. He discovered and so reported to the American Board that at the urging of such traders as William Aitkin and Lyman Warren the Chippewas had others beside Boutwell attending them; the Sioux, for their part, had no one but the unordained laymen, the Pond brothers. After visiting the Sacs and Foxes in Iowa and checking on the Sioux situation by interviewing chiefs and traders as far west as Lake Traverse, Williamson recommended the assignment of teachers, preachers and, yes, farming instructors; he added a bid for the establishment near Fort Snelling of a boarding school as a "strong fortress" in the campaign to force the natives into the white man's mold.

That campaign was five years old as far as Lawrence Taliaferro was concerned. In August, 1829, he had founded a Sioux farming community and, unmindful of the gossip about Peggy O'Neale's husband, had named it Eatonville. In spite of what the agent called "violent opposition" on the part of recalcitrant traders like Alexis Bailly, the experiment had flowered to a population of one hundred and twenty-five, and under the supervision of Philander Prescott had produced almost a thousand bushels of corn in the season preceding the Ponds' arrival. Melons, squashes, pumpkins, beans, peas, potatoes cabbages and onions grew in the gardens, and Taliaferro had plans to add a root cellar and an icehouse to the dwellings erected in the early stages. Cloud Man was the Indian at the head of this utopia, and the story the Ponds later told had the old chief persuaded of the necessity for white man's providence after a blizzard during which he spent three days buried in a snowbank; delivered from that ordeal, Cloud Man had promised himself never again to face a winter without the security of an adequate supply of stored food. (Something else might have sold him on emulating white man's ways—blood ties. His granddaughter Nancy was a souvenir left by Lieutenant Seth Eastman during his first tour of duty at Snelling. Raised by her mother in Cloud Man's village, Nancy married an Indian, but one of her sons grew up to mild fame as Dr. Charles A. Eastman—a mixed-blood of note. He did not inherit the painting talent of his soldier grandfather, yet his books *From the Deep Woods to Civilization* and *Indian Boyhood* give something of the poignancy of Sioux life in the days when the tribe was nearing the end of the trail.)

Nancy Eastman was a toddler when the Ponds came to live near her grandfather's experimental farm, and she gets no more mention from the Connecticut newcomers than her métisse playmate Mary Taliaferro receives in the agent's journal. But the Ponds appear frequently in Taliaferro's writings. Both he and Major Bliss were moved to see that the do-gooders stayed. "Laugh who will at these men," the journal says, "I have only to thank

143

my God for permitting me to receive them." The Ponds got some
lumber from the fort's sawmill, a ham from Mrs. Bliss, and
Taliaferro donated a window sash and a lock to secure the door
of the cabin they built beside Lake Calhoun. "They will plow
some this fall and again in the spring for the Indians," Taliaferro
wrote in July, "& go on thereafter to instruct them in the arts &
habits of civilized life."

Samuel and Gideon had an additional objective. They had
sought the security of the Fort Snelling area in order to learn
and record the Sioux language—a mission Samuel called "of
paramount importance" in order to communicate the word of
God; it was to be accomplished "no matter how our hands might
be employed. . . ." As the brothers began to devise an alphabet
with which to commit the Indian tongue to writing, they were
made aware of the wide difference between friend and foe. Bliss
and the Indian agent encouraged them—even though Taliaferro
offered no payment for their farm chores. But across the river in
the hamlet of St. Peter's was Rolette's man Bailly. Afraid that an
educated Indian might be a better businessman, Bailly wanted
no part of anything that might enhance native life, and in the
summer of 1834 he did his level best to prejudice the Sioux
against the pious newcomers. So effective was he, Samuel wrote,
that "we congratulated ourselves on the arrival of Mr. Sibley"
who superseded Bailly in October and began to build a reputation as the Indians' friend. For had Bailly "continued in charge
of that important station and centre of influence" the Ponds might
well have been forced out of the Sioux country by natives whose
minds Bailly poisoned against them.

Sibley's arrival at Snelling came at the end of another season
of change in the West. Old St. Peter's veterans were going. This
summer Henry Leavenworth, now a brigadier general, led the
army's first dragoons on a peace mission into the Southwest and
died on the trail; Henry Dodge took over. Kenneth Mackenzie
was on his way to Europe for exile prescribed by Pierre Chouteau and Ramsay Crooks. He would be back, but the autocratic
reign of the King of the Missouri was at an end. Meanwhile,
Mackenzie's old partner Joseph Renville remained securely en-

trenched at Lac Qui Parle, awaiting a promised visit from Sibley to which he looked forward, he wrote, "not having the honor of knowing you." Sibley saw to it that he himself was not cut off from news of western activity by having Ramsay Crooks send him the *New York American,* which that fall rapped Henry Schoolcraft for "un-Christianlike" behavior on his excursion with Boutwell. (The Chippewa agent had abandoned a lieutenant and his detachment of soldiers, none of whom spoke any Indian tongue or had any knowledge of the country through which they were passing.) In the press, as elsewhere, the religious fervor knew few bounds, and presently the arrival in Oregon of Jason Lee was reported, and it was duly discussed at Fort Snelling as well as in the Boston headquarters of the American Board of Commissioners for Foreign Missions.

During the winter of 1835–36 that board found time, in addition to supplying the needs of Jason Lee and other missionaries throughout the heathen world, to mount an attack along the St. Peter's. A year and ten days after the arrival of the Ponds, Dr. Williamson brought his wife, his small son John, his sister-in-law, Sarah Poage, and a layman named Alexander Huggins to Fort Snelling. Two weeks later the Reverend Jedediah Stevens, his wife and his niece stepped off a boat and brought trouble with them. Stevens and a companion had come upriver in the fall of 1829 on an investigatory trip. Preening over this jaunt and the fact that he was commissioned by the Presbyterian Board of Missions, Stevens began to demean the religious skills of the self-effacing Ponds. Treating them as little better than manual laborers, he quickly had Gideon at work building a mission station on Lake Harriet. Williamson used the brothers' house to store his gear, and made plans to establish himself as a neighbor; he persuaded Sibley and some military families to organize a church at the fort. Even those stone walls were not impervious to the spirit of the times. Gustavus Loomis, who had been transferred from Crawford, had whiled away the winter isolation by conducting what Bliss' son called "a red-hot revival among the soldiers," temporarily converting "the biggest rascals in the garrison." (Backsliding came on the heels of spring when the first

boat brought with it an illegal barrel of whiskey.) Then Joe
Renville came in from Lac Qui Parle with his season's furs, and
Williamson's plans changed.

Renville was a rare man for his day and age—a Bible-toting
fur trader. Some time in his varied past he had acquired a folio
edition in French and he kept a clerk who could read it. He was
more or less a Catholic, enough so to take his Indian girl to a
priest at Prairie du Chien for a wedding ceremony. But either
his tolerance or the fact that the Preface was in Latin kept him
from fretting over the philosophy of its author, who was John
Calvin. As a matter of fact, Renville seems to have been a
remarkably even-tempered man, and any cursing he may have
done about the wiles of Kenneth Mackenzie is lost to the record.
A dozen years had passed since he had piloted the Long expedition up the St. Peter's, seven since Columbia Fur had dissolved.
He was about fifty-six this summer of 1835, a patriarch with a
largely grown-up family and more influence over the Sioux than
anyone east of Fort Pierre. His own headquarters on the slope
that overlooks the ten-mile beauty of Lac Qui Parle was widely
known as Fort Renville. Here since the split with his old partners
he had kept a firm hand on the upper Sissetons and the Yankton
buffalo hunters. On June 4, the day after he pulled into St.
Peter's with a band of Sioux in train, he went into council with
Hole-in-the-Day, who had been in wait at the agency to charge
Renville with responsibility for the death of three Chippewas.
Old Joe, whom most people thought looked more Indian than
French, first made Hole-in-the-Day understand that his three
tribesmen would still be alive had the Chippewas not committed
recent murders near Fort Renville. Then he added that he had
had the guilty Sioux executed and their guns broken. Taliaferro
backed him by lecturing both tribes and threatening to have
Bliss enforce the peace with live ammunition.

The next night Taliaferro's wife served dinner and the two
Indian experts sat down to talk religion. Taliaferro makes himself out to be the sly one in the discussion. The journal says he
had had "occasional Suspicions" about the way Renville "was
acting & had been acting." In spite of Joe's protestations that his

146

trade would be ruined by war, there had been accusations that he incited his people to do away with any Chippewas found poaching on Renville hunting grounds. Taliaferro had no sub-agent to assign to Lac Qui Parle duty, but Dr. Williamson had given him an idea. Why not enlist the missionary as an undercover agent? Renville's God-fearing nature was helpful to the scheme. As Taliaferro set it down in his ledgerlike diary: "after detailing to him the advantages that would result to him & his large family from having such a valuable acquisition as Doct Williamson & his family, he readily consented & he offered his protection, and every facility in his power if they would go."

Williamson agreed and was ready to leave when Renville started upriver on the 23rd. With this departure, the Ponds began to learn the facts of missionary life. It was, as always, white man's burden. But without credentials it was day after day of toil with no pecuniary reward and little enough of any other. Samuel tilled the three acres of ground around their two-room cabin and worked to gain Sioux trust and friendship, passing up no opportunity to learn a new word and write it down. Gideon may have daydreamed of Sarah Poage as he hammered away at the Stevens mission house, for he persuaded the Ohio girl to marry him two years later. But the impatient minister gave him little rest, and Gideon's free time was spent with his brother in compiling a spelling book. The task of mastering an unwritten language was as grueling as it was essential. Samuel said, "We found we could learn more of the French grammar in a week than we could of the Dakota in six months."

They were not alone in the general effort, but they were the only serious word hunters. Over at the fort Lieutenant Edmund Ogden and a few other shavetails amused themselves by getting Taliaferro's interpreter to translate while they sang out English words from a dictionary. The half-breed linguist, however, entertained himself by sometimes giving ridiculously inaccurate definitions. Thus the Ponds found the resulting vocabulary list of little use when it was offered to them. "We learned the language," said Samuel, "as children learn their mother tongue, for interpreters could not help us." And they earned no respect for their pains. When they had showed their specially devised alphabet to Dr. Williamson they were snubbed. The true-blue missionaries "would use it for the present till they could have time to discover what alterations were required," Samuel wrote, "for it was not to be supposed that untutored laymen could perform a literary work so well that a college graduate could not mend it. . . ." Not much later, the undaunted pair (someone once said of them that "they seemed the children of a king") turned over to Gideon's boss the *chef d'oeuvre* of their year at Fort Snelling. When this small opus, the first publication of the language of the St. Peter's, came from the press its title page bore the words SIOUX SPELLING BOOK . . . *by Rev. J.D. Stevens*. To have given credit to untutored laymen would have cast doubt in the mind of the public as to the scholarship of the work. And, of course, the proper signature must be that of a member of the group footing the printer's bill.

The brothers turned the other cheek. Not until after they had worked with Stevens a year or so did their charity break sufficiently to free themselves of him. Misericordia and magnanimity prevailed. The Sioux needed them. A young man named Walking Bell-ringer came knocking at their door. Could a mere Indian like himself learn to read? They told him he could. When he said he wanted to be a guinea pig in their experiments, "we taught him the letters, and showed him how to use them in the formation of words, and, as he was quick of comprehension, he learned in a few weeks to write letters that we could understand, and was, doubtless, the first Dakota who learned to read and write." The laymen had scored again. They made a friend of Cloud Man, another Indian whose intelligence belied the Fenimore Cooper prototype then in vogue. "He was a man of superior discernment, and of great prudence and foresight. He did not hesitate to tell the Dakotas that the time had come when nothing but a change in their mode of life could save them from ruin. . . ." Samuel added, "It would have been well for the Dakotas if they had more chiefs like him, but he was far in advance of his contemporaries. . . ."

But Cloud Man had no advantage in looks over his peers.

Mary Eastman saw him as an ugly old man. She was no more generous, however, with other Sioux males. The Fort Snelling Indians were unlikely to have been considered irresistible by anyone. By the time the Ponds came to live among them they had been so long exposed to whites that their once picturesque appearance had become motley. No longer totally dependent upon the wilderness for apparel, they combined what was available from the white world with the most serviceable of their traditional garments. As a result they sometimes looked like beggars wearing cast-off clothing. More often than not, the men wore cotton shirts with buckskin leggins, loose coats made of blankets instead of buffalo skin robes. Samuel found the Sioux costumes "well enough, comfortable and convenient," and was careful not to submit to the romantic images common among writers of the day.

In fact, Samuel wrote: "The women, when young, were few of them very beautiful or very ugly, and many of them made a fine appearance when in full dress." There were moreover, he said, "some slight points of resemblance between the red squaws whom we dispise and the white ladies whom we admire." Dressed for a tribal gathering, the girls wore little paint on their faces, but vermilion shone in the part of their hair, and a small red spot was dobbed on each cheek with the end of a finger. Ears were accented with shell earrings, and necks with as many strings of beads as they could manage to barter away from the traders. They loved silver—when they could get it—sometimes covering their dress fronts with metallic broaches. Above a broadcloth skirt embroidered with silk ribbons the Sioux girls frequently wore a bodice of printed cotton that hugged the body, had tight sleeves, and according to Samuel, "was sewed up only an inch or two on the breast" and "needed a few more stitches." His view, plainly, was that of a missionary.

There was an immeasurable gulf between the races that was filled by the mirage of evangelical optimism that summer—and every season for years to come. Samuel was an old man when he had remarked sadly on the "very few" of his savage friends who could grasp the concept of piety. Yet at twenty-seven, with only

a year in the wilderness, his dreams were bright. So, more surprisingly, were those of Lawrence Taliaferro who now, proudly
as always, counted his sixteen years among the Sioux and Chippewa. When Cloud Man and two of his lieutenants one day left
the Ponds and traveled the seven miles to the agency house,
Taliaferro welcomed their speeches of gratitude. "If I have your
thanks for the little I have done for your families, your saying
so in truth pays off your account in full, and I am in your debt."
He talked on of the future of Eatonville, of annually adding "a
house or two as our town increases in strength. . . . We have begun well," he assured Cloud Man's delegation. "Let us so continue and your exertions will be rewarded in the end with peace
and plenty." It was a vision that would not truly focus on either
object.

Of course the general truth about Taliaferro's Indians was
far from peace and plenty; considering that the opinions of people like Taliaferro, the Ponds and Henry Sibley were exceptions
to the current attitude, there was little reasonable hope for the
future. Not long before the council at the agency with Cloud
Man, Indian bands camped around the fort had been visited by
George Catlin, who came to an easy conclusion: "The Sioux
Indians in these parts, who are out of reach of the beavers and
the buffalos, are poor and very meanly clad," he wrote, and he
found the "same deterioration" in their "morals and constitu-
tions." Accurate enough as far as it went, his observation was the
superficial result of brief exposure, and the impression he gave
easterners was offensive to some who knew the Fort Snelling
natives intimately. Kindly Samuel Pond believed that "during
his short sojourn among the Indians [Catlin] discovered many
things that have eluded the careful research of others." Sibley
was indignant and said that "people in this area were absolutely
astounded at his misrepresentations of men and things." Catlin
did sometimes falsify, and the letters he wrote for publication
are romantic reading today, but the glimpse he gives us of Taliaferro's Sioux in the summer of 1835 cannot be dismissed entirely.

The agent and the first painter of the West met soon after
the *Warrior* on June 24 steamed up at 10 A.M.—"in a dashing

shower of rain," said Taliaferro. On board were Catlin and his handsome wife, one of the daughters of Joseph Street, and the widow of Felix St. Vrain (whose daughter Felicité was about to go into legend as the forbidden love of Kit Carson, down at Bent's fort); there were a dozen other tourists on the deck, including a half-dozen children. The company was tamer than that to which Catlin recently had become accustomed. In 1832 the painter had been aboard for the maiden voyage up the Missouri of Pierre Chouteau's *Yellowstone,* along with a delegation of Assiniboines and a gang of oath-spewing *engagés.* He had met the western Sioux under the auspices of Kenneth Mackenzie whose table, he said, "groans under the luxuries of the country. . . ." He had been with Leavenworth in Comanche country when the former Fort Snelling commandant had died of malaria. Concerned about his own health he had spent the next winter in Florida. Then, *"like a bird of passage,"* he wrote, "I started at the rallying notes of the swan and the wild goose, for the cool and freshness of the North." At the fort on the bluff, Catlin and his lady were made welcome guests in the commandant's house. "A room in the officers quarters was given him for a studio, and he worked away with great industry," said Bliss' son, who found that the sometime correspondent for the *New York Commercial Advertiser* "seemed to be a born delineator of Indians."

Catlin had announced himself. He "wanted to paint the splendid panorama of a world entirely different," and he went across the St. Peter's to a spot not far from the limestone house that Henry Sibley was building. There he painted a scene that showed Chippewas in a birchbark canoe, Sioux tepees on the bottomland and the stone walls of the fort pale and commanding in the summer light. But he was less interested in landscapes than he was in Indians themselves. He took advantage of the fact that many tribesmen were encamped around the fort, and made Taliaferro a willing ally. "With the presence of several hundred of the wildest of the Chippewas and as many hundreds of the Sioux, we were prepared in abundance for the novel—for the wild and grotesque—as well as the grave and ludicrous," Catlin wrote in *Letters and Notes on the Manners, Customs, and Conditions of the North American Indians.* Taliaferro, he said, "represented to them that I had witnessed the sports of a vast many Indians of different tribes, and had come to see whether the Sioux and Chippewas were equal in ball-play, etc., to their neighbors. . . ."

Catlin's route to the encampment of Fort Snelling tribesmen had been circuitous, and a decade had passed since, in Philadelphia, he had first met natives "from the wilds of the 'Far West' . . . in all their classic beauty . . . exactly [right] for the painter's pallette!" Already twenty-eight, already having abandoned a law career, he had become a thriving portrait painter, and a better one than Major Bliss' son remembered. Young John, who was no more than twelve the summer of Catlin's first Fort Snelling visit, wrote years later that when their house guest painted his father's portrait "all it required was a few changes in the way of a blanket and spear and some eagle quills, to have it passed off as the portrait of a warrior of some unknown tribe, quite ready to try conclusions with tomahawk and scalping knife." No Bliss portrait is known, but if the description has any relation to truth it may be that Catlin achieved the effect deliberately. For his likeness of William Clark in his old age is certainly recognizable, as is that of Sam Houston. He was not a first-rate painter, but the influence of his friends Sully, Willson and Rembrandt Peale shows in the miniatures that survive from his days as a journeyman portraitist. In any case his dedication to traditional painting palled as soon as he met the natives of classic beauty, and he saved his money for four years so that he could realize his "determination of reaching, ultimately, every tribe of Indians on the Continent. . . ."

Catlin's first contact with the St. Peter's Indians had been at the Prairie du Chien treaty of 1830, five years earlier. In the interim he had taken his palette as far west as Great Salt Lake. Now he was ready to concentrate on the upper Mississippi, and Independence Day was in the offing. Taliaferro, he said, solved "all difficulties" and told the Indians that if they would oblige Catlin "on the fourth of July and give us a ball-play and some of their dances, in their best style, he, [the agent] would also have the *big gun* fired twenty-one times [the customary salute for that day], which they easily construed as a high compliment to themselves." Cloud Man's "Band of Agriculturalists" did not wait until the holiday; on July 3 they gave their own performance at the painter's special request. But on the Fourth, Sioux and Chippewa joined in big doings. Major Bliss' cannons blasted the hot sky on schedule. Drums throbbed on the prairie between the fort and the agency. For two hours the tribes' best men played lacrosse, and the swarthy champion, He Who Stands on Both Sides, was later painted in costume, holding aloft his racket. For three hours Taliaferro's charges danced—the beggars, the buffalo, the bear, the eagle, the dance of the braves. In Samuel Pond's considered judgment no Sioux dance had any "easy or graceful movements. . . . The motions of the men were unnatural, abrupt and violent . . . designed to afford the actors an opportunity to exhibit agility, strength, hardihood, and powers of endurance. . . ." Catlin required nothing more. He sketched the dancers, painted the portrait of Black Dog as well as that of Blue Medicine, a conjurer introduced to him by Surgeon Nathan Jarvis; and he was delighted with the fact that Jarvis had supplied Blue Medicine with potions from his own cabinet with which Blue Medicine mystified his uncivilized patients.

Catlin left as the dog days came. In the month after the painter's departure there was a restlessness among the young men around the fort. Lieutenant Ed Ogden, considered something of a sport by his mates, had settled down and was wooing the daughter of Captain Loomis. But Sibley, in his twenty-fifth summer, was hurting. "I am now speaking without jesting," he wrote his mother in Detroit on August 1. "I cannot live the life I now lead very long without somebody to help me and to soothe down somewhat the rugged ills of life! [Perhaps he was feeling guilty about the Indian girl who was to give him a daughter.] I must in future learn to look for something less than an angel in the form of woman and be content to put up with a creature of mere flesh and blood. You know how foolishly fastidious I have been heretofore. . . ."

So it was with Jarvis, who found some distraction in teaching the fort's children and running the garrison library, which included four hundred volumes and an abundance of newspapers and periodicals. However, he too wrote home about his real frustration. "Mary," the surgeon wrote his sister, "all I want now is a *wife*. Can you pick me out one. As for me I never shall have a chance thro' a regular courtship for I expect to stay here a long time and must therefore like royal personages court by proxy! Therefore select one for me and describe to me her qualities and accomplishments." Was he also solacing himself through the charms of native girls? We do not know, but at least he failed to satisfy the missionaries. Although the Reverend Mr. Stevens praised Jarvis for his medical services, he wrote the American Board to say that the doctor was not a "pios" man and to ask that the backslider be added to the *Missionary Herald* subscription list.

Taliaferro had few of the problems of the younger men. He had a wife, and one whose attractiveness was noted by travelers. In fact the ungenerous Englishman who arrived on September 12 found in her one of the few acceptable things he encountered at the fort, and made note of her "very fair share of personal beauty." This admirer was George W. Featherstonhaugh (pronounced Frestonhaw, said young John Bliss). He and an assistant, Lieutenant William Mather, were government geologists assigned to study the St. Peter's valley. Although Featherstonhaugh reported himself "very much struck by the noble appearance of the fort upon entering the quadrangle," he became critical in short order. Bliss invited him to tea, but offered no better sleeping quarters than a storeroom. When Featherstonhaugh crossed the river and received an invitation from Sibley, he turned it down because he assumed Bliss would have been insulted. Anyway, Sibley was "both aristocratic and conceited," Featherstonhaugh wrote in his book, *A Canoe Voyage on the Minnay Sotor*. Nevertheless he accepted Sibley's offer to furnish a guide, and after five days conferring with Taliaferro and visiting the Ponds, Featherstonhaugh proceeded upriver where he was equally caustic about the hospitality offered by Renville. His work was no better than his manners. "His report does not give evidence of a master mind," said Taliaferro. "He attempted to pass current for that which he possessed not—superior talent and modesty in his profession."

The Englishman was the season's last visitor from the outside world. But all signs now pointed to an increase in future traffic on the Mississippi. Even more, the old wilderness isolation seemed suddenly in jeopardy. When Sibley's Prairie du Chien supply boat arrived on October 7, Taliaferro wrote in his journal: "Report is that Inhabtants of New Orleans & St. Louis (the more wealthy) in consequence of the salubrity of our Climate at S Peters during summer & Fall intend forming a retreat at the Falls of St. Anthony. . . ." Lo, the poor Indian.

CHAPTER TEN

THE WIDENING ARC

EARLY VISITORS to the fort tended to romanticize its isolation. They took the standard tour with its invariable climax at the Falls of St. Anthony and found, as Lieutenant Cooke put it, "immense masses of rock, disjointed and fallen from immemorial abrasion . . . a sublime confusion and roar of waters." In the level, miles-wide prairie behind the fort they saw, as did Cooke, "an agreeable circumstance, when it is considered that chasing wolves and racing are almost the only resource for amusement and exercise." They stood at the point of the diamond-shaped walls, a hundred feet above the junction of the rivers, and wondered at the view; an Englishman in 1833 said flatly that it was highly romantic. He marveled at the broad, sunken Mississippi Valley and the glacial path that had left the St. Peter's a narrow, sluggish stream snaking its way in from the sunset horizon. From the fort, the 1833 visitor wrote, "It is seen flowing through a comparatively open vale, with swelling hills and intermingling forest and prairie, for many miles above the point of junction." Across the stream he noted the steamboat landmark known as Pilot Knob and called it "a notable summit" below which were clustered cabins and sheds of a couple of traders and a few conical tents of itinerant Sioux. "A more striking scene we had not met with in the United States, and hardly any that could vie with it for picturesque beauty. . . ."

Gideon Pond had written home that he, too, had seen no region more beautiful. But though it should not be said that his summer's labor on the mission station did much to blight the natural attractions, the new pattern was being hammered out. At the foot of Pilot Knob, Sibley was changing the landscape permanently. He had crews at work building a house that still stands. The mason he had brought to his site just across the St. Peter's from the fort had cut blocks of limestone from the bluffs and with the help of Sioux labor had laid the walls of a two-story dwelling. While the men dug a cellar and hauled rock, the squaws gathered grass, rushes, willow branches and mud from the river. The walls went up, two and a half feet thick, cemented with mud, a little lime and animal hair. Beams, flooring and windowsills were hewn from oak and pegged together. Three rooms were laid out downstairs, the same number above. Partitions were constructed by the Sioux females, who laced willow into lattices which they plastered with mud mortar; they bridged the ceiling beams by weaving reeds and grass to hold the primitive plaster. With untrained crews the work was slow, and the finishing was not complete until 1836. But in this autumn of 1835 there was plenty of evidence that a signal change had affected the old life at St. Peter's.

Samuel Pond found his own way to express the beginning of the new era. His cornfield had produced a bumper crop, far more than the missionaries could use. He sold the excess to Sibley and bought a cow, for "though G. had worked all summer for Mr. S[tevens] gratuitously, we had [now] more money than when we landed at Ft. Snelling. . . ." His dream of self-sufficiency faded, however, because Stevens knew how to manipulate the brothers for his own ends. Playing on their sense of duty to the Indians, he persuaded them that they must consolidate all their attributes with the purpose of his mission station. So, Samuel wrote, "we reluctantly abandoned our house—turned over our cow, corn and potatoes, of which we had a large crop, to Mr. S. and G. remained with him, while I went off with the Indians on a hunting expedition." It was a work trip, not an escape. "The language was the game I went to hunt," he reported, "and I was as eager in pursuit of that as the Indians were of deer." With fifty Sioux hunters, and carrying no book except a Bible, Samuel trudged some seventy miles north of the fort into the headwaters of the Rum and spent a month in snowbound tepees pursuing his word hunt. Returning to the Stevens mission, he found that Dr. Williamson had sent a call for help from Lac Qui Parle. The new mission at Fort Renville was making slow progress and required the linguistic prowess of the Ponds. Samuel tarried long enough at Lake Harriet to help organize a school for Sioux children and young *bois brûlés,* and then set off west up the St. Peter's valley.

While he had still been with the Sioux hunting party another missionary, this one a Congregational dominie from the American Board, had made it every inch of the way west—not just to Jason Lee's station on the Willamette but a hundred miles farther down the Columbia to the Pacific itself. That traveler, who shared the Ponds' New England background, was Samuel Parker, recruiter for the western missions. Riding the highways and back roads in the East, Parker already had signed up that ill-starred couple, Dr. Marcus Whitman and the golden-haired Narcissa Prentiss, who soon would marry. (The following year Narcissa and Eliza Spalding would be the first women to cross the Rockies.) Parker enlivened the missionary zeal of the 1830's, and he did something else. Like the Pond brothers, he instinctively understood Indians and conveyed their problems with objectivity.

This kind of understanding was no more in fashion than it had ever been. Andrew Jackson, who knew more about the natives than most, had consistently used his power in the White House to appease the animosity and greed of the whites at the expense of the tribes. In his annual message that year he told Congress, "All previous experiments for the improvements of the Indians have failed. It seems now to be an established fact that they cannot live in contact with a civilized community and prosper." His policy was to abrogate old treaties, offer compensation, but get on with the business of moving every eastern Indian into the Great American Desert. After all, the redskins were being asked to do no more than white Americans were doing voluntarily, eagerly. "Doubtless it will be painful," the President had said in 1832, "to leave the graves of their fathers. . . ." Yet a good example was being set. "Our [own] children by thousands yearly leave the land of their birth to seek new homes in distant regions. . . . Can it be cruel in this government when by events it cannot control, the Indian is made discontented in his ancient home to purchase his lands, to give him a new and extensive territory, to pay the expenses of his removal, and to support him a year in his new home?"

In the security of a region dominated by Fort Snelling and not yet coveted by land-hungry whites, Lawrence Taliaferro believed that Jackson "perfectly understood Indian wants and Indian character." The agent preserved a message relayed through him by the President to Little Crow, citing it years later as an example of Jackson's ability to communicate with the peoples he so often had fought. The language is the usual, from the Great Father to the potential juvenile delinquent—"let us smoke the same pipe and eat out of the same dish." When Taliaferro has something to say, listen, "for you hear my words. . . . Keep the 'Seven Fires' of your Nation in peace and good order, and I will try to do the same with the twenty-seven fires of my Nation. Make your wants known to your faithful agent and you will hear from your true friend speedily."

Although the Ponds are discreetly silent on Jacksonian policy, they generally approved of Taliaferro's instrumentation. But they laid great stress on the fact that there was no Sioux clash with the whites in the Fort Snelling area until the Indians had been herded onto reservations and deprived of their normal occupations. When Samuel set off on foot for the two-hundred-mile trip to check on Williamson's problems, he found the winter-isolated bands full of industry. He comprehended their way of life and said that the natives made war on each other not because they were Indians, but because they were "men like other men. . . . If they were to live at all they must have a country to live in; and if they were to live by hunting they must have a very large country, from which all others were excluded." To expect a Sioux, Samuel wrote, "to change at once all his habits, to become a steady, plodding farmer, is as absurd as it would be to expect that his dog, whose ancestors had been trained to hunt deer through a hundred generations, should be suddenly transformed

159

into a docile shepherd dog, and should faithfully guard the flocks of his master."

He was learning as few newcomers to Fort Snelling would permit themselves to learn. This February trek was a wilderness seminar. He also picked up prairie winter tactics that had been learned by white men who were veterans, the masters of the fur trade. He gives Hazen Mooers—twenty years among the Sioux in 1836 and too cultivated, Samuel thought, to limit his life to savages—credit for "sage advice" that one day would keep him alive. A snowstorm caught Samuel as he trudged the prairie between the fort and his goal, and because he lost his bearings he "was five days without food." He had survived only by sheer luck when he encountered Mooers. Samuel listened earnestly to the trader's counsel, and wrote down two rules of winter travel "here recorded for the benefit of others: first, if attacked by what is commonly called snow blindness, lie down on the back immediately and put snow on the eyes until the pain ceases; second, when overtaken by a violent snow storm on the open prairie, encamp at once, and do not attempt to travel until the air is so clear that you can keep the right course."

Six feet tall and lanky, Samuel kept his course with strides so loping that even Indians failed to keep up with him. One native had been moved to worry about the plight of a lone missionary on the trackless prairie, "but he told me that after following me half a day he found my steps so long that he became discouraged and turned back." Thus Samuel plunged his way through knee-deep snow and arrived at Fort Renville. Although he found that Old Joe "had lost the vigor and vivacity of youth ... he was very dignified in his bearing, knew when to be reserved and when to be sociable, and seemed never to forget that he was a great man." But, the missionaries discovered, Renville had more religious knowledge than could have been expected of one who had never heard a Gospel sermon. Perhaps at least as important was his penchant for hospitality. He had been providing for the Williamson group throughout the winter, just as he now offered to provide for Samuel.

However, the volunteer Samaritan stayed but briefly, for he

realized that his lack of sacerdotal authority meant that he would continue to be a second-rate citizen among the ordained missionaries. "It was evident they needed help at Lac qui parle about the language," he wrote, "for though Dr. W. was studying with characteristic diligence and perserverence he made little progress." With Indians running in and out all the time, the young wife of Williamson's agricultural expert was picking up Sioux at a great rate, but she was uneducated and the "Dr. would not have thought he could learn any thing from her." Samuel trekked back to Fort Snelling and talked matters over with Gideon. When the younger brother—perhaps with his missionary heart fascinated as much by thought of Sarah Poage as by self-sacrifice —volunteered to serve Williamson, Samuel tried for a time to continue his work with Cloud Man's villagers. It was no go.

"As G. was now gone [to Lac Qui Parle] Mr. Stevens thought I should be compelled to remain with him, and he gave me to understand that, as he was a licenced preacher and I only a layman, he should expect me to spend much of my time in manual labor, and interpret for him in his intercourse with the Indians, but I did not come here to interpret for any one,—certainly not for one with as little ability natural or acquired as Mr. S. so I determined to go to Connecticut and obtain a licence to preach. I did not think a licence would add any thing to my authority or ability to preach the Gospel to the Dakotas, but it might relieve me from some embarrassment in my intercou[r]se with my clerical associates, though regularly educated clergymen should still regard me some as West Pointers do one who is appointed to military office from civil life."

Thus the missionaries—their failings as human as those of anyone else.

Taliaferro was almost desolate, and his journal says that he "feared looseing" the Ponds as they left the fort in opposite directions. The absence of "these two disinterested and worthy young men," he wrote, "will be a serious loss to the Indians who are much and deservedly attached to them, and I shall loose two faithful & trustworthy assistants in improveing the condition of the Mdewakanton Sioux." He was still convinced that *"to civ-*

ilize, is to *Christianize,*" that the ways of education and agriculture must be accepted by the Indians before they possibly could grasp the concept of the white man's religion. In his journal he fairly explodes: "to expound the Bible to a set of ragged half starved indolent beings is the heit of extravagance, and *folly.*"

The year before, in the Rockies, Samuel Parker had not been utterly persuaded that the indolents he met had to be civilized before being offered wise words. Unlike Jason Lee, he had paused to instruct the Flatheads and Nez Percés in the elements of Christian belief, and in his journal, which was soon to be published, Parker expresses pleasure at an Indian request for a lecture on the sanctity of marriage. Marcus Whitman, Parker's enlisted physician, had taken east two unwashed Nez Percé boys after the father of one of the lads beseeched the white doctor to teach his son religion. Now in 1836, while Samuel Pond was traveling east for his own religious edification, Whitman was bringing the Indian boys back to their tribe. And he was also, late in May, introducing his bride Narcissa to mountain man Tom Fitzpatrick, who was to lead the missionary vanguard as far as Wyoming's Green River.

May was moving time. On the 29th, while Whitman's party camped with Fitzpatrick on the Platte, Captain Nathan Jarvis wrote his brother in New York that Fort Snelling "has assumed quite a formidable appearance." Three Sundays earlier the maiden voyage of the steamboat *Missouri Fulton* had brought to the limestone fortress a new commandant, Black Hawk's "old friend, a great war chief," Lieutenant Colonel William Davenport. With the Sacs and Foxes at last moved to Iowa and the Rock River now well settled by whites, Fort Armstrong had been abandoned. As Taliaferro noted in his journal, May 8, Davenport had arrived from Armstrong with one hundred and forty men, bringing the Snelling strength up to five companies. But what most interested Jarvis was the fact that the *Missouri Fulton* also debarked Dr. John Emerson, "who is my junior in rank and by the by no chicken, measuring 6 ft 4 inches in his stockings and large in proportion."

Neither Emerson's stature nor his assignment as Nathan Jarvis' replacement rates him a place in this narrative. The fact, however, that he brought a servant does. The frail, kinky-haired, flat-nosed slave who that warm Sunday wrestled Emerson's gear off the deck of the *Missouri Fulton* was named Dred Scott. In twenty years he would be famous, but then at forty or thereabouts he was an unremarkable bondsman whose African heritage was undiluted, who had been born on Virginia's southern border and who must have found himself that day farther north than he ever had expected to be. A decade earlier, Dred's owner had taken him from the plantation to St. Louis. In 1833 he had been bought by Dr. Emerson, who had recently been commissioned an army surgeon and was assigned to the First Regiment at Fort Armstrong. Only the evacuation of the Rock Island post tied Dred Scott's life to the Snelling garrison, for Emerson had bought land not far from the Rock River entry, and in letters from his new post he fretted a good deal at not being on hand to take care of his interests.

Nothing can be said certainly of Dred's activity while his master settled down to life at Snelling in the summer of 1836. But it seems unlikely in so isolated a place, where there were few servants of any kind, that he did not meet Harriet Robinson with dispatch. For Harriet was one of several slaves long a part of Lawrence Taliaferro's ménage. Taliaferro doesn't tell us the number of slaves he brought to the fort, but there were several, and collectively at least they made an impression on the Indians, who called them "Black Frenchmen." Aside from the fact that he kept them in bondage, Taliaferro seems to have treated them reasonably well, nor did he exploit them by hiring them out for his own profit. Ten years before, with his peculiar punctuation, he had written in his journal, "Let Col. Snelling have my ... Boy William until the 1st of October next—for his Victuals & Clothes." The same spring he noted, "Capt. Plympton wishes to purchase my servant girl Eliza. I informed him it was my intention to give her her freedom after a limited time but that Mrs. P could keep her for two years and perhaps three." As we shall see, Taliaferro's notions about slavery were not typical of a Virginian of the period.

Negroes had long been almost legendary among Taliaferro's Indians, as they were on many frontiers. The highly talented mountain man, Jim Beckwourth—a great liar, incidentally—claimed to have been a Crow chief; at any rate he set up housekeeping with a chief's daughter. So among the Chippewas there was Stephen Bonga, who was a respected trader and who once made the boast (it made some kind of sense to the Indians who could see that he wasn't a redskin) that he was "the first white child" born in his neck of the woods. Bonga's grandparents had come to the Northwest as the slaves of the British commandant at Mackinac. Gaining freedom, they had kept an inn and their children had found mates among the native citizenry. Pierre Bonga, Jr., was well known in the region of the Mississippi headwaters long before Pike came upriver. He was considered a giant, well over two hundred pounds. In 1800 he was one of Alexander Henry's voyageurs, and it was reputed that he could tote five ninety-pound beaver packs across a portage with no man's aid. Stephen Bonga, whose mother was a Chippewa, claimed to be able to swing nine packs, and he was big enough, apparently, so that no one disputed him.

Dred Scott didn't encounter the younger Bonga until 1837, probably, but among the Negroes even better known at the fort (a mulatto who said he had been brought west by George Monroe, a nephew of the President) was James Thompson. He had arrived at St. Peter's in the year of Snelling's departure as the property of sutler John Culbertson. Sold by Culbertson to a First Regiment captain named Day, Thompson gained his freedom when a missionary at Prairie du Chien appealed to the *Western Christian Advocate* for funds to achieve the Snelling veteran's manumission. According to Reverend Alfred Brunson, "the money came in showers," and the freed Thompson became the interpreter as Brunson preached the Methodist faith at Kaposia. (The truth about the former slave's later activities lies somewhere between two stories: Brunson remembered Thompson as a backslider who later ran a whiskey shop opposite Fort Snelling. The freedman's own version when he was at death's door was that he remained a pious Methodist and was instrumental in the erection of the sect's first church in St. Paul.)

In spite of the fact that Fort Snelling stood on free soil by virtue of the Missouri Compromise, no slave brought here prior to Thompson is known to have been turned loose. Major Bliss had as part of his retinue, his son said, "a nice-looking yellow girl and an uncommonly black man." The girl (John Bliss keeps her anonymous) "became such an attractive belle among the soldiers" that she was packed aboard the *Warrior* for sale in St. Louis. Her fellow slave, Hannibal, who made side money selling spruce beer to the garrison, must have met Dred Scott in the classic factotum posture; while Scott was tugging Emerson's luggage off the deck, Hannibal was loading up for the Bliss' departure the next day on the *Missouri Fulton*. Hannibal was given his freedom five years later.

But this June, in St. Louis, a former Snelling slave won her freedom in a court case that Dred Scott years later would mark well. While James Thompson still had been doing chores around the fort, Lieutenant Thomas Stockton had bought a girl named Rachel as a house servant. After a year on the banks of the St. Peter's Rachel had gone with Stockton to Fort Crawford, where she was kept three years before being sold in St. Louis. Now, in 1836, in the case titled *Rachel v. Walker,* the Negro plaintiff was ordered to be manumitted on grounds she had been held in bondage on soil where slavery had been banned by Act of Congress. At Snelling that summer no apparent heed was paid to this release of a forgotten slave girl, for the arm of civil law had yet to be implemented in the precincts of the First Infantry Regiment.

This was the summer that news of Texan independence burst —a meatier subject for barracks talk than a law few people took seriously. Vengeance for the Alamo. Americans under General Sam Houston had wiped out Santa Anna. The Mexican butcher was a prisoner. From Washington, D.C., Jackson had sent his congratulations to the Raven and his brave men. This was talk which even an illiterate like Dred Scott could relish as he eavesdropped, for in his years with Emerson he had become a seasoned garrison hanger-on, on whom the burden of servitude rested easily enough. It was talk which must have been stirred anew when George Catlin appeared for his second St. Peter's visit, for the Indian chronicler had lost a close friend at the Alamo— Joe Chadwick, who with Catlin had ridden under Henry Dodge against the Comanches. Taliaferro gives little enough of the painter's return: "Wednesday, 17th August. Mr. Catlin and an English Gentleman arrive . . . [and four days later] . . . off this day to the Pipe Stone Quarry." But in this stay at the fort it is unlikely that Catlin failed to talk with the agent and Dr. Emerson of common acquaintances in St. Louis, for it was a small world. Emerson, indeed, was about to marry the sister of the former Mandan agent, John F.A. Sanford, who on board the *Yellowstone* had supplied Catlin with Indian subjects; Sanford's wife was the daughter of Pierre Chouteau, Jr., Ramsay Crooks' and Henry Sibley's associate—a fact which made Sanford partisan to American Fur Company interests and therefore hardly to be more than tolerated by Taliaferro. Nonetheless there was talk of downriver—of that, no doubt. Talk also of Zachary Taylor at Fort Crawford, where Catlin had stopped. Eavesdropping, Dred Scott may have marked that name; his years of following the army were to take him with Taylor on the march toward the Mexican border.

Fetching Emerson's guests drinks that August week or not, Scott may well have missed the sight of Catlin and his companion riding off on horses borrowed from Sibley. But in the interval before the painter was seen again the surgeon's bat boy found time to make himself noticed by Harriet Robinson. He must have. He was going to marry that girl, and within less than two years would witness the birth of the first of their children whose names along with his would go down in U.S. Supreme Court history. This summer was as good a time as any—perhaps better—for courtship in the slave quarters. Every white man was wrapped up in the advance of settlement, which moved toward Fort Snelling as inexorably as a glacier. Michigan had attracted so many westering people that the peninsula projecting northward between two Great Lakes had achieved statehood. The

St. Peter's citadel had become virtually dead center of Wisconsin Territory—established on July 4, and extending from Lake Michigan to the White Earth fork of the Missouri. Jackson had named Henry Dodge governor. John Jacob Astor and Ramsay Crooks were laying out towns, and Astor was speculating on land as far west as Prairie du Chien. Dred Scott's master was only one of hundreds of spare-time dabblers in real estate in the Upper Mississippi Valley.

Pierre Chouteau was sufficiently interested in the terrain of the Upper Mississippi to share in financing a French intellectual who was determined to explore all of its values. Thus, with letters from Chouteau and introductions to the Fort Snelling commandant from the War Department, Joseph Nicholas Nicollet had arrived at the entry on July 2. He was a mathematician, a gifted astronomer, but mostly he was an early-nineteenth-century scientist, a European fascinated by the American unknown whose range of interests covered ethnology, geology, meteorology and botany. He had a gift for friendship. Almost immediately he was a favorite at Henry Sibley's house, at the agency, and at the fort where Davenport and his officers removed "all difficulties that might naturally be expected to present themselves to a solitary traveler." Nicollet had left the fort for Lake Itasca before George Catlin and his friend had passed through en route to the pipestone quarry.

During the scientist's absence, Catlin returned with the boast that he was the first white man to visit the red stone deposits which the Indians considered sacred ground. No question about it—he was not. But there is a question as to the number who had preceded him. Fur traders had been in this area (now bordered by the Minnesota-South Dakota line) long before Robert Dickson. Will Clark had noted the quarry on his expedition map: "Here the different Tribes meet in Friendship and collect Stone for Pipes." And the first recorded visit, in 1831, had been made by the restless Philander Prescott who observed that Indians "labored here verry hard with hoes and axes" to obtain pieces suitable for carving into calumets.

"This place is great, not in history, for there is none of it, but in traditions and stories," Catlin wrote when he arrived at his destination. He noted that Indians believed in "the mysterious birth of the red pipe, which has blown its fumes of peace and war to the remotest corners of the Continent," and that the Great Spirit, "at an ancient period, here called the Indian nations together. . . ." Standing on a red stone precipice, the Great Spirit "broke from its wall a piece, and made a huge pipe by turning it in his hand, which he smoked over them, to the North, the South, the East, and the West; and told them that this stone . . . was their flesh—that they must use it for their pipes of peace— that it belonged to them all, and that the war-club and scalping knife must not be raised on its ground. At the last whiff of his pipe his head went into a great cloud, and the whole surface of the rock for several miles was melted and glazed; two great ovens were opened beneath, and two women (guardian spirits of the place), entered them in a blaze of fire; and they are heard there yet . . . answering to the invocations of the high-priests or medicine-men. . . ."

Catlin caught the gist of the Indian traditions as he wrote this report for the *New York Commercial Advertiser*. The quarry for centuries had been a tribal mecca, lying equidistant between the Great Lakes and the mountains. He sketched the thirty-foot red stone cliff, and made note of the natives' excavations "ancient and recent," as well as "their sculptured hieroglyphics—their *wakons,* totems and medicines. . . ." En route to the site he had been threatened by Sioux who forbade him to desecrate their holy ground, but no one bothered him at the quarry itself. He and his companion trailed back to Fort Snelling for the last time. Taliaferro closed the episode cryptically by noting on September 6 only that the painter had unsettled the Sioux. Like Sibley and the Ponds, the agent may have been glad enough to be rid of a traveler so glib and, in his view, so insensible to Indian proprieties.

No one had any such complaints about Nicollet. On the 27th the Frenchman arrived at St. Anthony Falls after mapping the Mississippi headwaters and wrote a note to Taliaferro saying that nothing could cure his exhaustion "but the pleasure of meeting you again under your hospitable roof, and to see all the friends of the garrison who have been so kind to me." He had been gone from the fort for sixty-one days, accompanied by a St. Peter's voyageur named Desiré Fronchet and, after he reached Leach Lake, by trader Francis Brunet and Trying-to-Walk, a Chippewa. The map he made was the first topographical attempt to delineate the region. Burdened by a sextant on his back, barometer on his shoulder, portfolio in hand, and a basket containing thermometer, chronometer, compass, artificial horizon, tapeline, spyglass, powder flask, shot bag, and carrying a gun or an umbrella "according to circumstances," Nicollet had trudged through woods, marshes, prairies. Where Schoolcraft (that "writer of books" in Taliaferro's demeaning phrase) spent two hours, Nicollet spent days examining the Mississippi source and discovering a streamlet that carries the rise of the great river even farther. In addition he had collected samples and made notes of fossils, flora, fauna, minerals, geological formations, and meteorological conditions.

"He had succeeded well," wrote Taliaferro, "and returned with a map of the country, and though drawn with a pen, presented a beautiful picture of lakes, land and rivers." Nicollet was a man of many parts, perhaps by far the most interesting visitor to settle in at St. Peter's. Born in Savoy in 1790, he became a watchmaker's apprentice at ten, and after eight years began to pursue the trade on his own while studying at odd hours. Distinguishing himself in mathematics and languages, he made his way to Bonaparte's Paris, where he tested his theory of probabilities by publishing a study on the mathematics of life insurance. He became an astronomer, was promoted to a professorship and awarded the medal of the Legion of Honor. But with his theory of probabilities he also played the stock market, and eventually lost everything.

In need of a fresh start, he managed to find passage for America and reached New Orleans in 1832, the year and place of the arrival of Maximilian, Prince of Wied-Neuwied, whose similar scientific interests were to take him up the Missouri in the company of Kenneth Mackenzie. Nicollet makes no mention of the

Prussian princeling, but he made friends throughout the South, including the Dutch geologist, Dr. Gerard Troost, then beginning his great work in Tennessee; Troost invited the French scientist to "fossilize, mineralize, and study the form and structure of rocks and crystals together." (Interestingly, Nicollet was also a house guest, Taliaferro said, of Justice John Catron, who was to vote against Dred Scott in the Supreme Court.) At any rate, the urbane Savoyard came to Fort Snelling with conversational gifts that were no less rare than the degree of appreciation extended to him by the isolated population.

He had brought his violin, and he spent many evenings playing in the agency house, with the piano accompaniment of Mrs. Taliaferro. We get only glimpses of this valiant woman. In 1828 Philip Cooke on his downriver journey had met her and Taliaferro as their boats passed near the Des Moines Rapids. ("We beheld a friend, Mr. T., an Indian agent; and, surmounting a vast pile of furniture, &c. &c., his newly-married wife—a rough introduction to the Northwest, she thought, no doubt.") Taliaferro had found his bride in Bedford, Pennsylvania, a spa where he frequently sought to restore his health. Her physical charms were noted by more than one Snelling visitor, and her affinity for Nicollet was such that he spoke and thought of her as his sister. While her husband converted a storeroom to provide their guest with shelter, Mrs. Taliaferro fed him "wild rice, mush and milk" (says Taliaferro) after the evening's chamber music. What Harriet Robinson may have served for dinner parties given at the agency house in honor of Nicollet is left to the imagination. The agent's garden produced such delicacies as asparagus, and the standard meat courses could be varied with many kinds of fish from the multiplicity of nearby lakes and streams. According to the Taliaferro journal, the guest and his hosts more than once went up to the falls where Mrs. Taliaferro fished and "M Nicollet busied himself in procuring specimens of various kinds of formations."

Nights when he did not fiddle beside Mrs. Taliaferro's piano Nicollet stood on the walls of the fort making astronomical observations. Weather permitting, he devoted the work days to field trips. He spent four such days in late October, when Indian summer had reopened navigation, with a boatload of Snelling soldiers charting the course of the St. Croix River. By the end of the month Taliaferro, convinced, in his words, of the "vast importance of a more perfect knowledge" of the Snelling region, had persuaded Nicollet to extend his visit. "All opportunities for transportation on the Mississippi having ceased," the scientist wrote a St. Louis friend, "I could not go down the river without leaving behind my collections and regrets that would make me weep until spring. I remain therefore, and am going to roll up in a *maisonnette* being prepared for me, wrap myself in bearskins, and put on a cloak made from a woolen blanket when I receive visitors who come to me from Fort Snelling or the Sioux villages. . . . Have pity on me, write me. A reminder of your friendship will buoy up the courage already sunk beneath four inches of snow that fell a few days ago."

The prospect of winter at St. Peter's was dreaded by most. Not until Major Bliss had assumed command of the fort had stoves been available to supplement the heat of fireplaces. This winter Dr. Emerson, a benevolent slave owner, requested the quartermaster to issue a stove for his man, Dred Scott. The request was denied, purportedly on grounds that there weren't enough heating units to go around. That, said the surgeon, was a lie. Emerson, it seems, had insulted the wrong man, for a right cross came thudding into his face. Emerson heeled away, dashed across the parade to his quarters, got a brace of pistols, and gave chase to the fleeing quartermaster. When the commandant ordered both men brought in, the realistic fact that Emerson was the only medic north of Prairie du Chien was all (says legend) that ruled out a duel to the death. The civil rights of Dred Scott—that was the issue. Maybe there was just something restive in the Fort Snelling climate.

CHAPTER ELEVEN

————◆•◆————

VIBRATIONS

TENSIONS RODE that winter's prevailing winds. Courtly Joseph Nicollet—by whom everyone was charmed—became a lifelong friend of Taliaferro and Sibley, but he was not a catalyst. The agent and the American Fur Company man were separated by the same gulf that had been extant when Astor had dominated the fur trade personally. To the end of his days Taliaferro believed that, "in the aggregate," American Fur traders were scoundrels. Although he had not included Sibley in the generalization, no rapport existed between the two in spite of the enthusiasm each had for Nicollet. Sibley, in fact, had come to St. Peter's with the company view that the agent was a menace. His letters indicate that he was not flattered to be treated by Taliaferro as a man to be trusted and therefore at least a cut above the average trader.

For his part, Lawrence Taliaferro did not relax his guard. On October 21 he assessed himself generously in a paean which ends as if it were designed to be sung by erring employees of the American Fur Company:

"He would never take a *Bribe*—

"He would see justice done all traders—

"He guided and protected the Indians—

"He broke down foreign influence—

"He drove whiskey out of the country—

"He forced dishonest Traders out—

"He is too independent for a tool

"He is opposed to paying *old credits* lost or said to be lost in Trade for 20 years

"He keeps peace, & has the confidence of the Indians—

"He keeps off oppression by the Traders & causes the Indians by frequent councils to pay their just debts

"He advises the Indians to take goods instead of money as annuities—when called on for his opinion

"He has prevented a Set of Canadians & other persons from makeing slaves of the Indians—both of minds as well as persons

"He causes the Indians to be instructed how to raise corn & to use implements of husbandry—

"He has altogether too much influence over the Indians for us or our designs of enriching ourselves out of them & their lands—"

The pages of Taliaferro's journal are salted with such indictments. Don Lawrence in his righteous armor rode out every day to tilt with the enemy. His giants were real, not windmills; no whirling vanes knocked him from his charger. And upon his retirement at the age of seventy—with Astor dead, Crooks dead, and Sibley a frontier hero who snubbed him—Taliaferro was no less convinced that the Indians would have been better off without "the wiles of the American Fur Company." Throughout his life at St. Peter's he went regularly to the fort to share his conviction with the commanding officers. While Bliss was still the man in charge Taliaferro burdened his journal with a transcript of their dialogue about a plot by Crooks and his friends for a treaty advantageous to the trade. Bliss had heard that the plotters were besieging Washington. "I hear letters many of them," Taliaferro has Bliss say in the agent's contorted syntax, "have been written for the purpose of effecting the object we speak of. . . ." Taliaferro's rejoinder is for the record. He reminds Bliss of the 1830 treaty when the company tried to get the government to pay long-standing debts the traders claimed were owed to them by Indians. And makes a speech: "I then defeated their object. . . . For I view the allowance of all such claims as a fraud commited upon the Treasury—tho legalized by a Treaty. The company are much opposed to me on this ground & fear me—& would be glad to have me out of the country. I know too much— and they are fully aware of my independence and that I am not slow in opposeing malefic practices. . . . I am determined at some future day, Major, to address the President directly." Adding that Jackson "abhors iniquity, & deception," the agent assured Bliss that the President will protect him "against a host of such men as seek to rob the Treasury." ("O, white man," he cried thirty years later in his autobiography, "what degradation has your thirst for gold brought upon the poor savage!")

Determined to prevent fraud, Taliaferro in this summer of 1836 was nonetheless persuaded that Jackson's policy of Indian forfeiture of lands east of the Mississippi must be carried out. He held numerous councils to prepare the Sioux for the inevitable future. Patiently he explained to them the evil of the Seminole uprising which had broken out in Florida early in the year. His job was to prevent such an eventuality on the Upper Mississippi. It was also his self-assigned task to frustrate profiteers. "The Crisis is approaching," he wrote Will Clark in November. "We have designing & unprincipled men at work—Gold is their brazen goal, and they will act freely to destroy any honest man standing between them and the forlorn and helpless savage." It was fair enough, he told the aging Indian expert in St. Louis, to provide the tribes money to pay for damages individual Indians might have done to American property, "but never, never for a set of patched up and fraudulent claims for *Credits lost* or stated to be lost in the trade with the Indians for ten or twenty years back." By the end of the month he had devised a treaty proposal—liberal to the Indians, but paring their alleged trading debts to the bone—which he sent off to Washington. He was adamant that the American Fur Company should get away with as little as possible.

So adamant that his friend Nicollet tried to make him see that he was, as the scientist once put it, "too great a friend to the Indians." Although Nicollet believed that Taliaferro was highly thought of in Washington and that "your Indians love you," he cautioned the agent on grounds that he stuck too close "to the interest of the government to suit the times." There is here more than a hint that the French visitor was listening, with some sympathy, to Sibley's side of the controversy. For in the past year, unbeknown to Taliaferro, Sibley had been campaigning for the appointment of a new Fort Snelling agent who would cooperate with American Fur goals. His complaints about Taliaferro's prejudice against the company had been relayed in January from the War Department to General Clark. That same month his Prairie du Chien partner, Hercules Dousman, had arrived at St. Peter's to bring out in the open the kind of allegations that Sibley, for reasons of his own, chose not to issue directly. In his journal Taliaferro recorded that Dousman threatened reprisal, accusing him of turning the Indians against the company and "god knows what all." Taliaferro refused to be bullied and told Dousman he had "every confidence" that he and Sibley "could manage our own affairs."

He had, in fact, already written Sibley's boss, complimenting the St. Peter's trader "in the highest terms," Ramsay Crooks said, and adding that he so respected Sibley's honor he would take his word on anything. In view of this, Crooks told Sibley it seemed strange that he should be so annoyed by Taliaferro, even though all his complaints were "doubtless well grounded." Crooks' view was that Taliaferro had been invested with enormous, "unwarrantable" power and that the Indian department "is so sure its Agents are almost immaculate that the best founded representations are disregarded." The old story. Crooks, however, promised one more effort in Washington. If Will Clark would not recognize the reasons to fire Taliaferro, perhaps the Secretary of War, the company's longtime friend Lewis Cass, would.

But Taliaferro thought differently. Already he had set down in his journal the code that nourished him. Spelling, punctuation and sanctimony are his:

"So long as there is opposition in the fur trade—so long will there be continually engendered—*feelings,* and actions & words —calculated to disturb friendly intercourse. 16 years experience has taught me not by any means to be too familiar with persons engaged in Indian trade For a public officer, an *Agent more particularly* is watched with a jealous eye. his every word, act & deed is closely canvassed and scrutinized, and unhappily too often by interested & partial observers—to be done even justice

175

at their hands. this feeling has not been concealed it has been insinuated & at one time openly avowed that the Agent—favourd one sett of Traders more than another—without specifying exactly in what this favoritism consisted—but so it was.

"Now before a just god—to whom I am accountable for every act & deed done & thought on this earth I call him to witness—that I am incapable of such an act of degradation—and that all that I have ever done has been with an eye single to equal justice unto to *all*—and a jealous preservation of the diversified interests of the government and of my responsible charge. I thank my god that I am above a mean action. my government has fully sustained me in all that I have ever done during a public service of 23 years. I am gratefull for this repeated & continued confidence reposed in zeal, integrity, and abilities. to forfeit my Oath of office—I accept *no bribes*. no man dare offer one. To be intimidated may be the aim of some—but the *Devil* himself cannot induce me by artfull designs to—leave my *even ground* or turn one jot, or letter from that course which my Government expects its officers to persue. I am free to confess I have my weaknesses & follies, but I trust they are too well guarded by honorable feelings to do intentional wrong or injustice to any man, or sett of men on earth."

There can be no doubt that Taliaferro believed every word of his flashing and somewhat fractured rhetoric. Nor any that he took his duties seriously. Yet there is a problem in the fact that he so offended Sibley that the latter dismissed the agent's capacities out of hand. Certainly Sibley was partisan to affairs of the company as he was to his own pocket. Like Crooks he believed—in this era when monopoly capital influenced government and controlled business—in the necessity of Indian compliance to the exigencies of trade. But Sibley was no Kenneth Mackenzie, no Indian hater. Generally, he had a way with men, regardless of station. Still he also had, or thought he had, reason to waive aside Taliaferro's entire record. One may assume fairly a personality clash. Sibley did not like Taliaferro, did not like his treaty proposal, did not—above everything—want him to be a treaty commissioner. He wrote Crooks: "All these troubles might be easily prevented, if we had an efficient Indian Agent, but the wavering and uncertain measures of the present incumbent make him all but despised by the Sioux, who do not hesitate to speak of him (& sometimes to him) in the most contemptuous terms. . . . It is of great importance to us that Taliaferro be not appointed commissioner, inasmuch as he is known to be inimical to the Am Fur Co. and all connected with them, not withstanding his many fair professions." Sibley went on to say that Taliaferro had made it clear "he would not allow anything for Indian credits" were the treaty his responsibility. It was imperative, Sibley wrote, to get the right man for the commissioner's job. "Col Davenport is a fair and honorable man, but our Agent has too long had his ear to make his appointment as Comr a very profitable one to us." The question of profit was, of course, central to the issue. The treaty terms framed by Taliaferro prescribed an amount to cancel Sioux debts to the company "which would be less than an eighth of what it should be," Sibley lamented. He suggested that Crooks use his influence in Washington to have Governor Dodge appointed as commissioner, when and if the treaty became a reality.

In September, Taliaferro wrote Dodge that the Sioux had agreed to accept $560,000 as payment for their rights to territory east of the Mississippi. If Washington could be persuaded to act with dispatch, he thought, a deal at that figure might be consummated. But any lengthy delay would provide time for the men he called "vultures" to gather and persuade the Indians to demand more money in order to satisfy exhorbitant claims of the traders. While he was concerned with the Sioux, others were concerned with the Chippewas. The American Fur Company was more than usually concerned with both. For the tide of settlement, the very thing that made the treaties desirable, was encroaching on the fur trade; inevitably, Indian trappers were bringing in fewer pelts. And in the Prairie du Chien region there were fewer natives able to trap, or even to perform as customers, because smallpox had struck. Taliaferro had reported the disease affecting two Lac Qui Parle families in 1832, when it was apparently arrested. In 1837, it would assume epidemic proportions, proceeding up the Missouri River to kill at least 17,200 tribesmen among the Mandans, the Minnatarees, the western Sioux, the Assiniboins, and the Blackfeet. But now, in 1836, smallpox infected Chippewas and Winnebagos, and on October 25, Dousman wrote Sibley that business would be reduced thereby to a third of the normal volume. To recoup such losses the traders were intent not only on treaty provisions that might insure funds to cover legitimate claims but on tactics that would cut deeply into the Indian payments. Under Ramsay Crooks' leadership they could make good use of the winter ahead by lobbying among the natives.

Crooks himself was on a field trip that fall, running into more and more reports of the progress of a strange expedition that had begun making news in August. Just about the time Sibley got his news of smallpox from Dousman, Crooks opened a letter from Charles Borup, one of his Lake Superior traders, and read the news that, shortly after his own visit to Borup, a military party led by one James Dickson had arrived. On October 22, the day Borup had dated his letter, James Dickson's expedition rowed up to the company post at Fond du Lac on the St. Louis River, armed with letters of introduction from the old Astor man, Lyman Warren. Dickson headed an incredible army of sixty men who had enlisted to drive the Spanish out of the Southwest and set up an Indian state. He was pausing now at William Aitkin's headquarters on his march to the Red River Settlements, where he intended to recruit hundreds of *bois brûlés* to swell the ranks of his Army of Liberation. What deals he may have discussed with the American Fur Company are not known. But it is clear that he made Crooks' arch rival nervous. The Hudson's Bay Company had advised its London headquarters of his movements, and word had been passed on to the British War Office. Not only did Hudson's Bay fear losing its cheap labor to the cause of Indian liberation; there was concern as well that the none-too-happy half-breeds might join Dickson in conquering the Red River country.

This thought may have titillated the cooperative American Fur Company traders. The old problem of prohibition, enforced by Fort Snelling soldiers on occasions, had frustrated the company's competition in the Minnesota border country, for Hudson's Bay traders suffered no restrictions on liquor. Unable to keep Red River and Rainy Lake Indians from taking the furs across the border to the sources of alcohol, American Fur—behind Taliaferro's back—had made a deal with Hudson's Bay, agreeing to abandon its border competition in return for 300 pounds a year. In September of this year the Hudson's Bay president, George Simpson, had written both Aitkin and Crooks in the hope of negotiating a renewal of the pact. Crooks stalled. Was he waiting to see what luck General James Dickson might have in inciting the Red River *bois brûlés* to overthrow their ruthless Hudson's Bay rulers? It is a tempting prospect for which the record gives no support. Nevertheless, ten months passed before Crooks told Simpson that he and his partners would again agree to leave this part of Minnesota to the Canadians. Plenty of time, as it turned out, to take the measure of General Dickson. (Plenty of time, too, for Taliaferro to learn, as he reported the following summer to Washington, that Crooks' traders, stepping outside "the course of their lawful business," had turned over to British administration "a portion of our Indian territory." No Fort Snelling troops marched to the border, for Washington refrained from taking any action on Taliaferro's charges.)

Still, during the winter that Crooks postponed coming to terms with Simpson, Dickson took his men toward Fort Garry on the Lower Red River, making full use of American Fur hospitality as long as it was available. He talked glibly at each of the posts, but revealed little of his background. He had turned up—some said from England—in Mexico. He was vague in his talk about Texas, but there is some chance that he had fought for the cause of independence before his arrival in Washington in the winter of 1835–36. Here at capital levees he cut a handsome figure, in a not-quite-identifiable uniform and with saber scars that gave his bearded, mustachioed face a martial glamour. His secret was that he had been talking to Indian chiefs, including some Cherokees who at the end of 1835, after years of litigation, had been bulldozed into agreeing to abandon their ancestral land. They and other tribes would appear at Dickson's rendez-vous, just as soon as his army was recruited.

From Washington the bizarre Liberator had gone north to Buffalo and Montreal in search of gullible young men who would serve as officers and who, once Dickson's Indian empire was established, would become statesmen. The romantic bait had drawn a motley staff. Brigadier General John George Macken-zie was the half-breed son of none other than the King of the Missouri, one of the two children who had been left behind in Canada. Another officer was a *bois brûlé* son of Dr. John Mc-Loughlin, the great Hudson's Bay factor who now in the fall of 1835 was entertaining Narcissa Whitman at Vancouver. A captain was a Polish revolutionary who had escaped the Russian invasion after the crushing defeat of General Ramarino on the Vistula. And the young major of artillery was Martin McLeod who, though he did not yet know it, was headed for Fort Snell-ing and a career with Henry Sibley. Young Mackenzie had dropped out of the expedition because of ill health, but McLeod and others followed Dickson for two months as they struggled through the North Woods from Fond du Lac to the Hudson's Bay Red River headquarters.

In the pause at Fond du Lac, Dickson paid his respects to the resident missionary, Edmund F. Ely, and Ely in his diary of October 23 offers a glimpse of the Liberator. "Another boat . . . chartered by Gen. Jas. Dickson—& manned by his soldiers. . . . They are on an expedition against Mexico & it is the present intention, if a sufficient force shall be collected, to make a de-scent from the passes of the Rocky Mountains upon a Cer[tain] mexican City & destroy it. . . . The Gen. called on us in the Eve-ning [and I had] a long conversation with him, concerning his plans. He keeps nothing back, except the city in view. His plan is to form a Government in California of the scattered Indian tribes of the west—Cherokees, Creeks, & all others who may be disposed to join them." Ely later wrote that "Our conversation brought out the following points—that Dixon (and also the Pole) had been engaged in the Texan Army . . . That the idea of being called to fill some important position in the Affairs of the World, had possessed him—that the star of fate was guiding him (unauthorized by U.S.) in this bold stroke (a purely filibustering Expedition)." Dickson left Fond du Lac for Fort Garry, "calculating to recruit (a force of) Half Breeds—hunt their way across the buffalo plains, & thus (suddenly) and from an unexpected direction, to fall on the doomed city (whh I concluded to be Santa Fee), and from its pillage, to find himself abundantly supplied with gold for future wants."

Ely does not say so, but the filibusterer carried with him embellished broadsides to post in public squares: ACCOMPANIED BY A GREAT ARMY OF WELL-MOUNTED SOLDIERS WITH SHIELDS AND LANCES SENT BY GOD AND BY THE HOLY MOTHER OF GOD, MARY MOST HOLY, I, MONTEZUMA II HAVE COME TO SUCCOR AND SAVE MY COMRADES IN THE LANDS OF MEXICO. Montezuma II—the reincarnation of the last great Aztec ruler? Rather a man infected by the twin viruses of romance and ambition. He carried in his luggage a coat of mail. (So, too, would the King of the Missouri had he had his way. Four years earlier Mackenzie had written William Astor about his desire for armor with which to dazzle his savage clients.) The wonder is that Dickson's lavish dream was so readily stomached, yet what other visitor to isolated trading posts could have been half so entertaining? Besides, compared to the Jacksonian removal policy, his plan seemed almost to make sense. "It would make the proposed Indian Country of the American government," Bernard De Voto wrote tartly, "a bush-league idea, mangy and poverty-stricken. It would be the final Indian nation. Montezuma would form a military government to rule over it but no white man could own an acre of it."

But Dickson never transmogrified himself into Montezuma. Even the help of Ramsay Crooks' partners was of little avail. He left Aitkin's headquarters and eighteen days later he and his men were given shelter by Allen Morrison at Sandy Lake. They got a "highland welcome," said McLeod, and one almost can hear the squeal of bagpipes. They started up the Mississippi, breaking ice so their canoes could move freely. On November 19 they were at Augustin Belanger's post where they were "civily treated during our 6 days stay." McLeod had been keeping a diary which is revealing. On the twentieth, a month inland from Lake Superior, he was "dull & melancholy"; on the twenty-fourth: "Out shooting. No luck." They started across Lake Winnebagoshish on November 26 "on ice (15 miles) Walking difficult and exceedingly fatiguing as there is no snow as yet upon the ice." Next day, however, they were guests of Aitken's son Alfred and "dined al la Turque on excellent venison." They made it to trader John Fairbanks on Red Lake by December 1, but from there on they were in the Hudson's Bay rented bailiwick and had run out of fur trade hospitality. Ten days later their Indian guides deserted them near Thief River and the expedition began to disintegrate. Some of the Liberator's erstwhile followers turned back—not without the grizzly forecast that those who went on would be "casting lots to eat each other." The truth was not much better. "The whole distance we had travelled on foot from the 26 Novr . . . is about 645 miles . . . during that time we lived upon a pt of boiled rice each pr day and were 4 days without food of any kind except two ozs each of meat and a small Partridge divided between 9 persons."

They were at the Red River Settlements in time for Christmas, but the Hudson's Bay Company was not in a giving mood. It refused to honor Dickson's drafts and thus prevented him from hiring *bois brûlés* or purchasing supplies for an army. McLeod had described his general as "some what visonary," and added "n'importe I wish to go north & westward and will embrace the opportunity, but must 'look before I leap.'" The now jaded major of artillery did not leap when Dickson, persuaded at last that Hudson's Bay would not cooperate, decided that the Southwest still called him. The Liberator disappeared into the buffalo plains. He materialized as spring came to one of Mackenzie's Missouri posts, Fort Clark. There on March 21, Francis Chardon made an entry in the fort journal: "Pleasant weather. I was Presented to day with a Sword from Mr. Dickson—the Liberator of all Indians." On March 24, Chardon wrote: "Mr. James Dickson, the Liberator of all Indians, started with Benture for Fort Union." The visionary general vanished from history a few miles up the Missouri where a passing traveler left him—"as he is tired of walking, and has lain himself down to die."

On March 24, on the east shore of Lake Traverse, Martin McLeod was at another American Fur Company fort as the guest of Sibley's man, Joe Brown. Although McLeod had just missed laying himself down to die, that fate had come to one of his companions, the Polish captain; and another man with whom he had started south from Fort Garry had been lost in a blizzard. Two weeks recuperating from a month of harrowing winter travel in the Red River Valley made McLeod fit again, and he and his guide borrowed some horses, then crossed the shallow continental divide to the St. Peter's headwaters. On April 7 he rode up to Fort Renville where, he told his diary, he was well received by the proprietor. Old Joe's missionary neighbors were thriving, and a big log mission house built by Gideon Pond stood snugly on the slope above Lac Qui Parle. Things were humming among the religious. Renville was so paternalistic about Dr. Williamson's venture among his Indians that he had joined in a kind of assembly-line translation of the Bible into Sioux. In the big hall-like living room of Fort Renville, Williamson would read a verse and Joe, a gifted simultaneous translator, would immediately recite in Sioux. Gideon Pond, sitting nearby, then wrote it down. Also sitting, on the banquette that was built against the walls, were retired voyageurs and members of Renville's elite Indian bodyguard. Under such circumstances enough progress had been made so that McLeod, in an audience consisting of "half breeds, Indians, Canadians, and a few Whites" heard Williamson read in Sioux "a chapter from the Testament" in the same service in which a group of *bois brûlés* and full bloods sang the Psalms of David in their mother tongue. McLeod had one complaint. Gideon Pond and Sarah Poage (by this time only six months away from marriage) tried to convert him. In his diary he underlined the latter verb in some distaste, and said that "in the hypocritical cant of the day" Gideon had tried to make him see *"God's mercies* &c. &c. &c." in having weathered the blizzard which had taken the lives of his companions.

McLeod left Renville and the missionaries and went down the

St. Peter's to Fort Snelling, where he arrived on April 16. He had had enough of liberating Indians, and he appears to have had little interest, one way or the other, in Lawrence Taliaferro's battle with Sibley, Crooks, *et al* over the welfare of the Minnesota natives. Dickson's scheme for a Indian empire on the sunny California slope, all the youthful dreams of power and authority, had been blown away by the winds of March—abandoned as surely as the foundering Liberator had surrendered his sword to Chardon, who hated Indians as much as any fur trader ever did. McLeod came to Fort Snelling in the spring, but for him it was a year's ending, and he turned the calendar's last page and joined the exploiters. He would be around Fort Snelling for the rest of his life, much of that future to be spent with the American Fur Company—until it too went under.

CHAPTER TWELVE

TREATY AND TRIUMPH

THREE DAYS after McLeod walked up the bluff road to the fort, Nicollet may have sighed audibly as he recognized the end of the tedious northern winter. "I send you news," he wrote a St. Louis friend on April 19, "of the Bear of St. Peter's who is coming out of his lair to watch the ice depart and enjoy the first rays of heat that the spring sun has cast over a region appalled by snow, hunger, and a 20 to 30 degree temperature." The long winter had had its pleasant interruptions in the musical soirees with Mrs. Taliaferro, but these diversions had come to an end when the arrival of the first steamboat offered the agent's lady a chance to go east to visit her family. For reasons unknown, but apparently without rancor, Nicollet had moved then to the bachelor hospitality offered by Henry Sibley in the new stone house across the river.

By this time Sibley was well entrenched in wilderness splendor, as firmly in command of his own domain as was the presiding officer at Fort Snelling. His home was viewed by one visitor (John Charles Frémont by name, but he comes later in this narrative) as a hunting lodge. The walls which had been plastered by Sioux women were embellished with bearskins and other trophies of field and forest. At least twenty-two dogs came at their master's bidding, and a painting of Lion, one of Sibley's two lean pedigreed wolf hounds, hung over the fireplace of the main room. Books were important to the American Fur Company's new St. Peter's partner, and he ordered newly published volumes through Ramsay Crooks in New York. This year it would have been strange indeed had not Sibley and Nicollet dis-

185

cussed Washington Irving's *Astoria*, off the press the preceding October—for it had made Crooks himself (along with the others who a quarter-century before had gone to the Pacific for John Jacob Astor) a man with whom armchair pioneers must reckon.

One might say that the literature of the mountain West had a beginning in *Astoria*, but Irving's tribute to Astor had been preceded six years earlier by the publication of a small volume in which Nicollet expressed substantial interest. Having budgeted some of his winter hours for the study of the Sioux and their language, Nicollet was eager to read *Tales of the Northwest*, by William Joseph Snelling. The son of the fort's founder, now a well-known Boston writer, had found the materials for penetrating sketches of the Indians in his years at St. Peter's. In Nicollet's company Sibley talked of his similar experiences which he later set down in his own series of published sketches, some of them not unlike those of Joe Snelling. Already he had begun to recognize the half-breed Jack Frazer for the unusual character he was. As Sibley encouraged Frazer in the evolution that finally took the talented half-breed from warrior life to a respected role as one of American Fur's traders, he drew from Jack some of the stories he later would write.

At Sibley's limestone headquarters Nicollet found a passing parade of characters frequently as interesting in their own way as was Frazer in his. (Simon Fraser's Minnesota nephew was about to importune the missionaries for English lessons denied him when his father had vamoosed.) As spring progressed, men like Louis Provencalle came downriver with their boatloads of peltry to be consigned by Sibley for shipment to Crooks in New York. Louis, so dark of complexion he was called Leblanc in irony, was an illiterate who used pictographs in his bookkeeping. Joe LaFramboise, who had guided Catlin to the pipestone quarry, was renowned as a practical joker who found sport in embarrassing colleagues unencumbered with the rudiments of English. Fun for LaFramboise was to watch a friend with the smell of hides on him taking tea at a party given by the ladies of the fort —taking cup after cup because the tongue-tied outlander could not politely say no—and then to burst into laughter when the tea-glutted friend rose in anguish and cried, "Laframboise, *pour l'amour de bon dieu, pourquoi ne dîtes vous pas à madame, que je n'en veut point d'avantage?"*

Such men were Sibley's winterers. He was boss of what Crooks called the company's Sioux Outfit—a series of trading posts stretching as far west as the Sheyenne River on the ninety-eighth meridian. Through Crooks, he supplied these forts with goods for the trade and recruited the voyageurs who manned the boats and generally did the traders' dirty work. His role was not much different than that of Robert Dickson, thirty years before—except that Sibley had formalized his relationship with the garrison by assuming the sutlership in partnership with the quondam Menominee agent, Samuel C. Stambaugh. American Fur's man at the entry left few stones unturned. As Nicollet had been attracted to St. Peter's by the security of the fort on the bluff, Sibley had arrived to dominate a white community already in embryo.

While Sibley's guest, and using the fort as base for his scientific investigations, Nicollet observed the pockets of settlement that had become portents of the future at the same time they threatened the First Regiment's military autonomy. Scattered near Sibley's house, and near the still visible site of Leavenworth's Cantonment New Hope, was an increasing population of squatter families. Some of these belonged to traders like Jean Baptiste Faribault, who had come to the entry in 1820 and who did his winter's bartering upriver. But more belonged to jacks-of-all-trades, voyageurs who—having served their periods of servitude —chose to eke out existence from odd jobs, hunting, and hard-scrabble gardens. When Nicollet, an infinitely curious man, left the fort to head toward Sibley's, he had a panoramic view of the hamlet of these voyageurs. He could walk along the citadel's westerly wall and pause beside a young oak that had grown up on the edge of the bluff. Pike's island lay below, sprawling in the sluggish waters of the entry, greening with April's new grass, pied with clumps of budding trees. Beyond the island and across the St. Peter's narrow channel, Sibley's pale yellow house stood at the bottom of the far slope. The grassland behind rose in swells toward the horizon. Nicollet could see the Sibley ware-house, the stables, blacksmith's shop, and a few log huts scattered on the slope. What he saw was the hamlet Sibley tended to call New Hope, and which the Indians (and others increasingly) called Mendota, the Sioux word for "meeting of waters."

Turning to look west from the fort across the prairie, Nicollet could see Taliaferro's story-and-a-half stone dwelling which had been built by Captain Nathan Clark in 1823. Close by was the log Indian council house and the small home of the interpreter, outside of which Scott Campbell habitually sat and smoked his long clay pipe. A white fence framed the agent's garden, a flagstaff stood at the edge of the plaza that had been staked out for Indian gatherings. Across this flat terrain, a few days after his arrival, Martin McLeod guided Lieutenant James McClure, bleeding profusely from a shoulder wound caused by the accidental firing of McLeod's rifle. McLeod had found himself a stopgap job with Benjamin Baker, an independent trader who, almost fifteen years before, had erected a big stone building near the old Camp Cold Water. Here, probably a few days after he had stepped off the steamboat, Nicollet had met some of the refugees from the Red River Settlements who had become squatters on the reservation. A few of these had established small farms not far from Baker's house, a couple of others tilled the soil on the east side of the Mississippi. The five families who, in 1821, had settled in as the result of Josiah Snelling's generosity, were joined by others who had been arriving periodically. For some time they had been welcomed, in at least one case not without reason—the wife of the Swiss refugee Abram Perret was hailed by the women of the garrison because she was an accomplished midwife.

But any visitor, like Nicollet, soon learned that the military reserve was now less than tolerant of these extralegal residents. Snelling and his successors had disregarded army policy in permitting civilians to set themselves up on land deeded to the War Department by Indians. In agreeing to Pike's treaty of 1805, the Sioux had been assured that the reservation was to be used for military purposes exclusively. And white men could live on land which the Indians had not ceded only if there were no objections from the natives. Many Indians thus took a dim view of this growing population of settlers, for unlike the traders who offered the savages merchandise they coveted, men who farmed had virtually nothing with which to appease the Indians for their presence. Resentful natives understandably harassed the Snelling squatters. They frequently killed cattle for the sheer hell of it, not even bothering to butcher the carcasses. The settlers, in turn, made claims for damages against the government, a fact which made life difficult for Taliaferro and the fort's command. By the spring of 1837 the situation had developed to the degree that corrective action now seemed inevitable.

During this uneasy season Samuel Pond returned to the missionary life as an ordained minister, but in spite of his improved status he did not find that his relations with the Reverend Mr. Stevens were advanced substantially. He seems to have taken refuge in again lending Cloud Man's farmers a hand and in translating the story of Joseph and his brothers into Sioux, sending the manuscript out to Lac Qui Parle to be used by Gideon in edifying the Indian flock kept in line by old Joe Renville. Presumably Samuel shared his Indian knowledge with Nicollet as the weather warmed up and May slid into June; for in their alien ways both were scholars. But we are sure only that beginning in June, Samuel made his increasing Sioux vocabulary available to Stephen Riggs, another missionary, who was to publish a dictionary which owed much to the Ponds.

Meanwhile word reached the garrison that the First Infantry's decade of tenure on the bluff was about to end. The Florida war against the Seminoles was going badly, and Colonel Zachary Taylor's regiment was penciled in for its first real action since the Black Hawk fracas. Lieutenant Colonel Davenport marched his four companies out of the fort on July 15 and joined Taylor at Fort Crawford. There the commands changed as General George M. Brooke brought in Josiah Snelling's old regiment, and Martin Scott, now a captain, returned to the St. Peter's with two companies of the Fifth. Surgeon John Emerson appears to be the only soldier in the garrison to be unaffected by the shift.

He and Dred Scott stayed on. Dred, in fact, got married. Taliaferro fails to record the date, but some time that summer, most
likely, the agent gave Harriet Robinson in marriage, performing
the ceremony himself. We have the assurance of his autobiography that the giving was literal; in agreeing to the wedding he
manumitted his servant girl—a point not heeded in the legal
conflict which made Dred Scott famous.

Taliaferro's charitable act was minor compared to the duties
which now occupied him. Not only had his plan for a Sioux
treaty been accepted, but the War Department had decided to
do business with the Chippewas, and Fort Snelling was named
as the site. As the garrison thermometer registered in the high
nineties the agent began counseling with various Sioux bands in
an effort to set them up for a peaceful reception of their enemies'
arrival. Sub-agent Miles Vineyard had been delegated to round
up Flat Mouth, Hole-in-the-Day and other Chippewa chiefs,
and Vineyard had gone up the Mississippi early in July. Immediately bands from both tribes began streaming in. Taliaferro
may well have been grateful for the reunion with Martin Scott
in this regard alone, for there were few soldiers better equipped
to handle—with only eighty men—a gathering so fraught with
explosive potential. Martin Scott is one of those frontier heroes
who should have found a chronicler. He came west too early to
be discovered by any of those who helped to make the reputa-
tions of the mountain supermen like Carson and Bridger; his
military exploits in the Mexican War were largely forgotten when
he was killed at the head of his regiment in the battle of Molino
del Rey.

However, take the word of an English traveler that he was,
in the 1830's, a celebrity who "may be accounted a public character," and that he was also "one of the first Nimrods of the
United States ... who, perhaps, has seen more of every variety
of hunting than any other person." That he was the first to be
able to toss two potatoes in the air and fire a shot through both
of them may be debated. But Captain Frederick Marryat, who
enters this narrative next year, said that he could hardly believe
his eyes as he watched Scott perform the feat. A teetotaler

("high-souled," said his commanding general), Scott was the best soldier in the Fifth Infantry in the view of one Fort Snelling enlistee. His character rating may have been missed by the Indians, but not his fast draw, nor his marksmanship. More than one native had seen Scott emulate William Tell by shooting an apple from the head of his Negro servant. A good man to keep two tribes of treaty-making savages in line.

The Sioux gathered at the fort as witnesses; their formal negotiating would occur in Washington in spite of the efforts of Sibley and Crooks. American Fur had lost this round to Taliaferro and had to be content with a massive gathering of Chippewas on which to work its wiles. Experience taught that a delegation of chiefs conferring in the capital was less apt to cooperate with traders' demands than a tribal powwow in which the young men could be influenced to sympathize with the company claims. As a result Sibley and the North Woods experts, William Aitkin and Lyman Warren, had left no stone unturned to insure as many concessions from the Chippewas as possible. Earlier in the year the three men had signed their own agreement with the tribe, consummating a deal that gave them exclusive rights to cut timber and build a sawmill on Chippewa-controlled pinelands. In June, Warren had written Sibley that he had the assurance of the chiefs that they would not sell these lands to the government when they came to the fort to treat. Thus, no matter how the government negotiations affected the fur trade, there was the promise of new profits in lumbering to offset the decline of company business.

As the July sun blazed, the Chippewas came downriver in their canoes and set up their lodges under the trees, and by Thursday, the twentieth, there were a thousand or more tribesmen milling about the bottomland and on the bluff. To guarantee the security of the prairie, on which the treaty was to be staged, Captain Scott had mounted his artillery pieces on the roof of the fort's magazine and had them trained to cover the meeting ground. More than three hundred Sioux observers came from the villages of Little Crow, Black Dog, Good Road, Shakopee and Sleepy Eyes; and tepees, feathered warriors, gala-costumed

191

women and children studded the terrain. All the missionaries, one of them reported, were there. The Methodist Alfred Brunson said that the Presbyterians (meaning Samuel Pond among others) took special interest in the Chippewas among whom Brunson had been laboring. "After catechising them as to their religious experience and attainments, they took occasion to address the Sioux . . . endeavoring to excite the ambition of the Sioux to emulate, and, if possible, exceed the Chippewas in this matter." For Brunson the treaty was an opportunity to proselytize and to show off the prayer-meeting fervor of his Chippewa converts.

But for the traders, he wrote, it was a chance "to get as good a price out of the government . . . as possible . . . always having an eye to the payment of their claims against the Indians, some of which, it was said . . . had been paid two or three times already." Taliaferro agreed substantially with this interpretation, but Sibley, of course, did not. Both men were excessively vigilant when Governor Henry Dodge arrived and the proceedings opened. Taliaferro had had erected the usual leafy bower to shield the white officials, including Dodge and the secretary of the treaty commission, Verplanck Van Antwerp. Martin Scott's men stood guard. Among the crowd of onlookers were many of the squatter-farmers, old voyageurs from the New Hope hamlet and, one hopes, the half-breed children from the neighboring villages, including Nancy Eastman, Mary Taliaferro and Lieutenant McClure's young daughter, also named Nancy. Somewhere about, attending their masters, must have been Captain Scott's Negro orderly and Surgeon Emerson's man Dred.

A bugle call, drifting on the hot air, brought the meeting to order. Under the canopy of leaves that stood seventy yards from Taliaferro's office, Dodge rose to wade into the tried-and-true treaty psychology: What the whites wanted was only a small part of the Chippewa domain and this small part had little worth to the natives. "This country, as I am informed, is not valuable to you for its game, and not suited to the culture of corn, and other agricultural purposes," Dodge intoned. As the veteran Indian fighter moved toward his peroration, the speech that was the standard government pitch was translated by the Negro half-breed Stephen Bonga, who came to the rescue of the inept official interpreter. Yet though Dodge had no inspired thoughts, he had presence. The Wind, son of Chief Wet Mouth, assured him that he had seen "a great many Americans, but never one whose appearance struck me as yours does."

Opinions of all kinds were aired. Chief Buffalo pretended that Dodge's proposal took him by surprise and said he'd have to think matters over. The Lone Man demonstrated that American Fur emissaries had not been idle when he made a speech in praise of the traders. On Friday the Indians parleyed on their own, and cloudy weather kept them in their lodges until 3 P.M. Saturday, when they met to do a little plain and fancy bartering among themselves. Taliaferro and the missionaries saw to it that Sunday was observed as the Lord's Day. Then on Monday the Lone Man and the Wind got practical. The grub furnished by the fort commissary was far from satisfactory. Beans. A little pork. "My Father," the Lone Man assailed Dodge, "what has happened to you? Have you cut off your breasts, that you cannot suckle your children?" He said plainly, in the transcript that comes down to us, that more generous fare would make the Chippewas "more pliant and ready to yield." What he meant was that whiskey was the missing lubricant. The Wind pointed to the livestock belonging to the squatters as well as to the fort and said, "You have everything around you, and can give us some of the cattle that are around us on the prairie. At the treaty of Prairie du Chien the case was as difficult as this. The great Chief then fed us well with cattle." Dodge succumbed to the demand for meat, but offered no alcohol. Before the end of the proceedings 6,123 pounds of beef had been consumed by the Indians. Peter Garrioch, a Red River settler who was among the onlookers, wrote that 1,536 pounds of pork were also doled out.

On Tuesday, Taliaferro remembered, "we heard loud shouts and yells in the direction of the Chippewa camp, near Baker's trading post at 'Cold Spring.' Word soon reached us that Warren, a trader, had marshaled a large body of Pillagers, and were coming down like so many black devils to force the Commissioner to give to said Warren $20,000." Taliaferro was standing at Dodge's right when the latecomers, with Lyman Warren in the lead, momentarily broke up the conclave. While his Pillager Chippewas howled through the arbor, the old trader sat down, "fanning himself with his hat," and demanded that his claim be written into the treaty. Taliaferro, aware of the illegal deal to take over Chippewa pinelands, apparently construed Warren's move as an effort to get the timber area excepted from the treaty or, failing that, to extort a sum sufficient to console himself and his partners for the loss of logging prospects. The agent suddenly drew his pistol and leveled it at the perspiring trader. Describing this scene in his autobiography, Taliaferro says that Hole-in-the-Day urged him to shoot Warren, but that Dodge restrained him, at some cost to his Virginia sense of honor.

The incident was not the only demonstration, according to Taliaferro, of the traders' determination to profiteer. As the proceedings drew to a close, Sibley's partner, Hercules Dousman, prevailed upon Dodge to honor a bill for $5,000 which the American Fur men said had been advanced for the construction of a sawmill. The fact that the mill was for the benefit of the Sioux rather than the Chippewas was ignored; Taliaferro labeled it "a plain fraud traded on the helpless Indians." Although Hole-in-the-Day and others protested, there were strong voices in favor of the demands of Dousman and Warren. These Indians had been well coached. "Nobody," one of them said revealingly, "no trader has instructed me what to say to you." He added: "I have been supported by the trader, and without his aid, could not get through the winter with naked skin. . . . Do us a kindness by paying our old debts." The treaty terms did so to the extent of $70,000. While Van Antwerp wrote down the details of the final agreement, the Chippewas turned out on the prairie behind the fort and danced—pausing periodically as one brave or another boasted of his exploits in battle with the Sioux. An eyewitness noted that Martin Scott, ready for trouble, barred the doors of his bastion, but that the Sioux contained themselves, "looking on with apparent indifference." Then the treaty was signed by the chiefs, and witnessed by Taliaferro, Henry Sibley, Lyman Warren, and Joseph Nicollet.

Now Taliaferro, having had little influence on the deal with the Chippewas, faced the Sioux challenge; he was determined to hold the American Fur demands to a minimum. Sibley and his partners were desperate. Crooks estimated the company's sales for the season just ended at no more than one-tenth of normal. Dousman told Sibley that their profits out of the Western Outfit amounted to only $1,588.77 on an investment of $72,000. King Rolette wrote Crooks that only by getting a generous treaty settlement for the Sioux could the partners end up in the black. He construed Taliaferro's plan to take a Sioux delegation to Washington as a move to deny American Fur its claims; but he was confident in early July, he assured Crooks, that he and the other traders could persuade the Sioux to hold out for a meeting at St. Peter's, as had the Chippewas. Lyman Warren backed him up; in a letter to Sibley he suggested they convince the Sioux that a fair treaty was possible only if the tribe insisted upon being present in large numbers—that strategy might "force government to hold [the Sioux negotiations] at St. Peters." But Taliaferro's influence on the tribe prevailed. He persuaded the most powerful chiefs "to counteract the designs of these officiously interested men who eat of their dainties, wipe their mouths and say, 'I have committed no sin.'" There were threats, by traders he does not name, to prevent any Sioux from leaving for Washington unless there was "a guarantee . . . for the payment of their indebtedness. . . ." However, Taliaferro would make no promises. He said "the path was open" for just claims, but that American Fur would get no help from him in its effort to pad its bills.

On August 18 he turned agency responsibilities over to Martin Scott. To insure an unharassed getaway, Taliaferro chartered the services of a steamboat whose captain agreed to keep his engine running for an immediate departure. "Captain Lafferty was prompt," the autobiography says, "the traders and others astonished at the *coup de état*." With the help of interpreter Scott Campbell, almost a score of Sioux statesmen were marched aboard, "and with steam up, off glided the steamer down stream."

The boat stopped en route to add Big Thunder, Wahkouta, Wabasha and Jack Frazer to the delegation, making a total of twenty-six to represent the St. Peter's tribe in the capital. On September 15, Taliaferro and his charges arrived in Washington and became front page news in *Niles' National Register*; in the reporter's observation, the St. Peter's Sioux were "greatly attached" to their agent.

They found that they were not the only Indians in town. Joseph Street led a group of Sacs and Foxes to join the Fort Snelling party. Joshua Pilcher, the veteran Missouri trader-turned-agent, brought in representatives from that river's tribes, and a Winnebago embassy was shepherded by agent Thomas Boyd. Washington reporters were moved to adjectives. "Their forms are of the most noble mould," one wrote, "and the grace and majesty of their movements, despite the gaudy and grotesque trappings which encumber them, are subjects of general remark. Several are more than six feet high, straight as an arrow, with thews and sinews that seem to set fatigue at defence, but with hands and feet of the most regal proportion." Cosmetics, then and for a long time to come, fascinated eastern writers. "The 'ground color,' to speak in painters' phrase," said one reporter, "is a bright vermilion: on this they daub spots of white and green. Some dandies, however, draw a circle of white or black around one eye, which gives a ferocious expression to that orb."

They gathered gawkers wherever they were taken, and they stole the show from the actors when they attended a performance at the National Theatre. The play was *The Mountain Sylph*, and forgettable. The star was not—not in Indian memories. She was billed, in the fashion of the day, as plain Miss Nelson, for familiarity on the part of stage-door Johnnies might be encouraged were a lady's first name to be made too public. But plain Miss Nelson brought the Indian delegates to their feet. They began tossing war bonnets to her as she stood transfixed onstage. They gave her buffalo and white wolfskin robes. And she, sylphlike, returned the favors with ostrich plumes from her headdress. A few days later, the Fort Snelling Sioux drew a crowd estimated at five thousand when they staged an exhibition of tribal dances in the public square at Fourteenth Street near Franklin Row.

But no one had forgotten the seriousness of the mission, least of all Henry Sibley. He had no intention of letting Taliaferro block reimbursement of the company for what he considered to be the Indians' just debts. And he was at least as determined to do what he could to head off the agent's plan to pay the tribesman for their land in goods and provisions instead of cash. Ramsay Crooks had been in Washington to lobby unsuccessfully against this scheme, but Sibley was not convinced that everything possible had been tried. He had written Crooks that he would follow Taliaferro to the capital, and he was now on hand, working hard at presenting the company's case. As businessmen who dealt with Indians to make a profit, he and his partners had little to gain from tribesmen who were provided annually with food and merchandise at regulated evaluations. American Fur wanted the total amount of the sale price of Sioux land to be paid in money.

Taliaferro saw to it that Sibley and company failed in this direction. He had introduced his chiefs and their companions to Secretary of War Poinsett, and to President Van Buren. Then, as joint treaty commissioners, he and Poinsett had begun the series of meetings that were held in Dr. James Laurie's Presbyterian church on Fourteenth Street. A stage had been built around the pulpit, and on it, in the presence of several hundred curious Washingtonians, the Sioux were seated to the right of the Sacs and Foxes. The opening sessions were wasted largely in what someone called "a war of recrimination and sarcasm." Neither the Sioux nor the Sac-Foxes were any more interested than usual in peace talks between the two tribes. Cloud Man, with accustomed ritual, put the blame on the opposition. "My ears are always open to good council," he said, "but I think my Great Father should take a stick and bore the ears of these people. They appear to shut their ears when they come here into the council." Keokuk answered in kind for the Sac-Foxes. Black Hawk was there, but his days of influence were over—even though his autobiography, published four years earlier, lent his name a sheen of greatness among some whites. Joe Snelling had numbered himself among these when he reviewed the book. "We have seen Black Hawk in that country," Snelling wrote, "and have always heard him mentioned as a dangerous and formidable warrior." He dismissed as a canard the doubts of those who accused the old war chief of distortion. "No one but a Sac Indian could have written or dictated such a composition," he said, and added that nobody "ever knew of an Indian warrior to boast of feats he never achieved." From Boston Common the early days at Fort Snelling had taken on a rosy hue.

Even Black Hawk's more active participation would not have done much for the hopeless peace talks, so the subject was dropped, and the order of business shifted at last to the sale of land. The Chippewas had sold about a third of what is present-day Wisconsin and almost one hundred square miles of Minnesota. The Sioux now ceded their rights to an area east of the Mississippi that was less than half as large. In Dr. Laurie's church, in the presence of Sibley, Alexis Bailly, Faribault's sons Alexander and Oliver, Joe LaFramboise, and several other traders, Poinsett and Taliaferro offered the Sioux annuities, schools and the aid of technicians to the value of almost a million dollars; traders' claims of $90,000 were included. Yet American Fur was dissatisfied. The *bois brûlé* Alexander Faribault, believing that blood ties might speak louder than words, attempted a walk-out. In the doorway of the church, however, he and his fellow traders discovered that the Indians had not followed them. A quick speech to the chiefs by Taliaferro "had set them to thinking," the agent wrote later; the treaty "was promptly authenticated in the presence of four hundred spectators. . . ." Sibley was downcast and went back to his hotel to write to Crooks, asserting that the "whole treaty is but one series of iniquity and wrong. . . . This is the boasted parental regard for the poor Indian." So spoke every trader of the era. Indians submitting to governmental paternalism which protected their finances were not the best customers.

There was one other frustration—one in which Sibley had marginal interest that would develop. His partner in the Fort Snelling sutlership, Sam Stambaugh, had joined with Jean Baptiste Faribault's son-in-law, Alexis Bailly, to pry some side money out of the Indian department. They produced the un-ratified Leavenworth treaty of 1820 and asked that the grant of Pike's island to Mrs. Faribault, stipulated by the old document, be recognized and confirmed. There is no solid evidence, but there are indications that the American Fur Company had already dealt in some collusion with the Faribaults to gain possession of the island. In any event, Stambaugh and Bailly sought to persuade Poinsett to make it clear that the land surrendered by the Sioux did not include the 1820 claim. As became increasingly apparent, it was important to the Faribaults, as well as Sibley and Crooks, that private ownership of the island be established so that it could be sold at a profit instead of being available to the first preemptor to come along in the wake of the Sioux treaty. Poinsett begged the issue. He ruled the matter out as a subject to be dealt with in the treaty provisions. Yet he appears to have been willing to set aside the Faribault claim to be considered by itself, as if the Sioux had not just sold *all* their lands (including islands) east of the Mississippi's right bank. Thus he inhibited American Fur's scheme for immediate gain, while leaving the door open for more direct action four months later.

Meanwhile Sibley got some news that made the future seem brighter for the American Fur partners. Four days after the Sioux put their marks on the treaty, Taliaferro announced that he hoped to resign as agent and to get another government job in a climate less detrimental to his health. "Our friend," Sibley wrote iron-ically to Crooks, "is on the lookout for some other and more lucrative office, to which he, no doubt, thinks his *late* services eminently entitle him, and I trust he will receive some appoint-ment, which will deprive us of his valuable assistance in our part of the country henceforth and forever." Sibley's optimism was justified in company terms, but it was slightly ahead of schedule. Taliaferro did not quit the St. Peter's that fall. He took his dele-gation to Wheeling, and thence followed the Ohio-Mississippi watercourse to the fort. He was welcomed by another veteran of Josiah Snelling's stewardship, Major Joseph Plympton, for whom Martin Scott had assumed temporary command.

Plympton's arrival had brought to a head the uneasiness among the families squatting on the Fort Snelling reservation. They had witnessed the Chippewa proceedings and had seen in them the portents of the Sioux treaty in Washington. In consequence, the householders had signed an appeal to President Van Buren written by Duncan Graham. The letter pointed out that the families had settled with army permission and "were only exercising the privileges extended to them by the benign and salutary laws which have peopled the western country with a hardy, industrious and enterprising class of citizens." If the Washington treaty should cause them to have to move, they asked "a reasonable and just allowance in the treaty for our improvements." Somehow, however, their request went astray. And instead of Presidential interest, they received the attention of Major Plympton who believed, he wrote his Washington superiors, "that many persons will be applying at the War dept. for favors which will continue their encroachments upon what I have always thot. to be a military reservation. . . ."

Plympton saw the prevailing laxity toward the squatters as "an evil . . . which has at this time a strong commencement," and he took the first steps toward clearing the reservation of the undesirables. He ordered a lieutenant to survey and map the area and to take a census. He found, as a result, a total headcount of one hundred and fifty-seven white inhabitants, including children. Nobody bothered to count the *bois brûlés,* some of whom, like Jack Frazer, had become as civilized as most of the other residents. Plympton made his report to the War Department and awaited instructions. The status quo was maintained through the winter. No settler was evicted. Taliaferro was still entrenched at the agency, and Sibley was back in his hunter's castle across from Pike's island. In November, Nicollet, the friend the two men shared, went to Washington "with all my baggage, instruments, pebbles, plants, birds, reptiles, quadrupeds, medicine bags, moccasins, calumets [he said in a letter] and in company with Mr. P. Chouteau. . . ." Life was back to normal at the fort. But the old days were over.

CHAPTER THIRTEEN

YEAR OF THE LONG WAIT

TALIAFERRO says that he returned from the Washington treaty not a day too soon, "for the ice made a few days thereafter." A vintage winter, 1837–38—the Mississippi a frozen highway to Prairie du Chien and beyond. The ice, however, was pavement to be used only on the most urgent errands. The veterans of the Fifth, back at the fort that they had erected on the river bluff, once again were locked in prairie cold. Much would be made of what little news might find its way to them from the outside world. They fired up the stoves they had not possessed in their earlier tour of duty and faced their wintry isolation. The Fifth had no Gustavus Loomis to exhort them in a season of evangelism, but the men warmed to the old outlet of dramatics, exchanging their uniforms for vainglorious costumes and, as a member of the garrison put it, "making a generous sacrifice of their cherished whiskers and mustaches." When not entertained by these thespians, officers and their wives alike resorted to what Taliaferro once called "a System of tatling which has been reduced to a Science." They must have had, however, some serious subjects as well.

Surrounded by voyageurs and traders who were natives of British America, fresh from service at Ford Howard on the border, they were unlikely to ignore the Canadian rebellion led by Louis Joseph Papineau and William Lyon Mackenzie in the fall. They would wait impatiently before they heard that Papineau's patriots had been routed in Montreal and Mackenzie's forces defeated at the bridge in Toronto. But they also had more practical matters to mull over. Frontier officers were by nature speculators

201

and frequent dabblers in investments. This year they had the effects of the Panic of 1837 to second-guess. Most of all, however, the chief subject of discussion was the summer's two treaties which, when ratified by Congress, would make millions of acres available to the first to claim them. Already Surgeon John Emerson had land in Illinois, and in October he had gone south (hiring out Dred Scott to a fellow officer) to check on his investments. For his part Major Plympton, in the winter-wedged fort, looked covetously at the land directly across the Mississippi. And he was far from alone. In fact, one newcomer to the Snelling domain had jumped the gun.

Young Franklin Steele, who before he was through was to own the fort itself, was too impatient to submit temperately to the long wait for ratification of the treaties. He had made his first bid for a fortune in real estate at the end of the summer. Legend —one that he apparently fostered—says that Steele was chosen by some young men of Lancaster, Pennsylvania, to take a token of their esteem to Andrew Jackson in the White House. He so impressed the President, the story goes, that Old Hickory urged him to investigate the Upper Mississippi, pointing out the potential value of its waterfalls. No matter; acting on someone's information Steele had arrived to spend the rest of his career in and around Fort Snelling. Alert to the worth of the timberlands, he had hired a crew of workmen to pole a scow from the fort to the falls of the St. Croix, where he provided shelter from this cold winter by erecting two log cabins in which to wait for ratification. His act was no more legal than the position of the squatter-farmers, yet as long as the Indians did not demand his ouster he could hold his beachhead and thereby prevent anyone else from claiming the same site.

While the newly felled timber of Steele's roofs creaked under the burden of January snow, Sam Stambaugh renewed his Pike's island campaign in Washington. Now he came out in the open. He did not want to have simply the bequest of the island to Mrs. Faribault recognized; that point, according to him, had been established when the Secretary of War had failed to reject the claim he had made during the treaty proceedings. On January

17, Stambaugh proposed that the government purchase the Faribault rights to the island "for the purpose of annexing it to the military reservation of Fort Snelling." There is sufficient evidence of typical frontier chicanery here to merit attention. Stambaugh represented a client who wanted to sell to the government land which already had been ceded to the United States. Although the Faribault claim of 1820 had not been recognized by Congress— nor had the family even established squatter's rights by continuing to live on the island—Stambaugh was attempting to extort payment in return for the abandonment of the claim whose perpetrator, Leavenworth, was now dead. Machinations of this sort were not new to Stambaugh, for a half-dozen years earlier he had helped to persuade the Menominees to cede the mill rights on a Wisconsin River island to a white speculator. And he had been involved in the efforts of Fort Howard squatters to exact compensation for grogshops they had built on the Green Bay reservation.

Now Stambaugh pointed out to the War Department that Pike's island marked the head of navigation on the Mississippi and was the most likely site for settlement because steamboats could so easily draw up beside it. Lying immediately below the fort, it offered ideal locations for the sale of whiskey to troops and Indians alike. Such hazards could only be removed by including the island in the military reservation. The goodhearted Faribaults, he said, were willing to clear the way for such government action for as little as $12,000, a mere tenth of the value of the island were it to be developed commercially. Working quietly in Washington, he was optimistic that his deal could be made without protest from government representatives at St. Peter's.

And as it turned out, Taliaferro did not become involved immediately. He had gone east during the winter and was in Pennsylvania with his wife, pursuing his hope of transfer to another branch of government service. He had applied for an assignment as an army paymaster· "If not this then a Majority in the Commissary Staff. If not either of them then to stand as *I am* for another season in hopes of better prospects." Perhaps he felt that

203

with the Indians on government dole, as a result of the treaties, his chief importance as their mentor had come to an end. Yet concern for his own health was also a motivation. Almost two decades in the Old Northwest had made him think he would "much like a Station at St. Louis." He was tired of the long quarrel with the American Fur Company—and unaware of its behind-the-scenes interest in the island controversy.

A year was to pass in which there was no response to Taliaferro's request for relief and no direct action on the Faribault claim. In the meantime the controversy over the squatters continued. During the winter, Plympton had worked out a plan for the military reservation, and in March, just before the rivers opened up at the foot of the bluff, he sent a runner to Fort Crawford with a map to be forwarded to the War Department. He warned the farmers that their eviction was inevitable and as a result, when the frost oozed from the ground several of them were ready to break soil in the treaty lands across the river. Still the first steamboat to arrive that spring did not bring the hoped-for news of ratification.

Spring did bring the end of Dred Scott's Fort Snelling residence. With Harriet ripe with child, Dred was put aboard the *Gipsey* by Emerson and sent downriver to Jefferson Barracks. En route, north of the free-soil latitude of thirty-six degrees, thirty minutes, Taliaferro's former servant girl gave birth to a daughter who was called Eliza, the given name of Dr. Emerson's recent bride. This child who was thus born in free territory—and technically, at least, not a slave—became nevertheless a party to the trials that at last brought Dred Scott's case before the United States Supreme Court. Although he remained Emerson property after he left Snelling, Dred worked for a number of masters in the next ten years and got as far as the Mexican border with Zachary Taylor while the servant of Mrs. Emerson's brother-in-law. Soon after, he was turned down by the Emerson family when he asked for his freedom, and in April, 1846, he petitioned for permission to bring suit on grounds of residence in Illinois and at Fort Snelling. Although a Snelling soldier and the widow of a Fifth Regiment officer testified—and although

Dred's "detention at Fort Snelling" was termed a violation of the Missouri Compromise—the failure of the Negro's champions to win him freedom is too well known to be detailed here. Suffice it is to say that Dred Scott was not at the fort during the remainder of Surgeon Emerson's tenure, nor was he likely to have been aware of the events which followed his departure.

Spring and early summer brought many boats to the St. Peter's entry, but none carried the news for which Taliaferro and Plympton waited. On May 25 the *Burlington* churned in to bring the return of Joseph Nicollet at the head, this time, of an army exploring party which included a young lieutenant, John Charles Frémont. The future "Pathfinder" became Sibley's guest, but appears to have won no lasting favor with Ramsay Crooks. When Frémont was being ballyhooed for President in 1856, Crooks took exception to the claim that the former had been first through the famous South Pass of the Continental Divide. Crooks had been there himself in 1812, decades ahead of Frémont. The army explorer, Crooks wrote angrily in 1856, was no more fit to head the nation than the mountain men who were the real pathfinders of the West. But now, in the spring of 1838, Frémont was a Fort Snelling transient and, along with Nicollet, a grateful member of Sibley dinner parties.

At last the War Department had been persuaded to examine the western terrain itself, instead of little more than the course of rivers. Behind this second Nicollet expedition can be seen the letters written by Taliaferro and the influence in the capital of Pierre Chouteau, Jr. Nicollet this time had been fully commissioned by Colonel J. J. Abert, chief of topographical engineers, and his assignment was to map and explore the land between the Mississippi and the Missouri. With Frémont designated as his assistant, Nicollet had been briefed by that great architect of western expansion, Senator Thomas Hart Benton himself. A pattern was being established. Not only did young Charles Frémont soon marry Jessie Benton, who was to use her father's good offices and her own large talents to foster her husband's career, but here, based at Fort Snelling, Frémont began the first of three seasons that provided a foundation for his topographical reconnaissance in the next decade. Here the army's first full-scale trans-Mississippi expedition tuned up. The party was provisioned, the fort's shops checked equipment, horses and wagons were saddled and loaded up, and early in June, Nicollet's entourage could be seen through the Snelling telescope as it was silhouetted on the far rim of the prairie.

Within a few days of its departure, the *Burlington* was back again at the landing below the fort. Again no news of ratification. But Captain Throckmorton's passengers this time included General Henry Atkinson, on a tour of inspection, as well as the peregrinating Captain Frederick Marryat, whose fame as an English novelist had exploded into rancor among his American readers when he had publicly espoused the loyalist side in the Canadian rebellion. Americans looked on Papineau and his *Patriotes* as promulgators of a second Revolutionary War and sympathized with the effort to wrest all of British America from the United Kingdom. Taliaferro did no more than note Marryat's arrival in his journal. His Indians could not understand why they had not yet received the payments and annuities promised by treaties they had signed almost a year ago; the agent predicted trouble if the government did not act soon. The Sioux had been drifting in for weeks, the western bands booting their horses, dragging travois; women, children, dogs trailing as they came across the prairie. Their mood may have made an old hand like Taliaferro ill at ease. Not Frederick Marryat. He found them a cinch to deal with, he says, "for they knew I was an *English* warrior, as they called me, and they are very partial to the English."

Perhaps. The old partiality might have been fanned into a minor explosion by a traveler as indiscreet as Marryat; the Indians were restive. He had not been long at the fort when Taliaferro wrote Governor Dodge, "We are on thorns as to the fate of the Sioux & Chippewa treaties, as upon these hang the future peace & tranquility of this fair land." Yet in Marryat's memory the mood of the natives was just fine. In his book he described the Sioux he met during his stay as models of Indian behavior. He visited Samuel Pond's friends at Eatonville and found them very neat and clean, he wrote, "indeed, particularly so, compared with other tribes of Indians." He noted their penchant for "a great deal of mirth and humour" in playing lacrosse outside the fort's gates. Moreover he found them honest, "except on the point of stealing horses . . . no more to be considered as stealing than is our taking merchant-vessels on the high seas."

Jack Frazer had been a passenger on the *Burlington,* and Marryat discovered him to be a remarkable fellow, "a fine intellectual-looking man." Marryat heard the story of the half-breed's life, and Jack toyed with the English traveler, displaying his tomahawk with its twenty-eight notches while asserting that he had given up wanting to kill anyone except his father. Taken aback, Marryat asked why and was told Jack's favorite story of the paternal promise of a white man's education, on which James Frazer had reneged. Marryat "could not help admiring the thirst for knowledge and the pride shown by this poor fellow, although mixed up with [the Indians'] inveterate passion for revenge." He seems to have been more impressed with another *bois brûlé,* old Renville. Joe was there with his winter's furs for Sibley, and he had brought along his elite guard as well as the Lac Qui Parle Sioux who were interested in their share of the treaty proceeds.

Renville's Indians, says Marryat in *A Diary in America,* set up their war tent near Sibley's warehouse. There they put on the usual choreography, while Taliaferro fumed over the delay in treaty news. They also donned their finest costumes which this year, somebody told Marryat, outdid any finery heretofore seen at St. Peter's. If this was true, it may be that Renville's braves had made a better than average bargain with the Crows on the Missouri plains. For the Crow women were the most expert tanners and embroiderers and did a big business in shirts, leggings and robes. At any rate, Marryat was determined to acquire one of the costumes because he had seen George Catlin's New York exhibition, "and I knew he had not one in his possession." Marryat went to Renville and asked him to pry loose "a sort of kilt of fine skins, ornamented with beautiful porcupine quill-work and eagle's feathers; garters of animals' tails . . . head-dress of eagle's feathers and ermine's tails, etc." In the guest room in Sibley's limestone house Marryat sat by while Renville called his warriors to order and acted as interpreter. The old English empathy worked again, according to Marryat. In spite of the fact that the Indians were hungry, they had turned down a bid of two barrels of flour from one of the fort's officers for the costume Marryat coveted; still, they were willing to let him have it because he was English. There may be some truth in this tale, but Marryat doubtless exaggerated. It was late in the game for the Sioux, under Renville's influence or not, to have any faith in a return to British patronage. Impatience at the tardiness of ratification may have given them some delight in refusing to bargain with one of Plympton's underlings in favor of doing business with the flamboyant traveler.

June wore on as Marryat continued to enjoy himself so much that he noted he could have stayed a year at St. Peter's, were not life "so short and the Mississippi so long." Before the end of the month the *Burlington* made another upriver trip and this time brought a celebrated lady whose lifetime spanned that of the nation. She was the fort's most elegant guest to date, Mrs. Alexander Hamilton; and she had been a widow, in a sense a heroine, since that dark day not long after Zeb Pike had set out to dicker for the site upon which the citadel now stood. In this frustrating summer the garrison made much of her. Given only a day in which to do the honors, Plympton waited at the landing with a carriage at 9 A.M., then escorted his guest up the bluff road, across the flowering prairie past Baker's post and the neighboring squatters; on to the falls whose waterpower he covertly hoped to make his own. Here the garrison wives served lunch alfresco. After a leisurely return to the fort in the afternoon, Mrs. Hamilton was led to a chair placed on a carpet at the edge of the parade ground. The frontier troops stood West-Point-straight in the sun, then passed in review. A reception followed in Plympton's quarters—at which Taliaferro and Sibley must have set aside animosity for the courtly opportunity so seldom offered at St. Peter's. Dusk had fallen when the *Burlington,* with its somewhat glamorous passenger, could be seen from the lookout as it disappeared down the Mississippi.

Two weeks passed before another steamboat, the *Palmyra,* ended that summer's tension. On board the 101-ton packet was a month-old copy of the Washington *Globe,* in which there appeared the news that Congressional approbation of the 1837 treaties at last was a fact. The garrison now had far greater reason for celebration than the visit of Mrs. Hamilton had provided. Taliaferro had even more so. "All sunny like a new day," his journal for July 15 reads, "countenances brightening with smiles of pleasure and real delight." Those smiles did not stay in place on every countenance. All the events of the day after the arrival of the *Palmyra* are not clear in the record, but one thing is sure —Joseph Plympton failed to secure his interest in the Falls of St. Anthony. He may have been declaring his hope of personally acquiring the west side of the cataract when, in March, he excluded the area from his delineation of reservation limits. He may also, as many St. Peter's civilians believed, schemed to be the first to claim the east side at the moment of treaty ratification.

A favorite story of later years asserted that Plympton had taken Martin Scott into his confidence and that Scott, early in the year, had gone up the left bank of the Mississippi to the falls and planted potatoes in a clearing, a common enough way of establishing proprietorship of otherwise unclaimed land. This story makes much of the fact that Franklin Steele was a passenger on the boat that brought the ratification news. Waiting for no one, Steele disembarked and rushed to St. Anthony Falls with enough lumber to throw together a shanty. Next morning he was "in residence" when Scott—or Plympton, depending upon the story—arrived. By virtue of having a shelter in which to live, Steele's claim got priority, and it is a matter of record that, no matter what shenanigans went on, Steele assumed control of the waterpower accessible on land ceded by the Sioux.

Inhibited by his status as an army officer, Plympton was stymied on the west side, where the saw- and gristmills erected by Josiah Snelling was still government property. Plympton's map, submitted to Washington in March, may not have included this site in the fort holdings, but the mill buildings, having been built at War Department expense, could be leased by U.S. authorities even though they stood on what remained technically Sioux land. Plympton, however, could make no such deal in his own behalf while he was still in uniform, and he bided his time, apparently counting on the eventual extinction of all Sioux land rights. In the meantime, Henry Sibley and Kenneth Mackenzie, the latter now a St. Louis merchant, became interested. But Secretary Poinsett avoided the possibility of encouraging competition at the falls and turned down their application to lease Snelling's mills. Taliaferro wrote that he headed off a similar scheme on the part of Stambaugh. Thus Franklin Steele, by dint of immediate action after the ratification notice, lined up for himself the earliest opportunity to profit from the sale of Sioux-Chippewa lands east of the fort.

Ten days after Steele's coup, Plympton took another step toward the removal of the unwelcome settlers from the west side of the Mississippi. His reservation boundary line ran through Lake Calhoun on the west, meandered northeasterly to a point above St. Anthony Falls, followed the river south, then four miles or so north of the fort turned due east and cut off a large elbow of the Mississippi's left bank as buffer territory—insurance that no liquor dealer legally could set up shop within an hour's walk of the garrison. Now, on July 26, he issued Order No. 65, prohibiting anyone not connected with the military from erecting buildings or fences of any kind, "or cutting timber for any but for public use, within said line, which has been surveyed and forwarded to the War Department. . . ." His determination to rid the reservation of squatters was based as much as anything on excluding all but soldiers from making use of the fast-disappearing woodlots which provided fuel for the fort. Prohibition of the sale of alcohol on the reservation was army policy, but the conservation of firewood was a necessity.

The Selkirk settlers, whose presence so long had been tolerated, might have taken this edict as a signal to move en masse had the government answered their appeal for restitution. Failing immediate response, they stayed put and refused to give up hope. The transition that began with ratification augured well for them. Had not millions of dollars been appropriated to make land available to other pioneers? Was it unreasonable to assume that a government so encouraging of settlement in general would fail, in the end, to acknowledge the years of labor they had put into their farms? They did not think so. Their very presence so far in advance of the agricultural tide was proof that a stable, civilized life among the Sioux was possible. That authorities thought in similar vein seemed to be indicated in certain political shifts that followed the treaties of 1837. In preparation for statehood, Wisconsin pulled in its western territorial boundary from the Missouri to the Mississippi. The organization of Iowa Territory, which ensued, encompassed the region Wisconsin no longer claimed. Civil law came close to Fort Snelling in the person of Joseph R. Brown, who was named justice of the peace in Wisconsin's sprawling Crawford County.

And this appointment in itself reflected the complexion of the transition. It fortified a squatter in the belief that he, too, had a rightful place in this era of metamorphosis. For Joe Brown, remember, was the fourteen-year-old fife-and-drummer who had come west with the Fifth Infantry in 1819. Mustered out as a sergeant, employed briefly in the fort's sutler's shop, Joe had joined the fur trade and had bartered with the Sioux as far west as the Sheyenne. He had established a lasting relationship with Sibley, but had cut away from a full-scale company connection to pursue his own vast dreams. In 1837, Franklin Steele had found him already logging pines on the St. Croix. Once George Featherstonhaugh had slandered him for his dalliances with female Indians, but now he was the squire of Grey Cloud Island in the Mississippi and a frontier J. P. The squatters would be making use of him in the months to come.

Now, however, they stood by as Taliaferro wound up the ratification ceremonies. After the news of Congressional action the agent went downriver to St. Louis to arrange contracts for the purchase of farm horses, oxen, cows, and agricultural implements for the benefit of the tribes. He hired blacksmiths and seven men to act as supervisors of farms to be opened at that number of Sioux villages. In September—when St. Louis papers were dressed in mourning because of Will Clark's death—commissioners appointed by the War Department joined Taliaferro in dispensing the money payments prescribed by the treaty. The long wait was over. But Plympton's problem with the squatters was not, for government wheels that year ground as slowly as ever before or since. October brought the news that Black Hawk had died, three weeks after Clark. And the end of autumn also brought the last visitors to the St. Peter's. Nicollet returned from his excursion west. And Ramsay Crooks, on a tour of inspection of American Fur's domain, spent a few surprisingly unhistoric days with Sibley. From downriver there also had come Cordelia Eggleston. In November she was married to Samuel Pond, and Sibley, Dr. and Mrs. Emerson and other guests crossed frozen Lake Calhoun in a sleigh to attend the ceremony. Winter had returned, and Taliaferro had gone to Virginia on family business. He would be back—but not for long.

CHAPTER FOURTEEN

———•••———

THE DAY THE ROOFS CAME OFF

RETURNING from the East in the spring of 1839, Taliaferro was at the now-booming town of Prairie du Chien when he was told that Congress had appropriated funds for the island which lay beneath the southerly guns of the fort. The report that the Faribault claim had been honored made it his special duty, he wrote Poinsett in April, to review the facts of a situation that had begun soon after his arrival at St. Peter's. He pointed out his personal involvement in the case, reminding the War Department that he had been a witness to the Leavenworth agreement which involved the island as well as the ground on which the American Fur Company's New Hope establishment was situated. Poinsett should be aware, he said, that he had told Leavenworth, because the island could be covered easily by artillery and small arms fire from the bluff, that it was the logical spot on which to take out government livestock in case of attack. And he stressed to Poinsett that the Secretary's predecessor, Calhoun, had personally vetoed Leavenworth's scheme, that the so-called treaty had been ignored by Congress, and that Calhoun had directed the agent to notify Faribault and others—more than fifteen years before —that any claims they thought they had were invalid. The matter, said Taliaferro, "was supposed to be at rest, until S.C. Stambaugh volunteered to become the agent of this fictitious claim."

But it was not at rest. Unbeknown to Taliaferro, Ramsay Crooks had been aiding and abetting Stambaugh throughout the winter. On March 29, Crooks had written Sibley his belief that a contract to purchase the Faribault claim for $12,000, which had been signed by the Commissioner of Indian Affairs, had closed the deal. In May, in another letter to Sibley, Crooks made clear a new facet to the American Fur Company's interest; the amount to be paid to Faribault, he said, would make it possible for the company to persuade the government to pay handsomely for American Fur's New Hope establishment. "No doubt," Crooks said of the latter property, "it is admirably calculated for the Indian Agency." Convinced of Taliaferro's determination to end his tenure at St. Peter's, American Fur was looking to the future. Its partners were entrepreneurs of the period—interested in profit under any and all circumstances. If they could sell the Sioux Outfit's headquarters at New Hope (title to which they had acquired through a surreptitious deal with Leavenworth beneficiaries), they would be well rewarded on a minor investment. And Sibley's operation could be moved to the recently ceded treaty lands where preemption cost nothing.

Again, however, the fur partners were less wary of Taliaferro than they might have been. The agent, for his part, was tired but still alert. His journal continued with warnings to himself that "now the main object of Tom—Dick & Harry—" was to get rid of him "so that those who come after me can the more easily be bribed or threatened into silence. . . ." No more than ever would he be silent. His letter to Poinsett resulted in a directive to Major Plympton to conduct an investigation "on the subject of the ownership or occupancy of Pike's or Ferribault's island" because, wrote the Indian commissioner, it was apparent "that some doubts exist as to the individual in whom the title is vested." Plympton got together with Taliaferro and they summoned Bad Hail and other Sioux who had been present at the Leavenworth negotiations. Plympton was as vexed by the machinations in Washington as was the veteran agent. Both had been in on the founding of the fort, and Plympton had no doubts about the long occupancy of the island by the Snelling garrison. He reported to Washington that he and the Indians were in substantial agreement on what had occurred in 1820. He had been away on special duty when Leavenworth had made his deal, but he stressed his knowledge of the controversy: The island had been "used by the military, as belonging to this post, to my knowledge, from the 23rd of August, 1819, to the present date," he wrote; "and I never knew until within the last few months, that any individual pretended to claim this island. . . ." Plympton supported his report with a recapitulation of the facts by Taliaferro which asserted that Stambaugh was a perpetrator of a fraud against the government; if the Faribault claim was entertained, Taliaferro said, so must those of claimants to the land on which stood the American Fur buildings, and he underscored the point by urging "that *cupidity* . . . be defeated and the designing knaves unmasked."

Plympton and the agent were convinced that the case was locked up. Taliaferro, believing he had done all he could at St. Peter's, several days later sent in his resignation, effective at the end of the year. But American Fur tenacity knew few bounds. Hercules Dousman encouraged Stambaugh to continue pursuit of the matter in 1840. Jean Baptiste Faribault gave power of attorney to Ramsay Crooks. Poinsett's successor as Secretary of War in 1842 recommended that the claim be paid. As late as 1857 the subject was being debated in the Senate. There, at last, it died in committee. Pike's island remained government property until 1871 when it was patented to Franklin Steele, the fort's greatest real estate expert—who now, in 1839, had become sutler to the garrison.

Unlike the longtime squatters on the reservation, the man who had sat out the winter at the falls of the St. Croix knew how to have things his own way and make a good deal of money as well. Steele had invested a thousand dollars on the St. Croix (the story goes) and, after ratification, had sold his interest for thirteen times that amount. There were other preemptors, of course, and Plympton, Scott, Emerson and Stambaugh were numbered among them in one of Stambaugh's numerous letters to the Secretary of War. Having abandoned the sutlership, Stambaugh was deeply involved in the stir that had been caused by the treaties. In addition to his advocacy of the Faribault interests, he had been retained to plead the cause of the fort's extralegal farmers, and he tried to thwart Plympton's plan to include the area east of the Mississippi in the military reservation. For the squatters, who were now resigned to the inevitability of removal, wanted to be permitted to resettle as close to the fort as possible.

Some of them had legitimate reasons. They did not trust the Indians, and wanted to be in range of the fort's lookout. They also wanted easy access to a steamboat landing, and the Mississippi's bluffs were so generally precipitous that there were few places other than the St. Peter's entry where a paddle-wheeler could pull up. It was Stambaugh's contention that "no steamboat landing can be procured by the settlers within a distance of twelve miles of Fort Snelling. . . ." Too far away, obviously, to cause a hostile Indian to fear swift intervention by U.S. soldiers.

Still, the most militant antagonism to Plympton's proposed reservation boundaries came from whiskey sellers. Emerson considered their threat so serious that he appealed to the Surgeon General. "Since the middle of the winter," he wrote in April, "we have been completely inundated with ardent spirits, and consequently [have witnessed] the most beastly scenes of intoxication among the soldiers of this garrison and the Indians in its vicinity. . . . The whisky is brought here by citizens who are pouring in upon us and settling themselves on the opposite shore of the Mississippi River, in defiance of our worthy commanding officer, Major J. Plympton, whose authority they set at naught." Emerson urged that the reservation be at least twenty miles square, excluding settlers from the mouth of the St. Croix northward. Nothing smaller, he felt, was adequate to frustrate the temptation that the average soldier found in alcohol.

There had been no change in the caliber of army recruits. By and large they were illiterate, and many were European immigrants forced out of overpopulated regions and equipped with little or no civilian skill. Some were outlaws. Dissatisfied, emptyminded, some had signed on to kill Indians, and they found at Snelling no opportunity to appease the lust. Denied violence, they chose drunkenness as the next best thing. When liquor became available just across the Mississippi, they became expert at scaling the fort's stone walls. In May, 1839, some of these acrobats sneaked back to barracks with liquid assets sufficient to cause a minor mutiny. Plympton corralled the miscreants in the guard-house, but the punishment cowed few on the enlisted men's side of the parade ground. Ten days later a gang went over the wall and made its way to a whiskey shop on Grey Cloud Island; the next morning forty-seven were behind bars and wrestling with hangovers. Inspector General John Wool was at the fort, and he fired off a report that underscored everything that Plympton and Emerson had been trying to tell Washington. The whiskey sellers were "destructive to the discipline of the troops [and] hazardous of the peace and quiet of the country." The alcohol peddlers, said Wool, were a nefarious lot so intent upon plying their trade that he was moved to predict the possibility of armed revolt on their part. He seconded Emerson's motion that the reservation be increased to an area twenty miles square.

Wool made a point of the effect of liquor on the Indians, and so did others. Gideon Pond, back from Lac Qui Parle, carried his memory of the 1839 Indian degradation for years. In the newspaper founded by Samuel and himself he wrote a vivid description of native behavior:

"Twelve years ago they bade fair soon to die, all together, in one drunken jumble. They must be drunk—they could hardly live if they were not drunk. Many of them seemed as uneasy when sober as a fish does when on land. At some of the villages they were drunk months together. There was no end to it. They would have whisky. They would give guns, blankets, pork, lard, flour, corn, coffee, sugar, horses, furs, traps, anything for whisky. It was made to drink—it was good—it was *wakan*. They drank it—they bit off each other's noses—broke each other's ribs and heads—they knifed each other. They killed one another with guns, knives, hatchets, clubs, fire-brands—they fell into the fire and water, and were burned to death and drowned—they froze to death, and committed suicide so frequently that, for a time, the death of an Indian, in some of the ways mentioned, was but little thought of by themselves or others."

Taliaferro indicates in his journal his awareness of the menace, but there was little he could do to prevent dissolute natives from patronizing unscrupulous white men. Nor did he record as great a degree of debauchery as indicated by the missionary zeal of Gideon Pond. He was no less vigilant because he had tendered his resignation, and he was determined in his last summer at St. Peter's to protect the Chippewas and the Sioux from each other, as well as from the whites. There had been a minor clash between the tribes the previous year, and he knew his Indians well enough to expect one infraction to beget another. On June 8, with a thousand Sioux gathered at the fort to receive their annuities, he got word that Hole-in-the-Day was headed down the Mississippi with his Chippewas. Calling the Sioux to council, he told them that if they were to have visitors they were not to *"infrindge* the rights of hospitality"; then he rounded up Steve Bonga and sent him north to tell Hole-in-the-Day "to hold still where he is and not to come here." But the Chippewa chief had come too far to turn around willingly. He assured Bonga that he planned to stay no more than three days and that he would keep his young men from making trouble as long as the Sioux behaved themselves.

Two weeks later Taliaferro knew he had reason to worry. "I *have my hands full,"* he wrote, and added that *"trouble* on trouble" could be expected "with Indians at war." Hole-in-the-Day arrived on June 20 with five hundred followers, perhaps half of whom were armed. "They came down the Mississippi in bark canoes," said an eyewitness, "and as they shot around the bastion of the Fort, presented one of the most vivid and picturesque scenes that is possible to imagine of savage life." The writer was the garrison's new chaplain, the Reverend Ezekiel Gear, who had lately operated a mission among western New York Indians, and should have seen the Snelling Indians more objectively than most travelers. Gear knew that both Taliaferro and Plympton were apprehensive. The Chippewas had no business at St. Peter's. La Pointe was the place at which their annuities were to be paid. But the North Woods Indians were again protesting that the Lake Superior post was a thirteen-day march with no waterways to follow in the way the Mississippi led them so easily to Fort

Snelling. They told the commandant and the agent that they would rather give up their annuities than risk losing their small children on a journey so long and one which offered no chance to find food en route.

Hole-in-the-Day's party was joined in the next five days by the arrival of more and more canoes "announced by vollies from many guns." More than a hundred Chippewas arrived from the Crow Wing; one hundred and fifty from Leech Lake; and most of the St. Croix bands joined the encampment across the Mississippi from the fort. On the twenty-fourth, Taliaferro counted an aggregate of 1,756 natives representing both tribes. He and Plympton, Gear wrote, "most kindly entered into [the Chippewas'] views and feelings," relayed their complaints to Governor Dodge of Wisconsin and Governor Lucas of Iowa Territory, and urged the tribesmen to accept the necessity of the La Pointe trek. Next year, the Indians were told, the Great White Father would see to it that the annuities were distributed at a place more convenient. Promises and diplomacy worked. The Sioux were in a placating mood because they had no annuity troubles. They staged a great lacrosse game, eighty players to a side, for which men and women of the garrison saddled up and rode out to the playing grounds. Two days later both tribes put on exhibitions of their dances, and that evening they joined in foot races.

So much good feeling was manifest that there was no limit to the fraternizing, and Sibley found in the conclave the materials for a romance which he wrote for the *Spirit of the Times*. His hero was the Sioux's fastest runner, a brave named Track-Maker. "He was tall, beautifully formed, and as a natural consequence, he was much of a favorite among the copper-colored girls," Sibley wrote. "It so happened that in mingling with the Chippewas, he had won the heart of one of their maidens, to whom, if I was a novelist or dealer in fiction, I would give the cognomen of the 'Bounding Fawn,' or the 'Budding Rose.'" Had the Chippewa girl not been young and pretty, he added, unnecessarily, Track-Maker would not have been so frequently seen with her after dark. At any rate, the romance provided Sibley with a frame for his account of the ensuing events.

The prairie heat was classic that summer. Taliaferro recorded 100° on July 1, and 110° the following day. Emerson, mulling over his medical responsibilities, wrote a friend that it was the driest summer in the fort's history. It was sullen weather, and the air was filled with what Sibley called "no small excitement." Access to alcohol was prohibited until shortly before Hole-in-the-Day got ready to leave. There was nothing wholesale about the night's revelry, but portents darkened appreciably. Hole-in-the-Day broke camp and moved up to the falls, on his way home. As he did so, two braves slipped away to the grave of a Chippewa murdered by Sioux the year before. The record is not clear, but the Sioux adage that whiskey induces tears may have been operative; the two braves wept at the burial plot and were moved by the spirit of the dead to avenge their slain relative. They went to nearby Eatonville and lay in ambush until dawn. Any victim would suffice. The unlucky Sioux that day was the Badger who, accompanied by Cloud Man's young son, was out looking for a horse. He fell without knowing what hit him, and was swiftly scalped before the two Chippewas escaped. Cloud Man's boy dashed for the village and spread alarm; and before Taliaferro was apprised of events, runners had reached all the Sioux in the neighborhood. One war party was already on Hole-in-the-Day's trail, and another had left Little Crow's band to pursue the Chippewas heading up the St. Croix with William Aitkin who, as usual, was not without liquor.

On the Mississippi, above the falls, Sioux under Shakopee and Good Earth caught some of the Chippewas making a portage. Most of the warriors were hunting, having left women, children and old men to wrestle the canoes and gear overland. The latter were nonetheless fair game for Indians bent on requital. "It was while making this portage, and encumbered in the manner already related," Sibley wrote, "that they were fallen upon by the enraged Sioux." In the lead was Sibley's hero, Track-Maker; among the Chippewa women was Bounding Fawn (or Budding Rose, if you will), who did not fail to recognize her recent nocturnal partner and sprang forward, crossing her wrists in token of surrender. "Who can depict the horror which overwhelmed the young Sioux?" Sibley asked his readers. (His pseudonym, for the record, was "Hal, a Dakotah.") "Convinced that he could do nothing to save her, he touched her lightly with his spear, and bounded forward." Track-Maker simply left the dirty business to the warrior behind him, and Bounding Fawn was duly dispatched—along with seventy or more Chippewa women and children. Track-Maker was alive to tell the story to Sibley, but he professed a wish to regain his lost love in death, a desire not difficult for a reckless brave to fulfill.

Meanwhile the Little Crow warriors on the St. Croix had caught up with the Chippewas, who were led by Strong Ground. The pursuers found the enemy encamped in a hollow, sodden with drink after a day's celebration under Aitkin's aegis. Lining up at dawn on the slopes above the camp, the Sioux waited briefly as the trader and several white companions began to move out. Then they opened fire and, according to Little Crow's report to Taliaferro, "might have killed *every* soul of the Chippewas had there been no white people along." Actually, things weren't quite that easy. Strong Ground managed to spur his warriors out of their hungover state, and their firepower drove back the Sioux after a few Chippewas had fallen in the opening round. Aitkin claimed that he had been hit, but Taliaferro dismissed his longtime adversary's wound as "a *Scratch* from a *bush or stick . . . supposed* by some to have happened in his *flight.*" Writing later to Sibley of "your infernal Sioux," Aitkin said the tribesmen "very nearly made me Close all my worldly Concerns," and he enjoined his fellow trader to "not Ever Speak in their favour hereafter." Lieutenant McPhail had brought a detachment up from the fort to succor the wounded, but he had no stomach for the aftermath; he steered clear of the battleground, he told Taliaferro, because of the *"excessive* stench from the carcasses."

If the fracas provided a tale for Sibley's pen, it was also a fitting climax to Taliaferro's last summer at the fort. Little could be said for the slaughter except that it was typical of Indian warfare before friction on the Plains needled the tribes into organized uprisings. As the government's agent Taliaferro had no weapon other than persuasion to use in maintaining peace. And no matter who commanded the fort, it was not army policy to intervene with force when Indians attacked each other. When Taliaferro had remonstrated with the Sioux chiefs after their return, Chief Good Road recalled the advice of President Van Buren, given when the Sioux had last visited Washington. The President had told them, according to Taliaferro, to return "to your people and keep peace with all nations—go to war against none. . . ." Unfortunately he had added, "If struck upon by your enemies, then you may revenge it. We [Americans] have been struck upon & we have revenged it." Understandably, the Indians considered this carte blanche. Good Road said his sincere wish for peace had been shattered when the two Chippewas killed the Badger. "We thought of the many insults offered our people," Taliaferro's journal quotes Shakopee, "& the murder in *cold blood* of 3 Lodges of our *women* & children last year by the Hole in the Day."

The Sioux danced the scalp dance nightly for the rest of the summer. They had had missionaries among them for five years, but in spite of the travails of the Pond brothers and their peers the percentage of converted natives around Fort Snelling was miniscule. And although the fort now had an official chaplain, few civilians had had the benefit of ministry, for the majority —squatters, voyageurs, breeds—were nominal Catholics. The bloodlines were Irish, Scottish, and Old French, some of the latter native to the Sioux-Chippewa country for two or three generations. Only now, as the scalp-bearers returned with their bloody trophies, were the St. Peter's papists exposed to mass. On the Fourth of July, Bishop Mathias Loras was "offering prayers to heaven, in favour of my adopted country, when . . . I perceived through the windows" the Sioux celebrants. The bishop turned to the gathered worshipers and asked them to pray for the savage neighbors among whom these errant Catholics had lived so long.

His presence among them, Loras wrote that month, "was a

cause of great joy to the Catholics, who had never before seen a Priest or a Bishop in these remote regions; they manifested a great desire to assist at divine worship, and approach the Sacraments of the Church. . . ." The bishop had found one hundred and eighty-five Catholics at St. Peter's, and more than one hundred of them wanted the simple rites of baptism, confirmation, and marriage. Although most of them now lived under Plympton's threat to their homes, they were intent upon staying as close to the fort as possible; and they were confident enough of the future to prevail upon Loras to promise them a parish priest. Squatters they might be, but in sacerdotal recognition they heard the sound of permanence.

In this desire to fix themselves to the region of the fort, these immigrants from Canada missed the drumbeat that was stirring others in the Mississippi Valley. In May a handful of citizens of Peoria, Illinois, had organized as the Oregon Dragoons and had headed west carrying a guidon inscribed OREGON OR THE GRAVE. At least nine other Oregon settlement societies were forming in 1839. In Missouri, old acquaintances of John Marsh began to receive letters from the erstwhile Fort Snelling schoolteacher who had found his last frontier in California's San Joaquin Valley— his insistent tattoo brought the first settlers across the Sierras. The nation was getting its second wind and was on the threshold of a great decade of increased expansion. Tall tales of incredibly balmy climes along the Pacific roused many east of the Mississippi, but many more responded to the prospect of virgin land in territory politically organized, as was Wisconsin. There settlers were beginning to arrive at a rate that in ten years would multiply the population from something over 3,000 to 165,000, including the squatters now clinging futilely to their homesteads on Fort Snelling's military domain.

Early in October, Taliaferro obliquely noted the fate of the squatters when he made one of the last entries in his St. Peter's journal: "The line [of the final demarcation of the reservation] extends much further east than any survey hitherto." His words meant to the fort's unwanted civilians that even those who had

223

moved across the Mississippi were still on soil claimed by the government; they would have to pull up stakes once more. But Taliaferro too was pulling stakes. He had no heart left for the St. Peter's winter which would be the last the squatters would spend on the reservation. He had lost his zest for the fight against traders whose dealings with Indians were always self-seeking. The treaties which brought annuities to the tribes, making them no longer masters of ancestral domains, had changed the face of the wilderness. There was little now that a single white man in his rectitude could accomplish alone, for the influence of the chiefs whom Taliaferro so often had counseled was diminished; a brave with his own government allotment did not need to listen to his tribal leaders. With the breakdown of the ancient social structure, the challenge for a man like Taliaferro was over. On October 7, he noted in his journal the unexpected arrival of a steamboat which would save him the discomfort of a canoe trip downriver. The Indians, said Samuel Pond, "long deplored the departure" of the man whom they had dubbed "Four Hearts."

Taliaferro had scarcely reached St. Louis when Major Plympton gave the squatters final notice. The heads of households soon met in the home of Abram Perret and commissioned Joe Brown, former drummer boy, to write their protest to Wisconsin's territorial delegate to Congress; the territorial legislature supported the protest, and Delegate James D. Doty pointed out to the Secretary of War that the army could not extend the Fort Snelling reservation eastward into Wisconsin without the consent of the legislature. Nevertheless, Poinsett did not rescind his order to the territorial marshal "requiring that the intruders on the land recently reserved" be removed. When spring arrived, a deputy marshal from Prairie du Chien boarded the first upriver steamboat and ended the long hassle with direct action. After giving the settlers several days' notice, he requisitioned a military detail from Plympton on May 6, 1840. "He went to work, assisted by soldiers," wrote Father Galtier, the squatters' newly assigned priest, "and unroofed, one after another, the cottages, extending about five miles along the river." Thus evicted, the squatters moved across the reservation line and began anew, and thereby founded the community that has become St. Paul, Minnesota's capital.

The fort remained. Regiments came and went. Snellings' monument was still the entry's citadel, but the wilderness was gone. Only Pike's island escaped the men and the tools that now began to obliterate all that had been primordial.

CHAPTER FIFTEEN

———◆•◆———

AFTERWARD

FORT SNELLING had reached its meridian. Eighteen years remained in which the duties of the garrison focused more and more sharply on the well-being of its white neighbors, less and less so on that of the Indians. Even as soldiers were tearing the roofs from the squatters' hovels, three companies from the fort had been sent downriver to join General Atkinson's roundup of Winnebago bands which had bolted their Iowa reservation and gone back to their Wisconsin homeland. Indian removal was on everyone's mind, and the subject approached one of its frequent climaxes during the Fifth Regiment's last months at St. Peter's.

William Henry Harrison's victory over Van Buren had brought a new man into the War Department and with him another new scheme to solve the Indian problem once and for all. When John Bell (who had been chairman of the Committee on Indian Affairs in the House of Representatives) became Secretary of War, he already had conceived a far-reaching plan to establish an Indian Territory between the St. Peter's River and the Canadian border. Here all homeless tribes, and some which had not yet surrendered their lands, could work out their own form of government, throw off the trappings of savagery, and finally, perhaps, develop an Indian state to be admitted into the Union.

To sell his plan to the Sioux, Bell had named James D. Doty, the Wisconsin territorial delegate who recently had been elevated to the governorship and whose career had long been supported by the American Fur Company. Early in July, 1841, Doty and his wife debarked at the entry, and the commissioner conferred with Henry Sibley, Jean Baptiste Faribault and his son Alex-

ander. Up on the bluff Doty was outfitted, and with a detail under Lieutenant Henry Whiting he proceeded seventy-five miles
up the St. Peter's to the crossing known as Traverse des Sioux.
On the last day of the month, in the presence of Whiting, Sibley,
the Faribaults, and old Joe Renville, Doty consummated a deal
to convert thirty million acres into a permanent home for the
restless Winnebagos, certain Chippewa and Ottawa bands of
northern Michigan, some derelict New York Indians, Sacs, Foxes,
Potawatomies, and the Sioux themselves. The treaty also made
specific provisions for half-breeds; and, as usual, for tribal debts
to the traders—this time in the amount of $50,000.

However, in spite of the fact that Ramsay Crooks called the
treaty "the first great object most desirable to secure"—and that
Sibley and Dousman lobbied in Washington, and Pierre Chouteau, Jr., offered to do so—the Senate refused to go along with
Doty's negotiations. For Lawrence Taliaferro, in retirement, was
still a nemesis of the American Fur Company. He supported the
opposition led by Senator Thomas Hart Benton, who believed
that an attempt to establish Indian self-government was uncon-
stitutional and impracticable. Out of office, Taliaferro's militant
interest in the welfare of the Indians rather than in the prosperity of the traders remained fixed. Benton presented the former
agent's testimony, and the committee failed to recommend passage of the treaty; on the Senate floor it was rejected almost unan-
imously. As a result, American Fur received no part of the
$50,000 in claims which had been honored by Doty's negotia-
tions, and that loss proved to be the last of a series which brought
Ramsay Crooks' firm to its knees. That fall of 1842 the American
Fur Company went into bankruptcy, ending an era in the Old
Northwest. Sibley's Sioux Outfit continued under the aegis of
Pierre Chouteau, Jr. & Company, and there was little change in
fur-trade ethics. But the master craftsman of field tactics, Crooks
himself, henceforward confined his activity to the New York
market. Yet it must not be inferred that the attack begun by
Taliaferro and Josiah Snelling a score of years before had brought
him down; his scruples were no worse than those of any other
big businessman of the nineteenth century.

227

Far more unscrupulous, in fact, were the whiskey dealers who now menaced the Indians under Fort Snelling's jurisdiction. By 1845, the alcoholism that so offended Gideon Pond had impressed itself so urgently on Inspector General George Croghan that he wrote lengthily on the subject after leaving St. Peter's in August. After nine tours of the Snelling area since 1827, Croghan knew whereof he spoke. "Confound not together the licensed trader and the whiskey dealer of the frontier," he told the War Department. "The latter is but the unprincipled scoundrel who makes the Indian drunk that he may rob him of his blanket, rifle, traps, and whatever else he can lay his hands on." The former, Croghan said, was well represented by Jean Baptiste Faribault, whose dealings with Shakopee's band he considered impeccable. But on the east bank of the Mississippi, instead of such traders as Faribault there were the grogshops run by dealers in "a poison made by compounding together bad whiskey, water, tobacco juice, and red pepper." Croghan cited Little Crow's village as a typical victim which, he said, "but a few years ago ranked among the foremost in point of respectability of all the Sioux tribes; now it is reduced to the lowest depth of degradation, disunity, debauched, and poverty stricken, and all through the agency of the whiskey dealers."

No Fort Snelling commander ever had the means to stop Indian traffic to the ceded lands across the Mississippi, and not for years was there effective control of the exchange between the liquor peddlers and army personnel. "The dangers and difficulties which the old soldiers risked to satisfy their insane craving for strong liquor," a Fifth Infantry fifer wrote, "is well-nigh incredible. . . . How often have I scaled the walls of old Fort Snelling . . . travelled through deep snow to an old log hut on the left bank of the river five miles above the fort . . . [and bought] the most villainous 'fire-water' that man ever had the courage to swallow, a compound of turpentine and alcohol requiring a copper lined throat and a stomach of gutta percha." The concoction cost three to five dollars a gallon, while the ingredients "couldn't have cost more than ten cents."

The excessive profits matched the excessive appetites, and the commandants at the fort had increasing disciplinary problems as settlement across the river mushroomed and the grogshops multiplied. Returning after a decade and a half, Captain Seth Eastman could not have failed to note the new excesses when, in the fall of 1841, he brought soldiers of the First Infantry to replace the Fifth for the second time. But Eastman had talent to distract him from the tedium of day-to-day responsibility. In the years of his absence from the St. Peter's he had taught art at West Point and had been elected a member of the National Academy of Design. During a year of service in the Seminole War he had begun to paint the Florida natives. Now he was back at Snelling for a stay of seven years—a period in which he became a master painter of the Indian. In one year alone he turned out four hundred pictures, and before he was transferred to Texas he had finished at least seventy-five major canvases, an accomplishment acknowledged when he was assigned to illustrate *Indian Tribes of the United States*, edited by Henry Schoolcraft. Clearly Eastman was more than a frontier example of the Sunday painter, yet he was also, a government official said, "a most efficient Frontier officer" who broke up a rebellion during the Winnebago removal and sent that restive tribe to its Minnesota reservation.

A couple of months after this incident the painter-soldier left the fort when, in 1848, the First Infantry was pulled out and replaced by the Sixth, fresh from service under Zachary Taylor in the Mexican War. The men of the Sixth soon found they had work cut out for them. The Winnebagos would not stay put. They had to be chased back when they left the reservation in 1849. That same summer there was similar action in Iowa where Sacs, Foxes and Potawatomies had returned from their new reservation on the Missouri. There were so many widely scattered instances of trouble that the garrison was reinforced with a dragoon company, the first mounted soldiers to be assigned to Fort Snelling. Gradually it was becoming apparent that strategically placed though the citadel was, new outposts were needed to help the garrison do its job. Not only did United States Indians need policing, but *bois brûlé* buffalo hunters from the Red River were ranging deeper and deeper across the border, killing as many as twenty thousand head on their annual forays. An expedition from Snelling was sent north to warn them to stay at home, and American half-breeds and Indians were given carte blanche to repel the hunters' invasions by force. But this rather casual approach could not work, and the inevitable forts to serve as adjuncts to the works at the entry were hammered up, one by one: Fort Gaines upriver on the Mississippi in 1848; Fort Ridgely on the St. Peter's in 1853; and Fort Abercrombie on the Red in 1857.

By this time a final treaty had been signed with the Sioux, and the St. Peter's bands were concentrated in a twenty-mile strip through which the river flowed from its source to the Little Rock fork. Much of the present state of Minnesota was open to settlement, and the land-hungry swept across the Mississippi. The emigrant tide had reached the Pacific, but its crest rose high in the continental heartland. At St. Paul's landing downriver from Snelling, 30,000 settlers arrived by boat in the summer of 1855. By 1857, an official census gave Minnesota Territory a total of 150,037 inhabitants. Among these arrivals was Lawrence Taliaferro, but he had not come to stay. He found, he wrote, "none to know him—not an invitation did he get to 'break bread' with any of the poor made quickly rich. . . ." With his friends gone from the Snelling area, the former agent decided to return to the army life of his youth, and he served in Texas, Kansas and Pennsylvania until his retirement in 1863.

Still secure on the bluff above the entry, the fort at which Taliaferro had served so long was surrounded by civilization, its mission accomplished. The Old Northwest, with whose protection it had been charged, had vanished in the swift spread of settlement. Within the fort, acting secretly, one man read the portents and swung his weight in Washington. He was Franklin Steele, the post sutler. In July, 1857, he bought Fort Snelling from the War Department, agreeing to pay $90,000 for the structure and six to seven thousand acres of reservation. The event was a sorry moment. Steele dickered with real estate speculations, grazed sheep on the prairie where officers had chased wolves, and brought his flocks within the citadel walls at night. But his secret deal had roused Congress to an investigation. A confusion of actions followed, to be interrupted by the Civil War. The fort was commandeered for the duration and retrieved from Steele's proprietorship after he had been paid rent so exorbitant that he made a whopping profit. From thenceforward, however, it remained an army installation until 1946, when it was turned over to the Veteran's Administration.

SOURCES AND ACKNOWLEDGMENTS

THIS IS a book for readers interested in the American past which is based on research in the National Archives, and in those of the New York Public Library, the New York Historical Society, and the Minnesota Historical Society. I owe much to many persons in these institutions, and at least as much to those scholarly authorities who have compiled excellent bibliographies of all the subjects dealt with in this volume. I am also grateful for the facilities of the New York Society Library. As noted in the Prologue, my greatest debt is to the letters and journals of Indian agent Lawrence Taliaferro, in the possession of the Minnesota Historical Society; they are cited below as Taliaferro Papers. That society also has the papers of Henry H. Sibley, as well as numerous other pertinent manuscript collections which were consulted. Photostatic reproductions of letters written by John Jacob Astor and Ramsay Crooks, 1813–1843, are in the New York Public Library. A voluminous collection of American Fur Company papers is in the New York Historical Society. In Washington, in the National Archives, my search was centered on Record Group 75 (Indian Affairs), Record Group 92 (Quartermaster General), Record Group 94 (Adjutant General's Office), Record Group 98 (Army Commands), Record Group 77 (Chief of Engineers), Record Group 49 (General Land Office), Record Group 107 (Secretary of War), and Record Group 159 (Inspector General).

No purpose, it seems to me, is served in such a work as this one by citing chapter and verse, nor the sources to which I am indebted for clarification, enlightenment, and insight. Therefore the citations which follow cover the basic topic treated in each chapter. Still, at this point it also might be said that great help came from books not easy to confine to chapter headings. They include, first of all, Marcus L. Hansen's *Old Fort Snelling, 1819–1858*, an admirable text which provides illumination for anyone interested in life at the St. Peter's entry. William W. Folwell's *History of Minnesota* is regional history of high order. Grace Lee Nute's *The Voyageur* is unique, her *Calendar of the American Fur Company Papers* is an indispensable tool; and Kenneth W. Porter's *John Jacob Astor, Business Man* now has been joined by David Lavender's account of Ramsay Crooks, *Fist in the Wilderness*; thus there are two fine biographies of American Fur Company leaders, neither of whom can be ignored in reading about the Fort Snelling era.

For a number of years I have had the privilege of the advice and encouragement of Russell W. Fridley, director of the Minnesota Historical Society, and I thank him once more. I also owe profound thanks to the talented Lucille Kane, the society's curator of manuscripts, and to her assistants Kathryn Johnson and Janet White; Thomas Diehl was helpful in identifying newspaper sources, and the illustrations in this volume are due to the good offices of my friend Eugene D. Becker, curator of pictures; for specific and sometimes osmotic help, my thanks to Theodore C. Blegen, Michael Brook, James Taylor Dunn, Bertha Heilbron, June Drenning Holmquist, and Alan R. Woolworth. I had the aid and comfort of two editors: Betty A. Prashker, whose interest brought this book into being, and Judith Bailey Jones who gave more than should be asked of a wife.

Chapter I—River Travelers

Alvord, Clarence W., *The Mississippi Valley in British Politics*. Cleveland, 1917.
American State Papers: *Indian Affairs, I.*
——— *Miscellaneous, II.*
Bakeless, John, *Lewis and Clark*. New York, 1947.
Blair, Emma H., *Indian Tribes of the Upper Mississippi Valley and Region of the Great Lakes*. Cleveland, 1911.

Carter, Clarence W., *Territorial Papers of the United States, X.* Washington, 1930.

Coues, Elliott, *Expeditions of Zebulon Montgomery Pike.* New York, 1895.

Cruikshank, Ernest, "Employment of Indians in the War of 1812," *American Historical Association Annual Report for 1895.*

───── "Robert Dickson, Fur Trader," *Wisconsin Historical Collections, XII.*

De Voto, Bernard, *The Course of Empire.* Boston, 1952.

───── *Journals of Lewis and Clark.* Boston, 1953.

Dillon, Richard, *Meriwether Lewis.* New York, 1965.

Hollon, W. Eugene, *The Lost Pathfinder, Zebulon Montgomery Pike.* Norman, Oklahoma, 1949.

Jackson, Donald, *Letters of the Lewis and Clark Expedition with Related Documents, 1783–1854.* Urbana, Illinois, 1962.

Kellogg, Louise P., *The French Regime in Wisconsin and the Northwest.* Madison, Wisconsin, 1925.

───── *The British Regime in Wisconsin and the Northwest.* Madison, Wisconsin, 1935.

Lavender, David, "Ramsay Crook's First Ventures on the Missouri River," *Missouri Historical Society Bulletin, XX.*

Lipscomb, Andrew A. and Albert Ellery Bergh, eds., *The Writings of Thomas Jefferson.* The Thomas Jefferson Memorial Association, Washington, 1905.

Mahan, Bruce E., *Old Fort Crawford and the Frontier.* Iowa City, 1926.

Marshall, Thomas Maitland, ed., *The Life and Papers of Frederick Bates.* St. Louis, 1926.

"Personal Narrative of Captain Thomas G. Anderson," *Report and Collections of the State Historical Society of Wisconsin, IX.* Madison, 1882.

Scanlan, Peter L., *Prairie du Chien, French, British, American.* Menasha, Wisconsin, 1937.

Smith, Margaret Bayard, *First Forty Years of Washington Society.* New York, 1906.

Chapter II—The Nameless War

Astor-Crooks Papers. NYPL.

Bulger Papers. Copies, MHS.

Carter, as in Chapter I.

Cruikshank, as in Chapter I.

Devans, R.M., *Our First Century*. Springfield, Massachusetts, 1879.

Robert Dickson Papers, 1790–1822. Copies, MHS.

Gilpin, Alec R., *The War of 1812 in the Old Northwest*. East Lansing, Michigan, 1958.

Gregg, Kate L., "War of 1812 on the Missouri Frontier," *Missouri Historical Review, XXXIII*.

Kellogg, Louise P., "The Capture of Mackinac," *Wisconsin Historical Proceedings, II*.

Mahan, as in Chapter I.

Michigan Pioneer and Historical Collections, XV, XVI.

Neill, E.D., "A Sketch of Joseph Renville," *Minnesota Historical Collections, I*.

Niles' Register, II, III, VI, VII, VIII.

Pratt, J.A., "Fur Trade Strategy and the American Left Flank in the War of 1812," *American Historical Review, XL*.

Scanlan, as in Chapter I.

Taliaferro Papers.

Tohill, Louis A., *Robert Dickson, British Fur Trader*. Ann Arbor, 1926.

Tucker, Glenn, *Tecumseh, Vision of Glory*. Indianapolis, 1956.

Wisconsin Historical Collections, IX, XI, XII, XIII, XIX, XX.

Wood, William, *Select British Documents of the Canadian War of 1812*. Toronto, 1920.

Chapter III—Nature's Rampart

American State Papers: *Indian Affairs, II*.

———— *Military Affairs, I*.

Armstrong, John M., "Edward Purcell, First Physician of Minnesota," *Annals of Medical History, VII*.

Army Commands, Fifth Military Department Order Book. MHS.

Babcock, Willoughby M., *Calendar of the Papers of William Clark in the Kansas State Historical Society.* MHS.

William Clark Papers, 1812–1839, St. Peter's Agency. Copies, MHS.

Ellet, Elizabeth, *Pioneer Women of the West.* New York, 1852.

Flint, Timothy, *Recollections of the Last Ten Years.* Boston, 1826.

Thomas Forsyth Letters, 1819. Copies, MHS.

Forsyth, Thomas, "Journal of a Voyage from St. Louis to the Falls of St. Anthony in 1819," *Minnesota Historical Collections, III.*

Gallaher, Ruth A., "The Indian Agent in the U.S. Before 1850," *Iowa Journal of History and Politics, XIV.*

Jameson, J.F., "Correspondence of John C. Calhoun," *Annual Report of the American Historical Association, 1899, II.* Washington, 1900.

John Lawe Papers, 1818–1832. Copies, MHS.

Leavenworth, Elias W., *A Geneology of the Leavenworth Family in the United States.* Syracuse, 1872.

Long, Stephen H., *Voyage in a Six-oared Skiff to the Falls of St. Anthony in 1817.* MHS, ms.

McLaughlin, Andrew C., *Lewis Cass.* Boston, 1891.

National Archives.

Neill, E.D., "Fort Snelling Echoes," *Magazine of Western History, X.*

——— *Fort Snelling while in command of Colonel Josiah Snelling, Fifth Infantry.* New York, 1888.

——— *The History of Minnesota.* Philadelphia, 1858.

New York Commercial Advertiser, 1819, 1820, 1821.

Porter, Kenneth W., "John Jacob Astor and Lord Selkirk," *North Dakota Historical Quarterly, V.*

Porter, Valentine M., "Journal of Stephen W. Kearny," *Missouri Historical Society Collections, III.*

Prescott Reminiscences, 1820–1851. MHS, ms.

Schoolcraft, Henry R., *Narrative Journal of Travels through the Northwestern Regions of the U.S.* (edited by Mentor L. Williams). East Lansing, Michigan, 1953.

——— *Personal Memoirs of a Residence of Thirty Years with the Indian Tribes on the Frontiers.* Philadelphia, 1851.

Sibley, Henry H., "Memoir of Jean Baptiste Faribault," *Minnesota Historical Collections, III.*

Smith, W.L.G., *The Life and Times of Lewis Cass.* New York, 1856.

Snelling, Henry, *Memoirs of My Life, From My Notebook and Journal.* Copy, MHS.

Statutes at Large, VII.

Taliaferro Papers.

Trowbridge, Charles C., "Journal of Expedition of 1820," *Minnesota History, XXIII.*

U.S. Infantry, Fifth Regt. Papers, 1819–1828, Copies, MHS.

Upham, Warren, "History of Mining and Quarrying in Minnesota," *Minnesota Historical Collections, VIII.*

Van Cleve, Charlotte, *Three Score Years and Ten.* Minneapolis, 1888.

War Dept. Papers, Selected documents pertaining to Ft. Snelling. Copies, MHS.

Williams, J.F., *Memoir of Col. Josiah Snelling.* MHS, ms.

Wiltse, Charles M., *John C. Calhoun, Nationalist.* New York, 1944.

Wisconsin Magazine of History, XXVII.

Woodford, Frank B., *Lewis Cass, the Last Jeffersonian.* New Brunswick, 1950.

Young, William T., *Sketch of the Life and Service of General Lewis Cass.* Philadelphia, 1853.

Chapter IV—People of Lakes and Streams

Blair, as in Chapter I.

Eastman, Mary, *Dahkotah; or, Life and Legends of the Sioux Around Fort Snelling.* New York, 1849.

Hagan, William T., *The Sac and Fox Indians.* Norman, Oklahoma, 1958.

Heilbron, Bertha, ed., *With Pen and Pencil on the Frontier, the Diary of Frank B. Mayer.* St. Paul, 1932.

Illinois Intelligencer, May 15, 1821.

National Archives.

New York Commercial Advertiser, June 11, 1821.

Pond, Samuel W., "The Dakotas or Sioux in Minnesota," *Minnesota Historical Collections, XII.*

Prescott, as in Chapter III.

Robinson, Doane, *History of Dakota or Sioux Indians.* Minneapolis, 1956.

Snelling, Henry, as in Chapter III.
Warren, William W. "History of the Ojibway Nation," *Minnesota Historical Collections, V.*

Chapter V—Edge of a World

Adams, Ann, "Reminiscences of Fort Snelling," *Minnesota Historical Collections, VI.*
Beltrami, G.C., *A Pilgrimage in Europe and America.* London, 1828.
Bliss, John H., "Reminiscences of Fort Snelling," *Minnesota Historical Collections, VI.*
Cooke, Philip St. George, *Scenes and Adventures in the Army.* Philadelphia, 1859.
Coues, as in Chapter I.
Eastman, as in Chapter IV.
Ellet, as in Chapter III.
Hagan, as in Chapter IV.
Henderson Democrat, June 12, 1856.
Jackson, as in Chapter I.
Nathan S. Jarvis Papers. Copies, MHS.
Keating, William H., *Narrative of an Expedition.* Minneapolis, 1959.
Long, as in Chapter III.
Lyman, George D., *John Marsh, Pioneer.* New York, 1930.
National Archives.
Office of Indian Affairs, Letters Received. Copies, MHS.
Prucha, Francis Paul, *Army Life on the Western Frontier.* Norman, Oklahoma, 1958.
Taliaferro, Lawrence, "An Auto-Biography," *Minnesota Historical Collections, VI.*
Taliaferro Papers.
Warren, as in Chapter IV.

Chapter VI—Theme of Conquest

Babcock, Willoughby M., "Major Lawrence Taliaferro, Indian Agent," *Mississippi Valley Historical Review, XL.*
Clark Papers, as in Chapter III.
Hagan, as in Chapter IV.

Journal of Proceedings at Prairie du Chien Council, Office of Indian Affairs. Copy, MHS.

Lyman, as in Chapter V.

John Marsh Papers, 1825–1828. MHS.

Mahan, as in Chapter I.

McKenney, Thomas L., and James Hall, *The Indian Tribes of North America* (edited by Frederick W. Hodge). Edinburgh, 1933.

National Archives.

Nichols, Roger L., *General Henry Atkinson, A Western Military Career.* Norman, Oklahoma, 1965.

Office of Indian Affairs, as in Chapter V.

Scanlan, as in Chapter I.

Schoolcraft (ed. by Williams), as in Chapter III.

State Papers, 1 Session, 20 Congress, 1, Doc. 1.

Taliaferro, as in Chapter V.

Taliaferro Papers.

Chapter VII—The Hinge of the Future

Abel, Annie Heloise, *Chardon's Journal at Ft. Clark.*

Adams, as in Chapter V.

American Fur Co. Papers. Copies, MHS.

Astor-Crooks, as in Chapter I.

Berry, Don, *A Majority of Scoundrels.* New York, 1961.

Chetlain, Charles L., *The Red River Colony.* Chicago, 1893.

Chittenden, Hiram, *History of the American Fur Trade.* Stanford, 1954.

Chouteau Family Papers. Copies, MHS.

National Archives.

Neill, History, as in Chapter III.

North Dakota History, II.

Office of Indian Affairs, as in Chapter V.

Prescott, as in Chapter III.

Selkirk Papers, 1806–1824. Copies, MHS.

Robert Stuart Letterbrook, 1825–1830. Copy, MHS.

Taliaferro Papers.

Tohill, as in Chapter III.

Van Cleve, as in Chapter III.

Chapter VIII—Valley of Violence

American State Papers, VII, VIII.

Astor-Crooks, as in Chapter I.

Blegen, T.C., and Sarah A Davidson, *Iron Face.* Chicago, 1950.

Clarke, Dwight L., *Stephen Watts Kearny, Soldier of the West.* Norman, 1961.

Cooke, as in Chapter III.

Elliott, Charles W., *Winfield Scott: The Soldier and the Man.* New York, 1937.

Hagan, as in Chapter IV.

Hamilton, Holman, *Zachary Taylor, Soldier of the Republic.* New York, 1941.

Jackson, Donald, ed., *Black Hawk, a Biography.* Urbana, Illinois, 1961.

Jarvis, as in Chapter V.

Lavender, David, *Bent's Fort.* New York, 1954.

Lyman, as in Chapter V.

Mahan, as in Chapter I.

Marsh, as in Chapter VI.

Meyer, Jesse S., *Life and Letters of Dr. William Beaumont.* St. Louis, 1939.

National Archives.

Nichols, as in Chapter VI.

Pelzer, Louis, *Henry Dodge.* Iowa City, 1911.

Scanlan, as in Chapter I.

Schoolcraft Memoirs, as in Chapter III.

Snelling, Josiah, *Diary, 1817.* Copy, MHS.

Street Papers, Calendar. MHS.

Strode, Hudson, *Jefferson Davis.* New York, 1955.

Taliaferro Papers.

Zachary Taylor Letters. Copies, MHS.

Van Cleve, as in Chapter III.

Chapter IX—The New Travelers

Ackermann, Gertrude W., "Joseph Renville of Lac Qui Parle," *Minnesota History, XII.*

American Board of Foreign Missions Papers. Copies, MHS.

Badger Papers. MHS.

Alexis Bailly Papers, 1820–1868. MHS.

Blegen, T.C., ed., *Unfinished Autobiography of Henry Hastings Sibley.* Minneapolis, 1932.

Bliss, as in Chapter V.

Boutwell, William, *Diary.* MHS, ms.

Catlin, George, *Illustrations of the Manners, Customs, & Conditions of the North American Indians.* Picadilly, 1876.

De Voto, Bernard, *Across the Wide Missouri.* Boston, 1947.

Eastman, as in Chapter IV.

Lavender, as in Chapter VIII.

Robert Lucas Papers, 1835–46. Copies, MHS.

Missionary Herald, XXX.

National Archives.

Neill, as in Chapter II.

North Dakota History, II.

Pond, Samuel W., "Narrative," *Minnesota History, XXI.*

Pond, Samuel W., Jr., *Two Volunteer Missionaries Among the Sioux.* Boston, c. 1893.

Pond Papers. MHS.

Riggs, Stephen R., *Mary and I.* Chicago, 1880.

Sibley Papers. MHS.

Taliaferro Papers.

Chapter X—The Widening Arc

American Board of Missions, as in Chapter IX.

Annals of Iowa, Series 3, XXI.

Babcock, as in Chapter VI.

Brunson, Alfred, *Western Pioneer.* n.d.

De Voto, as in Chapter IX.

Howard, Benjamin C., *Report of the Decisions of the Supreme Court ... in the Case of Dred Scott.* New York, 1857.

Jarvis, as in Chapter V.

La Trobe, Charles, *The Rambler in North America, 1832–1833.* New York, 1835.

National Archives.

Newson, T.M., *Pen Pictures of St. Paul, Minnesota.* St. Paul, 1886.

Nicollet Papers. Copies, MHS.

Nute, Grace Lee, *Voyageur's Highway.* St. Paul, 1941.

Pond, as in Chapter IX.

Sibley, Henry H., "Memoir of Jean N. Nicollet," *Minnesota Historical Collections, I.*

Sibley Papers.

Taliaferro Papers.

Warren, as in Chapter IV.

West, Nathaniel, *Ancestry, Life and Times of H. H. Sibley.* St. Paul, 1889.

Winchell, Newton H., "Joseph N. Nicollet," *American Geologist, VIII.*

Chapter XI—Vibrations

Ackermann, as in Chapter IX.

American Fur Co. Papers. NYHS, ms.

American Fur Co. Papers. Copies, MHS.

Babcock, as in Chapter VI.

Ely, Edmund F., *Diary.* MHS. ms.

National Archives.

Neill, as in Chapter II.

Nute, Grace Lee, "The Diary of Martin McLeod," *Minnesota History Bulletin, IV.*

———— "James Dickson, A Filibusterer in Minnesota in 1836," *Mississippi Valley Historical Review, X.*

———— "John McLoughlin, Jr., and the Dickson Filibuster," *Minnesota History XVII.*

Pond, as in Chapter IX.

Sibley Papers.

Taliaferro, as in Chapter V.

Taliaferro Papers.

Chapter XII—Treaty and Triumph

American Fur Co. Papers. Copies, MHS.

American Fur Co. Papers. NYHS, ms.

Brunson, as in Chapter X.

Frémont, John Charles, *Memoirs of My Life*. New York, 1887.

Gunn, George H., "Garrioch at St. Peter's," *Minnesota History, XX*.

Iowa Journal of History and Politics, IX.

Mahan, as in Chapter I.

Marryat, Captain Frederick, *A Diary in America* (edited by S. W. Jackman). New York, 1962.

Minnesota Historical Collections, III.

National Archives.

National Intelligencer, August 25, 1837.

Nicollet Papers. MHS.

Niles' Register, LIII.

Nute, McLeod Diary.

Petersen, W.J., "The Second Purchase," *Palimpsest, XVIII.*

Pond, as in Chapter IX.

Sibley, as in Chapter III.

Sibley Papers.

Taliaferro, as in Chapter V.

Taliaferro Papers.

Van Cleve, as in Chapter III.

Chapter XIII—Year of the Long Wait

American Fur Co. Papers, as in Chapter XI.

Annals of Iowa, as in Chapter X.

Frémont, as in Chapter XII.

Loehr, R. C., "Franklin Steele, Frontier Businessman," *Minnesota History, XXVII.*

Hopkins, Vincent C., *Dred Scott's Case.* New York, 1951.

Marryat, as in Chapter XII.

National Archives.

Neill, History of Minnesota.

Pond, as in Chapter IX.

Purchase of Island—Confluence of the St. Peter's and Mississippi Rivers (26 Congress, I Session, *House Documents,* no. 82— serial 365).

Schoolcraft Memoirs, as in Chapter III.

Sibley Papers.

Taliaferro, as in Chapter V.

Taliaferro Papers.

Williams, J.F. *History of Saint Paul.* St. Paul, 1876.

Chapter XIV—The Day the Roofs Came Off

American Fur Co. Papers, as in Chapter XI.

Annals of Iowa, as in Chapter X.

Annals of the Propagation of the Faith, III.

Billington, R.A., *The Far Western Frontier, 1830–1860.* New York, 1960.

Blegen, T.C., "War on the Minnesota Frontier," *Minnesota History, XXIV.*

Blegen-Davidson, as in Chapter VIII.

Fort Snelling Investigation (36 Congress, I Session, *House Reports,* no. 351—serial 965).

Loehr, as in Chapter XIII.

Lyman, as in Chapter V.

National Archives.

Pond, as in Chapter IX.

Prucha, Francis Paul, *Broadax and Bayonet.* Madison, Wisconsin, 1953.

Purchase, as in Chapter XIII.

Sale of Fort Snelling Reservation (40 Congress, III Session, *House Documents,* no. 9—serial 1372).

Sibley, Henry H., "Sketches of Indian Warfare," *Spirit of the Times,* March 11, 1848.

Sibley Papers.

Taliaferro, as in Chapter V.

Taliaferro Papers.

Williams, as in Chapter XIII.

Chapter XV—Afterward

American Fur Co. Papers, as in Chapter XI.

Fort Snelling Investigation, as in Chapter XIV.

McDermott, John F., *Seth Eastman, Pictorial Historian of the Indian.*
Norman, Oklahoma, 1961.

National Archives.

Prucha, as in Chapter V.

Sale of Fort Snelling, as in Chapter XIV.

Sibley Papers.

Skinner, Otis and Maude, *One Man in His Time.* Philadelphia, 1938.

INDEX

EVAN JONES was born in 1915 in Le Sueur, Minnesota. He attended school in Minneapolis and later worked on his family's newspaper in Northfield. His books and articles (published in such magazines as *Gourmet*, *Travel & Leisure*, and *Food & Wine*) reflect an interest in the American past and in cultural history. He coauthored several cookbooks with his wife, Judith Jones, and he is also the author of *The Minnesota*, recently reprinted in a new edition by the University of Minnesota Press. He died in 1996.